Amber's Donkey

How a donkey and a little girl healed each other

JULIAN AND TRACY AUSTWICK
WITH RUTH KELLY

EBURY
PRESS

1 3 5 7 9 10 8 6 4 2

Ebury Press, an imprint of Ebury Publishing
20 Vauxhall Bridge Road
London SW1V 2SA

Ebury Press is part of the Penguin Random House group of companies
whose addresses can be found at global.penguinrandomhouse.com

 Penguin
Random House
UK

With thanks to The Donkey Sanctuary for their permission to use the
photographs featured on page 1,4,5,6, and 8 of the plate section. All other
photographs are Julian and Tracy Austwick's own.

First published by Ebury Press in 2016
This edition published in 2017

www.penguin.co.uk

A CIP catalogue record for this book is available from the British Library

ISBN 9781785031694

Typeset in India by Thomson Digital Pvt Ltd, Noida, Delhi

Printed and bound in Great Britain by Clays Ltd, St Ives PLC

Penguin Random House is committed to
a sustainable future for our business, our
readers and our planet. This book is made from
Forest Stewardship Council® certified paper.

Contents

CHAPTER 1

Left for Dead

Ireland, January 2010

"Oh dear God."

Donkey Sanctuary rescue officer Sinead O'Donnell couldn't believe what she was seeing. Tucked away at the end of the overgrown garden was a donkey with the most horrific neck injuries. He was 100 yards away from the road where Sinead was standing, but she could clearly see the blood oozing out of the deep wounds. The poor animal was swaying, delirious with pain.

Sinead radioed Headquarters for back-up. "We need to get the Gardaí [the Irish police] here right away."

She knew animal welfare officers were not allowed to enter a property to rescue a mistreated donkey without being accompanied by a police officer; now, she just had to sit tight until they arrived. It was a bitterly cold day in January 2010, and Sinead tugged the zip on her fleece to the top and wrapped her scarf around her neck once more.

She couldn't imagine how cold the poor donkey must be. Although they are sturdy animals, meant for the outdoors, blood loss from injuries like the ones she'd seen would be sure to make his body temperature plummet.

It would take a while for the police to arrive as she was in the middle of nowhere – a tiny hamlet in the countryside, half an hour from the Irish harbour city of Galway. The Sanctuary had

had a tip-off from a member of the public the night before. The lady, who didn't want to give her name, had described how the donkey was tethered to a pole, looking very distressed. Sinead couldn't see the rope; she thought it must have been removed overnight.

Sinead felt a chill run down her spine. It wasn't just the cold getting to her – she hated being called out on cases like this.

The highest number of rescued donkeys is from Ireland – almost 4,500 have been saved. The Irish consider them 'lucky charms' to have on their land, so a lot of donkeys are essentially left to 'rot' at the back of someone's yard.

Sinead checked her watch. It was 2.53 p.m. She blew into her hands to keep them warm and then tucked them under her armpits. A police car appeared moments later.

"What have we got here then?" The garda asked, getting out of his four-by-four. His walkie-talkie exploded with crackles and voices. He turned the knob down to shut out the noise and concentrated on the job at hand.

Sinead didn't need to explain; she just had to point to the donkey.

The garda shook his head in disgust. He was young, in his mid to late twenties, with a wolfish grin.

"Let's see what they have to say for themselves." He geared himself up for the door knock. Sinead had found through experience that you could never predict how these situations would go. Sometimes the owners were apologetic; other times, they turned aggressive and back-up was required.

Paint was blistering off the front door. There was no bell, so the police officer banged, several times. They both took a step back, and braced themselves.

"Yes?" A middle-aged woman answered. She had the chain lock on, so they could only see half her face.

"Is that your donkey in the garden?" the garda asked.

"Yes," the woman answered, defensively.

"We have reason to believe that it has been mistreated and would like to take a closer look. May we come in?" he asked, politely, but firmly.

The woman eyeballed them for a moment. Without saying a word, she closed the door, removed the lock, and then swung it wide open.

The first thing that hit Sinead was the smell. It was of dirty bins or unwashed plates – rotting food – blended with stale cigarette smoke. It moved in waves, hitting her nostrils every few breaths. She covered her nose as she stepped into the hallway.

"We didn't know he was in such a bad way, we tried to help him …" The woman babbled excuses in her thick regional accent.

She was probably forty-five on closer inspection, Sinead thought. She wore a calf-length green corduroy skirt that bulged over her belly and then nipped in at the waist. Inside the skirt she'd tucked a cream blouse, and over the top of that she wore a blue, thick, knitted cardigan. Her unwashed hair was flecked with grey and hung straggly around her shoulders.

She led them through the house and into the garden. Sinead could see the property was as uncared for as the donkey. The walls boasted tidal waves of rising damp and the paint on the ceiling was peeling. The seventies-style furniture was covered with a layer of dirt and food crumbs. Cigarette butts overflowed from ashtrays dotted around the room. Sinead had never been so happy to step out into the cold again.

When she saw the animal she had come to care for up close, she was immediately struck by the size of the beast. He was much bigger than the average donkey – more like a small horse. He was dark brown, except for his white muzzle and

3

underbelly. Unlike in some other rescue situations, she didn't have to worry about him running off; he could barely stand. He was staggering in the wintry mud, like a newborn foal, unsteady on his feet.

"Oh dear God," she said for the second time that day. She clutched her hand over her mouth.

The wounds were much worse than she had thought from the road. There were three wide, deep gashes around his neck and throat. The fur around his cuts looked as if it had been burned off. The donkey must have been in indescribable pain.

"It looks infected, we need to get him some antibiotics right away." Sinead turned to face the police officer and the woman. The owner was hanging back by the door, retreating into her cave.

"How could you let him get like this?" she accused.

The woman furrowed her brow like a fan, searching for a way out.

"He had this rope around his neck, and we didn't realise it had got so bad, until me partner took it off last night," she said, panicking. "I think the rope must have grown into his neck."

"That's exactly what happened," Sinead snapped. It looked as if the owner had never once loosened the rope in the five years she'd confessed to owning him. As the donkey had grown, the rope had grown into his skin. Just like a garrotte. It looked like it had been millimetres away from severing an artery.

"He needs urgent medical care, we need to take him away, now." Sinead approached the woman with the Gardaí Relinquishment Forms.

"What are these?" the owner asked, flicking through the paperwork.

4

"It's an official statement whereby you admit to the mistreatment of your donkey and hand over all ownership rights to us," Sinead said, holding out a pen.

The woman looked like a rabbit caught in headlights.

Sinead had been here so many times before.

"There will be no criminal repercussions; we just want to get this donkey to safety ASAP."

Although the Donkey Sanctuary does work with the RSPCA and ISPCA to secure prosecutions, their primary concern is the safety of the donkey, and they will forgo court cases if it means a donkey's life can be saved.

She waved the pen under the woman's nose.

'Okay," she said sheepishly, signing the form.

Sinead sighed deeply. It was one challenge over; the next was to get the sick donkey to safety. She told the police officer she would be back shortly with the trailer.

She'd only been gone for 20 minutes, but Sinead returned to World War Three. The woman's husband had arrived home and was furious that his donkey was being taken from him.

"Who the f*ck are you to think you can come onto my property and take *my* donkey?" he raged, pointing his finger in Sinead's face.

"You need to calm down, sir." The police officer stepped in.

"Don't tell me to calm down, son!" he shouted.

The man was also middle-aged, unshaven, with a scar that ran from inside his hairline to the corner of his eye. He wore a reddish V-neck jumper, which had holes in the cuffs, and scuffed Timberland boots.

"You need to calm down, right now," the officer said again, holding his hand up.

"Or what?" The man egged him on.

"Or we might be forced to arrest you, sir," he threatened.

The warning seemed to work. The owner walked off for a moment to cool down and then turned around, to face the music.

"So what do you want from me?" he asked.

Sinead stepped in.

"Your donkey is very sick, we want to take him away and nurse him back to health.

"We are here to support both you and the donkey." She tried the softly, softly approach.

The man shook his head guiltily. "I didn't mean to cause him any harm. I even took the rope off and tried to clean the cuts with Jeyes Fluid."

Sinead gasped with horror.

Jeyes Fluid is an industrial-strength disinfectant for outdoor use – such as cleaning patios, drains or garden furniture. Some farmers use it to disinfect areas after livestock and animals have been there. It is *not* something you should pour in an animal's open wounds.

"It must have felt like burning acid," she whispered almost to herself, imagining the poor donkey's pain.

"I was just trying to make it better," the owner tried to explain.

Sinead had been here so many times before as well. A lot of the cruelty she'd witnessed over the years hadn't been done out of malice, but ignorance. Whatever the reason, she'd seen enough.

The police officer stood at the back of the room with his arms crossed like a nightclub bouncer, as Sinead persuaded the owner to sign his name next to his partner's.

"I was only trying to help," he mumbled again. His partner hid in the shadows, shamefaced

"Has he ever worn a head collar?" Sinead cut his mumbled excuses dead, more interested in how she was going to get the donkey into the trailer.

"Aye, that's right." He nodded.

The head collar wraps behind a donkey's ears and over the bridge of their nose. It can take a while for a donkey to get used to the sensation and they can rebel by rearing up or kicking.

But this poor donkey was so out of it he didn't put up any sort of struggle. It was like he had lost the will to live and was waiting to leave this earth. He looked at Sinead through his long eyelashes, which were coated in a layer of frost from the cold. It was a heart-breaking sight.

The owners stood back and watched as Sinead gently pulled the injured animal through the garden and onto the trailer. He stumbled several times, tripping over his feet.

"Nearly there, keep going," she whispered in his ear.

Those 100 yards were probably the furthest he'd walked in his whole, miserable life.

Sinead secured him to the back of the trailer and got ready to make the drive to the Sanctuary's headquarters in Liscarroll.

"Will he be okay?" The police officer had come to say his goodbyes.

"I don't know," Sinead sighed, answering honestly. She glanced back at the owners, but they had disappeared indoors. The curtain in the front window twitched, and Sinead felt their eyes watching them.

"You better get going." The garda patted the side of the van.

It was a two-hour journey south to County Cork, which gave her plenty of thinking time. As Sinead flicked between the radio stations, her mind drifted. She'd seen some terrible sights over the past fifteen years she'd worked as a welfare officer. Donkeys who'd had their eyes gouged out; been almost starved to death; beaten; burned. The images would sometimes haunt her at night – it was hard to switch off.

She prayed to God she'd rescued this donkey in time and that he hadn't got septicaemia – blood poisoning – from his wounds. If he had, his chances of survival would be very, very low indeed.

It was pitch black by the time they rolled into the Donkey Sanctuary car park, and the temperature had dropped into the minuses. The outside light in the yard pinged on and the team appeared out of nowhere.

"How bad is he?" The vet rushed to take a look.

"It's bad." Sinead shook her head. Her eyes were blurry from the drive and all the emotions.

The Sanctuary is a little safe haven for hundreds of rescued donkeys. It's tucked away in the beautiful rolling countryside just outside the village of Liscarroll. It's one of the many shelters the Donkey Sanctuary has dotted around the world. Since the charity was founded in 1969 by Dr Elisabeth Svendsen MBE, the charity has rescued over 18,000 donkeys and mules and currently has 4,725 on its farms across Europe.

Many of those donkeys were abandoned, or discarded in a field after having worked for their owners for years, hauling peat or pulling a cart. Donkeys feel pain just as much as the next animal, but they won't express what they are going through, which is why they are often abused. People don't see them reacting to pain as we would expect an animal to react, so they push them harder, often until breaking point. That's probably why people think donkeys look sad, because they have often led such a tough life.

Watching the vet go about his work, Sinead had to let go – she had done all she could. It was in the hands of the vets and the staff now, and hopefully the donkey would find the will to live and fight on.

There is a special quarantine area where the rescued donkeys are treated for their injuries and checked for diseases. There, they are examined by specialist veterinary nurses who deal with the donkeys when they first arrive. One such nurse was Tina Buckley, who was on duty that evening. Like Sinead, she'd worked for the Sanctuary for fifteen years, since she was eighteen years old. She'd also seen some horrific injuries in her time.

"So, what's happened to this one?" she asked the vet, as she prepped herself for the examination room. She threw on her overalls and rubbed the hand sanitiser between her fingers. Her preparations were not dissimilar to those of doctors in a hospital – only their patient was a donkey.

The vet didn't answer, but moments later Tina saw the patient for herself.

"Oh my Lord," she gasped. The smell of rotting flesh was everywhere. "What have they done to you?" Despite herself, she recoiled in horror.

The first thing the vet, Sue, did was to give the donkey several shots of antibiotics – around the wound, into his rump, and directly into his vein.

He didn't even flinch as the needle pierced his skin. Instead, he hung his head, as if he didn't have the strength to hold it up. His breathing was loud and strained.

"You can still see the rope." Tina pointed at the blue threads embedded in his wounds. "Oh Jesus. Every time he moved, the rope would have burned him." She imagined how it would have sliced, deeper and deeper, like a cheese wire.

Tina crouched to take a better look at the injuries around his throat. It was immediately apparent to her trained eye how close this donkey had come to death. "Any longer and it would have hit an artery." She looked up at the vet.

Sue shook her head in disgust. She told Tina they had a horrible task ahead – they had to clean the wounds by cutting away all of the dead skin.

The donkey was given a mild sedative to take the edge off his pain while they got to work on cutting out the infection. In spite of his injuries, he seemed sweet-natured. A lot of donkeys as badly hurt as him would have used their last ounce of energy to kick and bite, but not this one.

"He's a gentle giant," said Tina, stroking his nose.

It was a painstaking process, first clipping back his hair and then slicing away at the skin until it bled. The idea was to bring fresh blood to the wounds to flush out the infection. They could only do a small area at a time, and would have to come back to it the following day … if there was a next day.

"These blood tests will show if he's got septicaemia," Sue said, carting off the test tubes for examination under the microscope.

Tina knew the score by now. The isolation unit could hold 30 donkeys at one time, and it was always full due to the huge number of donkeys that are rescued. Just as in a hospital ward, there are often not enough beds to go around – so donkeys are often kept in 'holding bays' on people's farms, while they wait for a space to become free. Many of those donkeys do survive and go on to join the others in the nearby paddocks. But others, whose injuries are too severe, don't even make it through the night.

As she bandaged the donkey's wounds, Tina said a little prayer for her new friend, hoping he'd pull through.

She couldn't put her finger on it, but she sensed there was something special about him. Something that set him apart.

CHAPTER 2

Double Trouble

Good Hope Hospital, Birmingham,
March 2010

Julian and Tracy Austwick smiled nervously as the sonographer squeezed the jelly onto Tracy's tummy.

"Ooh!" Tracy winced as the cold ultrasound scanner touched her skin.

It was the couple's first scan at 12 weeks of pregnancy and they were both excited, but apprehensive at the same time.

"There's one heartbeat," the sonographer said, as she slid the scanner through the jelly.

Julian and Tracy smiled lovingly at each other.

"And there's the second heartbeat."

"What?" Tracy squealed in disbelief.

"Yes, you're having twins," the sonographer laughed.

"Oh my God." Tracy playfully hid behind her hands.

The parents-to-be then entered into a little debate about whose genes had brought this on.

"Your granddad is a twin, isn't he?" Julian prompted Tracy.

"Yes, that's right." Tracy nodded, still overwhelmed by the news. "All my family teased me that I was in the running for twins, but I never thought anything of it."

The whole drive home, Julian couldn't stop chatting about the news.

"Twins – that's job done, we have our instant family," he joked.

And then, a few streets later, the reality hit home that twins meant twice the amount of things they needed to buy!

The next few days were spent celebrating and telling friends and family the incredible news. Julian and Tracy did all the normal things any expectant parents would do, like dreaming up names. They didn't have a clue of the sexes yet, but Julian had talked himself into the idea that they were having a boy and a girl. Being an avid science-fiction fan, he wanted to call them Luke and Leia after his *Star Wars* heroes.

"No bloody way," Tracy choked. "There is no way our kids are being named after your favourite film."

That was the end of the discussion, as Tracy always liked to have the last word.

The pregnancy went like a dream from then on. The 20-week scan revealed the couple was having girls and, after getting over the initial disappointment of there not being a mini-Luke Skywalker on the way, Julian busied himself with preparing the girls' room, while Tracy carried on as normal with her cleaning job.

It was while Tracy was getting ready for work one morning that she noticed something a little strange.

"Eww, water's trickling out of me," Tracy squealed, as she shuffled from the bed to the bathroom.

"I'm sure it's nothing, love, the girls are probably just dancing on your bladder," Julian croaked back and rolled over.

After all, there was a long way to go still – four months. Tracy was not the sort to make a fuss. She didn't feel any pain so she just slipped a sanitary towel into her knickers and got on with her day.

By lunchtime, the water was still coming. Tracy gave the midwife a call, just to be on the safe side.

12

"You need to get to the hospital straight away, something's not right," the midwife ordered.

"What?" Tracy furrowed her brow in disbelief. She thought it was all a lot of fuss over nothing, so, after calling Julian with an update, she quickly nipped into town to finish her errands. Tracy put some money in the bank and picked up floor cleaner from the pound shop before calmly walking into the maternity ward at Birmingham Good Hope Hospital.

She explained the symptoms as the doctor examined her, while thinking of the million-and-one other things she needed to get done that day.

"I'm just going to get someone else to have a look," the doctor interrupted.

Tracy folded her arms across her chest protectively – she wasn't expecting that. Another doctor appeared and examined her. Tracy studied their expressions; she had picked up on a bad feeling.

The doctor stood back, clutching the clipboard into her chest.

"I'm ever so sorry, but your waters have broken," she announced.

Tracy sat bolt upright. She was listening now.

"We need to get you in an ambulance right away." The doctor signalled to the nurses to help move the patient.

"What?" Tracy's head was swooshing from left to right as staff crowded around her.

"If you go into labour now, the babies will die. There is nothing we can do for you here. We need to get you over to the main hospital, Heartlands, where they have all the resuscitation equipment."

Tracy was in complete shock. Labour? Resuscitate? The words skipped around in her head.

"But I'm not in labour, the water hasn't gushed out ..." Tracy was in denial as they wheeled her through the corridors.

Julian arrived as Tracy was lifted into the ambulance.

"What's going on?" he said, panicking.

"My waters have broken, follow me to Heartlands!" Tracy shouted through the closing doors.

SLAM!

Julian was left alone with his thoughts, his mind conjuring up worst-case scenarios. He followed the blue flashing lights. It was a good thing the ambulance was leading the way, as he didn't have a clue where Heartlands was, even though they had been living in Birmingham for four years. He'd never had to know – until now.

Tracy's sister, Debbie, came rushing into the ward not long after Julian arrived. At forty-two, Debs was ten years older than Tracy, and had been like a surrogate mum while Tracy was growing up. She quickly put on her mothering cap, pushing the doctors for answers.

Tracy's bedside was surrounded by confusion. Everyone's fears had been revved up to 100 mph and now they were back waiting at the traffic lights, waiting for answers. The doctors were frantically sidestepping each other like bad dancers, while Tracy was lying there, feeling absolutely fine.

It was stop, start, stop, start.

Julian tried to lighten the mood.

"There's no TV in here, we can't watch *Britain's Got Talent* tonight," he joked. It was his way of coping.

"Oh shush, you." Tracy shook her head with good-natured embarrassment.

As the hours crept past, Julian and Tracy started to question whether the doctors had possibly overreacted. Tracy was convinced she wasn't going into labour because she didn't feel any contractions.

"I've got to get out," she muttered, feeling claustrophobic in a ward full of mums with their crying babies.

"Calm down, love," Julian soothed her, just as a nurse appeared with a wheelchair. They were sending Tracy for a scan to see what was going on.

Julian trailed behind as they were led through corridor after corridor, snaking their way through the underbelly of the enormous hospital.

"You'll just need to wait here until your name is called," the nurse explained, and then, in the blink of an eye, she was gone.

Julian and Tracy felt very confused. The only time the couple had been to hospital together before was when Tracy had had her wisdom teeth out. They were now in a waiting room full of strangers. Julian caught himself studying the other couples.

That couple opposite look very panicky. There are a few women here on their own; it must be horrible for them to go through this alone, he thought.

"Tracy Austwick!" The gruff voice calling his wife's name sliced through his thoughts. A man in his early forties was beckoning them into the ultrasound room. Julian imagined the sonographer must be a surfer in his spare time as he was wearing three-quarter-length shorts under his scrubs and he had messy sun-bleached hair.

"Come on, love, everything's fine," Julian reassured Tracy, as she lay down on the bed.

It was the same procedure as before – the jelly on the tummy, the cold scanner sliding up and down – only this time there wasn't any smiling or laughing.

"Ah." The sonographer grimaced.

Julian and Tracy locked eyes.

"Hmmm," he carried on, like a mechanic examining an engine beneath the bonnet of a car.

"What's wrong?" Tracy asked. Until this moment, she hadn't really accepted her babies were in danger.

"One of your embryonic sacks has broken, the other one is fine," he said matter-of-factly. "There is enough water left for the baby to survive, for now. However, there is not enough fluid left for her to grow. There is a chance her arms and legs won't be able to develop and she will be handicapped," he explained.

"Handicapped?" The word speared Tracy's heart.

Suddenly, everything became very real for Julian and Tracy.

"The longer you keep the babies inside you, the better. Think of it like an oven: the longer they stay in, the greater the chance of them surviving."

Tracy couldn't speak; her tongue was tied with distress. Julian threw questions at the sonographer. He needed answers.

"Okay, we understand, but what about the other baby? If Tracy goes into labour, is there any way that baby can stay inside?" he asked.

"No, sorry, once the contractions start, both babies need to come out."

"So both of them aren't going to survive then?" Julian's voice trembled.

The sonographer turned to Tracy and said: "If, during labour, we can't do anything to save them, we will just put them on your chest.

"I'm sorry."

Tracy closed her eyes as if she was living that possible future there and then. The thought of her two babies lying helpless on her chest was too much to bear.

"Julian, I need to get some air, I need to get out of here," she pleaded.

They didn't say a word to each other as they left the room. Julian felt himself welling up but he wiped his tears away as quickly as they appeared. Tracy was always the strong one who never showed her emotions, so he wanted to be strong for her now.

They had both resigned themselves to the idea they would lose the girls, but neither of them wanted to say the words. It was like the elephant in the room.

"What happens now?" Julian asked the nurse waiting to collect them.

"I'm afraid Mrs Austwick will have to stay in hospital in case she goes into labour."

Her chances of getting air were dashed. Tracy looked at Julian with pleading eyes.

"No, lovie, I know you hate hospitals but it's for the best." He squeezed her hand.

Julian hated leaving Tracy alone. They hadn't spent a night apart since they'd met in 2004, working behind a bar in Stratford-upon-Avon. They had had to live in each other's pockets then, and they had remained as close ever since.

Julian couldn't switch off his thoughts as he lay in bed that night, alone. He decided to download an app on his mobile phone that calculated the percentage chance of the twins surviving. He tapped in 24 weeks gone ...

His heart almost stopped at the result.

Twenty per cent chance.

Jesus. It was all over.

He did his best to mask his sadness from Tracy when he visited her at Heartlands Hospital the next morning. She was already looking stressed because the nurses had ticked her off for moving around.

"I can't do anything in case I bring on the labour, I just have to lie here," Tracy said, gritting her teeth.

Tracy didn't know how to sit still. She was used to either cleaning her own house or other people's homes. Now she was being wrapped in cotton wool, and it was driving her crazy.

Julian and Debbie took it in turns to keep her company. The nurses came in every morning and evening to monitor how much water was being lost. Meanwhile, Julian had his own routine – checking his app morning and night. As the days crept past, the percentage slowly rose.

It was up to 30 per cent by the end of the week. Julian wanted to break the news to Tracy, but when he arrived at the hospital it sounded like she'd already had some good news. He could hear his wife cackling with laughter from all the way down the hospital corridor. He walked into the room to find Tracy and Debs laughing hysterically.

"What's going on?" he asked, bewildered.

It was hot, May Day 2010, and the windows were wide open.

"Come and listen to this." Debbie beckoned him over.

Julian didn't need to crane his ear; he could hear from the door.

"Arrrrrrrhh!" came the shrill scream of a woman giving birth.

Tracy's room was above the delivery room – and all you could hear was screaming and swearing.

"Ooooh, you bastard!" the mum-to-be yelled at her partner.

The three of them burst out laughing. It took them away from their problems.

"I'm going stir crazy in here," Tracy giggled, dabbing the tears of laughter from her eyes.

Her prayers were finally answered as the doctor confirmed nothing seemed to be happening, and it would be safe to go home.

Back in the comfort of their house, it was easy for Julian and Tracy to forget anything was wrong. As the days flew past, as the percentage jumped, and the scans revealed no changes, they carried on as normal.

That's why Julian couldn't quite believe it when Tracy woke him in the middle of the night on 16 June.

"I'm not feeling too good," she groaned, at one o'clock in the morning. She had felt a burning pain down below.

"Just go back to sleep, love, it's not happening now," Julian mumbled.

But something *was* wrong. Tracy sat up and switched on the bedside lamp.

"Lovie, something's happening."

She held her belly.

"Ah!" She doubled over with the pain of a contraction.

Reality came crashing down on them once again.

Julian sprang out of bed and helped Tracy into the car. It was the dead of night and Tracy would never forget the deafening sound they made as they screeched out of the driveway of their quiet cul-de-sac in Sutton Coldfield. The fan belt had come loose – it sounded like nails on a blackboard.

"Arrrrrrgh!" Tracy screamed with the pain of the contraction.

"Screeeeeech!" went the car as they pulled up at the traffic lights.

It was horrendous.

"Make it shut up!" Tracy cried.

Julian didn't try to reason with his wife this time. He put his foot on the pedal instead!

Tracy was laughing hysterically with the pain, and the comedy of the whole thing, when they arrived at the Heartlands Hospital. They were rushed into a birthing room and Tracy was greeted by the midwife.

"You won't be laughing for long," she said curtly.

Julian and Tracy looked at each other like scolded schoolkids.

Throughout their marriage, Julian and Tracy had always tried to see the light in the darkest of moments. They buried their worst fears until the doctor arrived, when they were forced to face the devastating reality – at 14 weeks premature, their babies were not likely to survive.

"We have two incubators free, so if we can do anything, rest assured we will," said the doctor. He smiled sympathetically.

"*If we can do anything …*" Julian repeated to himself.

"Because you're having twins, you'll need double of everything. Don't panic if one minute there is no one in the room, and the next, the room is full."

The doctor tried to reassure Tracy, but him saying "Don't panic" made Tracy want to panic even more.

"If there isn't anything we can do, we will put them on your chest, and you can hold them before they have to go."

There was that image again. Tracy couldn't bear to think about it.

The past two weeks had been a bit of a dream, where they could hope the pregnancy was going to carry on as normal. Now it was the end game.

The pregnancy had lasted just 26 weeks – the babies would be born 14 weeks premature. One of the twins had lost all of her water, so there was a high chance she was going to be handicapped, they believed. They'd named her Hope already because everyone had been saying: "I hope she's going to be okay." They didn't know what to call the other girl, or maybe they just couldn't bring themselves to get too attached.

Julian wanted to be strong for Tracy. All he could think about now was how it was going to affect her if the girls were stillborn.

He had to ask the doctor the question again: "Could we not just leave the one baby in who's doing well?"

It was a hard thing for Julian to get his head around, that one of the twins was likely to bring about the death of the other.

"No, I'm afraid we can't." The doctor sighed and, although Julian had already known the answer, he felt his heart sink that little bit further.

It was now 7 a.m. Tracy was given a bit of gas and air. If Julian's eyes ever closed with tiredness, Tracy's ginormous moans jolted him awake.

Debbie had arrived at the hospital and offered to do a sandwich run. Tracy let out another moan and the food was put on hold as the twins could be coming at any second.

The pair stayed glued to Tracy's side until the big moment finally happened at 3.40 p.m.

"Do you want to push?" The midwife mopped Tracy's brow.

"Yes!" Tracy screamed.

Within 30 seconds, there were two incubators and 15 doctors and nurses swarming around Tracy's bedside.

This is just the most amazing thing, Julian thought. He'd blinked and they'd appeared.

Between the pain and the pushing, all Tracy could envisage was her babies being placed on her chest.

Julian put the camera away because he didn't want to capture what was about to happen. He was now thinking about Tracy, and if she was going to be okay.

The only way Julian could describe the birth was like an alien emerging. Hope's head was elongated and her tiny body was black, as if she was bruised. Worse still, she wasn't moving.

That's it; she's dead. Julian shook his head.

The doctors whisked Hope away and Julian was certain he'd never see her again.

He squeezed Tracy's hand to tell her he loved her and he was proud of her. Tracy was barely conscious; she was panting heavily, trying to recover for Round Two.

But the twin they hadn't named yet just didn't want to come. She was happy inside her mum.

"We need to break your water," the doctor announced.

So they got to work and then suddenly there was this gush of liquid. Julian's eyes nearly popped out of his head; he'd not seen anything like it.

"Arrrrrrgh," Tracy screamed, pushing with all her determination.

But try as she might, the little thing didn't want to come out.

What a shame, she is so happy in there, Julian thought.

"Come on, Tracy, you've got to do it," the midwife ordered.

"I'm too tired, I can't." Tracy rolled her head from side to side in agony.

Julian stepped in. "You've got to do it or that nasty man over there is going to take you down into surgery," he threatened.

"Just shut up, will ya?" Tracy snapped. But it worked.

There's no chance I'm having one baby by natural birth and the other by Caesarean, Tracy thought.

"Arrrrrrgh," she screamed again, in anger now.

The baby appeared in a pool of blood and gunk.

She looked a lot better than Hope – she was the right colour and shape for starters – but her limp body was completely lifeless.

Julian watched in disbelief as an Indian doctor blew down what looked like a straw into his baby's tiny mouth. Her chest rose, and then it fell, and then the doctor tried again. Julian didn't expect for there to be any life, but he still couldn't bear to see the doctor fail.

It was agonising to watch; he had to look away.

The next moment, the nurses were wheeling her out in the incubator. It then suddenly dawned on Julian that it had been 20 minutes since they had whisked Hope away – maybe they had managed to resuscitate her too?

Julian had been so caught up in the drama he'd forgotten the doctor's words. Tracy, however, had never been able to shake the horrific image from her head of her lifeless babies being placed upon her chest. And so, when Julian looked across at his wife, it was to see her smiling through her exhaustion. She knew her babies were alive because they hadn't been placed on her chest.

The Indian doctor approached the couple. Julian hadn't let go of Tracy's hand the whole time. He now braced himself for the bad news.

"So both the girls needed to be resuscitated," he started.

Julian squeezed his wife's hand.

"But they are both alive."

"Oh thank God." Julian sighed the words. He hadn't realised he'd been holding his breath until then.

Tracy was still smiling; she'd known all along.

"They are in their incubators, all being well you can go and see them in a few hours."

The one thing Julian would always remember was how strongly the doctor's breath smelled of coffee. *Wow, maybe it was the caffeine that helped resuscitate my daughter*, he thought.

At 5pm Debbie and Julian finally stepped out for that sandwich.

"I better tell some people this has happened." Feeling the fresh air on his face, Julian was suddenly jolted back to normality. He messaged his parents, Tracy's parents and Tracy's brother, while Debs helped with breaking the news to the rest of the family.

It was 6 p.m. when Julian finally left Tracy's bedside to see the twins. He felt the palms of his hands building with sweat as he took the lift down to the incubator room. He was terrified because he didn't know what to expect. The last time he'd seen his girls, they were tiny lifeless bodies. Would Hope still be black? Would she be deformed?

Ping. The lift door slid open.

I've got to take a few pictures to show Trace, Julian thought as he walked through the sterile-smelling corridors. Tracy was so exhausted; Julian doubted she'd make it out of her bed that night.

Julian knew he'd arrived at the neonatal unit because he could hear the bleeping machinery from down the hallway.

It was like walking into a new world.

There were six incubators. There were tubes everywhere, there was a lot of bleeping and there were parents crouched over their babies, wiping their tears away.

Julian was hit by a blast of warm air as he looked for his girls. He expected the twins to be next to each other, but they were placed at opposite ends of the room. Hope was on the left and 'Twin B' on the right.

He walked gingerly to Hope's incubator.

Please be okay, please be okay, he prayed.

His heart was racing as he peered into the incubator.

Oh God.

Hope's body was black and blue. She had tubes coming out of everywhere. The big green ventilator pumping life into her mouth engulfed her tiny face. Her right foot was turned in, as if it was broken.

"Don't worry, she's all in one piece." The nurse had crept up behind him. It was as if she'd read his mind.

"Look, she has all her fingers and toes," the nurse whispered, showing him.

Julian gently placed his index finger into the palm of Hope's hand. She curled her tiny digits around it. Her whole hand was the size of his fingernail!

He then slowly made his way over to 'Twin B'. She looked much more in proportion – a perfect-looking baby, only a miniature one, weighing one pound and nine ounces.

Julian took a picture and video of the twins for Tracy.

He looked over his shoulder – *am I allowed to do this?* Even though they were his children, he worried about whether he'd be told off. It was all so strange, all so scary.

"You can talk to them, you know," the nurse said. She smiled encouragingly. "It would be good to let them know you're here."

"Oh yes, right." Julian nodded. They looked so fragile; he'd forgotten they were actual babies.

"Hello," he whispered. He didn't really know what to say.

Julian felt the tears well up in his eyes.

What a shame, he thought.

Even though they were alive, and in the best place they could possibly be, he was convinced he wasn't going to see them grow up.

If he was honest, he didn't expect them to last the night.

Suddenly, Julian felt overwhelmed with sadness. He hated being there on his own, without Tracy. Tears ran down his cheeks.

He prayed Tracy would get the chance to see them – before it was too late.

CHAPTER 3

A Diamond in the Rough

Devon, July 2010

"What are we going to call him?' Lisa Spence asked the rest of the team.

The name popped into her head a moment later.

"Shocks. We'll call him Shocks for the shocking state he was found in," the thirty-two-year-old decided.

The rest of the staff at the Donkey Sanctuary in Devon nodded in agreement.

Shocks had just arrived at Woods Farm in a lorry full of donkeys from Ireland. Woods Farm is one of the closest farms to the main Sanctuary, which is based at Slade House Farm near Sidmouth. The Donkey Sanctuary had bought Woods Farm in 1989, from a farmer who kept chickens as well as outdoor pigs and a small dairy herd. The current hay barn now stands on the site of the chicken sheds. It has an enormous 80 hectares (197 acres) of land and has provided sanctuary to many donkeys, specialising in the care of donkeys with breathing problems, laminitis, skin problems and those on diets. Shocks had made a miraculous recovery in six months. It had taken him several weeks to fight off the infection, and a good three months to be fit and healthy again, but he had pulled through. Sadly, there wasn't enough room for him to stay on in Liscarroll because the Irish Sanctuary needed to free up space for new rescue cases, so they'd shipped him across the Irish Sea so the Woods Farm staff could take care of him.

27

He was placed in a paddock with 100 other rescue donkeys from Ireland. The staff at Devon liked to keep the "Irish boys" together, because they were all very similar: young and, like typical Irish boys, cheeky and naughty.

They hoped Shocks would make friends because it is natural donkey behaviour to bond with others; donkeys don't like being alone.

But from the moment he stepped off the lorry on 16 July 2010, all he wanted to do was keep himself to himself.

"Maybe it's because he's spent all his life alone," Lisa pondered, after being filled in about his rescue.

She watched as some of the more brazen 'lads' played tug-o-war with a green Wellington boot. Shocks kept well away across the other side of the field, like an old man worried about being knocked into. He had this distant, unhappy look about him, like he was missing something.

The bright summer light exposed the white scars of his healing wounds. Lisa worried that the scars went much deeper than his skin.

She'd worked as a groom at the Donkey Sanctuary for 16 years. As for so many of the staff, once she'd started working with the cute, long-eared, furry animals, it was hard to think of a life without them.

But Lisa's job was not just to look after the wellbeing of the donkeys; she had acquired a unique talent – to spot potential.

There were 2,200 donkeys in total in Devon, and it was up to her to decide who mixed with who, which donkey would be one of the lucky few to be declared an 'adoption donkey' for the public to sponsor, and, of course, who would make a good riding donkey for their six additional-needs therapy centres.

Lisa also had the very rewarding job of deciding when a donkey was ready for rehoming. There is a rigorous list of criteria to be met before a donkey can be fostered. For a start, the new owner has to have at least 2,000 square metres of land. They must have a hard surface – donkeys' feet are very porous so they need to be able to get off the grass when it's wet. They must have access to a shelter – donkeys don't have waterproof coats like horses. And the 'foster parent' must have robust fencing – donkeys can be great escape artists!

One look at Shocks and you'd think he wouldn't make the grade for any of the above. A lot of the other staff had been whispering that, sad as it was, Shocks was a lost cause.

Lisa wasn't so convinced. Even though she rarely got to look him in the eye, as he spent much of the day with his head down or gazing into space, she sometimes caught him off-guard. It would only last a fraction of a second, but occasionally she managed to catch a spark in his eye. It was a sign of life, a desire to fight on.

Shocks certainly had some fight in him when the farrier came to tend to his hooves. His feet were improving after many years of neglect, but still needed a lot of TLC. The Irish Sanctuary had tipped Lisa off that Shocks wasn't very partial to men, and she caught the full flavour of it that morning.

The farrier was crouched down by his feet, ready to get to work on his overgrown hooves, when, all of a sudden, Shocks's whole body tensed like a tight rope. He reared up onto his hind legs, dangerously cycling his front legs in the air. The farrier tumbled back, covering his head with his hands.

"Easy, boy." Lisa pulled down on his head collar with all her might. Even though she was not much over 5 foot tall, she was a strong woman who knew how to put a donkey in its place. "What's got into you?" She tried to calm Shocks down.

His eyes were wild with fear, his nostrils flared. Something had scared the life out of him.

The farrier edged away, which seemed to help things.

"He doesn't like men; that's pretty clear," Lisa said, straining her arm to hold Shocks to the ground.

The scars of his past were showing themselves more than ever. Why else would he be so terrified of a man coming close? It made Lisa's stomach turn with anger that he was once treated so cruelly.

Lisa found that the best treatment for Shocks was to leave him be. She remembered a saying a friend had once told her: "Love is like a butterfly. The more you chase it, the more it will elude you. But if you turn your attention towards other things, it will come and softly sit on your shoulder."

She found that to be true for most things in life – including the donkeys she loved and cared for.

The more she left Shocks to his own devices, the more he took an interest in what Lisa was up to. Lisa divided her time between all the different paddocks and enclosures, but 10 a.m., just after her morning cup of tea, was always devoted to the Irish boys.

She'd come in, laden with food like carrots and apples, and occasionally with treats such as ginger biscuits and polo mints – donkey favourites – and give the cheeky chappies a pet or a good scratch behind the ears. It wouldn't be uncommon for her to have a fan club of at least 20 donkeys trailing behind her, all fighting for Lisa's attention.

Shocks would never join in, of course, but as the weeks flew by, she started to notice the way he looked over at them – longingly, like he wanted to join in, he just didn't know how to.

It was coming up to Christmas when Lisa witnessed something magical. She was in the paddock as usual, being harassed for attention. Lisa took her glasses off for a moment because they'd become steamed up with her warm breath in the icy air. She turned around and there was Shocks, quietly standing next to her. His eyes were lowered, like he was too shy to look at Lisa.

"Hello, boy." She smiled. Lisa slipped her hand into her fleece, and pulled out a ginger nut biscuit.

"Here you go," she said, holding her palm out.

Shocks's eyes lit up. He looked at the yummy treat for a moment, wondering whether it was safe to take it or not.

Lisa patiently waited for Shocks to build up the courage to take a couple of steps closer. He curled his lips into a point and then hoovered up the ginger nut in one swift inhalation.

Lisa giggled, wiping her hands on her trousers.

Finally, Lisa thought. It was the sign she'd been looking for.

As soon as she had a moment to herself, Lisa picked up the phone and dialled the Sanctuary's assisted-therapy centre in Birmingham.

She needed to speak to Amber Brennan, one of the chief riding instructors at the centre, where they offered riding therapy to children with additional needs.

They'd been friends for years, and she knew Shocks was just what Amber was after – a big sturdy donkey, who was also a bit of a challenge to tame.

The fact that Shocks wanted to please, that he wanted to make friends with Lisa, was enough of a sign to show he had a chance of being a riding donkey. Lisa had yet to be proved wrong in the many years she'd been "talent-spotting".

Amber was intrigued by the sound of Shocks. She looked after 21 donkeys in the Sanctuary in Birmingham, 15 of which were fit for riding. She was always on the hunt for a new addition to her team – few donkeys made the cut so, unbeknown to Shocks, it was an honour to be considered.

Amber drove to Devon as soon as she could get away. Amber, who was in her mid-thirties, always loved visiting Woods Farm because of the beautiful scenery – acres of fields nestled in the rolling Devon hills.

"Hello!" Amber waved cheerily at Lisa as she pulled into the car park.

It had been some time since the old friends had caught up. Amber towered over her friend, being 5 foot 8 inches in height. She had elfin-like short plum-coloured hair, with a sweeping side parting.

Lisa rested her hands on her hips, squinting in the bright sunshine.

"I've found the perfect donkey for you." Lisa jumped straight in as soon as Amber was out of the car. "I know you like a challenge," she teased her friend.

Amber laughed a real belly laugh. She was a larger-than-life character who was very popular with all the children she helped at the riding centre.

Lisa and Amber made their way up the lane to the big paddock where all the Irish donkeys were kept. The pair leaned on the fence, peering out across the grassy field. It didn't take a second to spot Shocks; he was the loner in the corner.

"That's Shocks there." Lisa pointed.

Amber's heart melted.

"I want him" were her first words.

Lisa grinned; she'd known Amber would take to him.

"He's a really solid, big chunky lad. Really nice sort, isn't he?" she asked in her soft Devon accent.

"He's perfect." Amber couldn't take her eyes off Shocks.

It was the fact that Shocks was a loner that, weirdly, made him so perfect for the job at hand. If he'd made friends in Devon, Lisa wouldn't have been able to let him go, because donkeys can go into shock if they are separated from their best friends. The official term for the life-threatening condition is hyperlipidaemia. It's better known amongst the staff at the Sanctuary as 'dying of a broken heart'.

"You know you've got your work cut out with him, I don't think you will see instant results," Lisa warned Amber.

Amber smiled knowingly. It might take time, but she had a gut feeling about this.

Shocks was a star in the making.

CHAPTER 4

Race to Recovery

Heartlands Hospital, Birmingham, June 2010

"So what's 'Twin B' going to be called then?" the nurse joked, as Tracy checked on her girls.

It had become a bit of a joke at the hospital, as a couple of weeks had passed since the birth, and 'Twin B', in the end incubator, still didn't have a name.

The truth was, Tracy never thought she'd get to this point. Hope was now a normal pinky colour and Twin B was developing at rocket speed. Tracy peered into the incubator, willing for some inspiration.

Twin B was sleeping under a blue lamp to prevent her from jaundice. Many newborns have jaundice – a condition whereby their skin turns yellow, when a substance called bilirubin builds up faster than their bodies can break it down. Twin B was cocooned, in what looked like bubble wrap, to keep her warm – like a gorgeous little present. She had a tiny eye mask on to protect her from the bright light.

There was a chorus of bleeping – one noisy machine for monitoring the heartbeat, another to measure oxygen in the blood, others still for blood pressure, temperature, breathing rate. Tracy couldn't think for the noise.

"Do you want to hold her?" the nurse asked, manoeuvring the spaghetti of tubes and wires that connected her baby to some of the machines.

Tracy made a hammock with her arms, ready for her little girl. Her daughter was small, but her warmth spread over Tracy like a hot bath.

Tracy's eyes filled with tears.

You weren't ready to come, you shouldn't be here, she thought, staring at the ventilator that was still pumping life into her daughter.

She looked at the laminate floor for a moment, blinking the tears away. Tracy didn't want to rain teardrops on her baby. She couldn't let her emotions get the better of her, otherwise her wall of strength would come down.

A word danced on her lips.

"Amber," she whispered. It felt right. "Hello, Amber." She curled down and welcomed the new name with a kiss.

"Why Amber?" the nurse asked. The care in the neonatal unit was so intense it was as if the nurses had eyes in the back of their heads.

"Because I think she's going to take after her mum and have red hair like me." Tracy looked up through her auburn fringe.

"Hope and Amber: they sound good together."

Tracy beamed.

Julian loved the name and, for the first time in weeks, it felt like a cloud had lifted.

Tracy had returned to their two-bedroom house the day after the birth. She felt more human there, in the comfort of her familiar surroundings and next to Julian at night, than she did sleeping on a hospital ward.

Soon every day became the same routine.

Julian would come to the hospital straight after work. First he would push the buzzer to get into the neonatal unit; the entrance led into a small room that was filled floor to ceiling with lockers. Julian would take off his dirty clothes, which would be dusty from his day of carpet fitting, and slip one of the protective plastic aprons over his change of clothes. More often than not, Tracy would already be inside, hooked up to the breast-feeding pumps, producing milk for the baby feeds.

Then came the grinding sound of the hand gel machine. Julian hated the noise with a passion; it went through him like nails on a chalkboard. For some reason, Julian always caught himself glancing at the sign above, which gave step-by-step instructions on how to wash your hands – even though he'd done it countless times before.

Julian would sit with one of the girls, Tracy with the other.

"Everything okay? What's happened overnight?" would be the first things each of them always asked the nurses when they arrived for a new day. The nurses would respond by reeling off a list of details, from changing nappies to giving the twins a wash.

It was like Groundhog Day – which had become strangely comforting for the both of them. As long as there was a routine, then that meant everything was okay as far as the twins' wellbeing was concerned. Julian and Tracy tried their best to have no expectations. Every day with Hope and Amber was a gift.

They didn't want to talk about serious things, like the future, in case there was no happy ever after. Instead, they found solace in the tiny community that they were building in the neonatal unit. Nurses became like comforting old friends, and the other families were sounding boards.

Julian and Tracy would compare notes with other couples. It was therapeutic for them to know they were not alone. Even if they didn't chat, it was reassuring just to see the other parents there every day. They might lock eyes, or simply nod hello, but that was enough to take the edge off the pain and fear that was gnawing away inside them.

There was a gentleman who had been there since Amber and Hope arrived on the unit. They hadn't exchanged a single word with each other – he often appeared lost in another world. Julian concluded he must be Muslim, as he would sit for hours mumbling Arabic prayers at the end of his baby's incubator. Sometimes the man would cry, which was heart-breaking to watch.

Just as in any community, they all kept an eye out for each other. If Julian or Tracy walked into the neonatal unit and saw that one of the other children wasn't there, their hearts would stop.

"What's happened?" Tracy whispered into Julian's ear as she spotted an empty incubator one morning. Her stomach clenched at the thought of a little life being taken away. Even though their main concern was Hope and Amber, they were all in this together.

"Wait here." Julian went to investigate.

Julian didn't feel comfortable asking the nurses if the baby had died, so he slipped out of the room to check the whiteboard. Above the nurses' desk was a list of all the baby names. His eyes scrolled down, willing baby Josephine to be alive.

Relief. There she was; she'd just moved to another room.

There was a system of four rooms, which the babies moved through as they became stronger. The neonatal intensive care unit was the starting line, and then came the high-dependency care room. The transitional care room was the end goal, where the baby went before it was ready to go home. Transitional care gave parents a chance to take care of the babies themselves, such as breast-feeding and changing nappies, but with the nurses still close by. It was only a matter of metres in distance from the start, but a milestone in terms of recovery.

Julian and Tracy couldn't believe it when the doctors announced that Amber was ready to move to the next room – she was leaving her sister Hope behind. Their progress was like racing cars: the twins were head to head, and then one would edge a bit in front, until one car took the lead. It made sense that it would be Amber; after all, she hadn't endured any of the complications that Hope had suffered in the womb.

Amber was going to be taken off the ventilator and put on a CPAP machine. Another mystery term for Julian and Tracy; they had been overwhelmed by medical words over the past few weeks.

"A CPAP machine will help Amber to breathe," the nurse explained. "Air goes in through a mask and gently inflates your baby's lungs and helps to keep them open."

Julian and Tracy looked at each other, bewildered.

The nurse smiled encouragingly. "This is positive progress," she said.

Julian and Tracy trailed behind as Amber's incubator was wheeled into the adjacent room.

"You'll be there soon," Tracy whispered to Hope on their way past.

But as quickly as their hopes were raised, they were torn down. Amber didn't even last a day out of the intensive care unit. And she never, ever returned to the high-dependency room.

Julian and Tracy didn't even need the doctors to tell them there was something wrong – they could hear an awful rasping sound every time their baby breathed in and out.

"It's called a stridor." The doctor explained the noise.

Any difficulty in breathing meant Amber was back on the ventilator; back in intensive care. Julian and Tracy were relieved their baby was still alive and hoped Amber would recover soon. But it was just the start of the problems.

The following day, Tracy was cradling Hope in her arms when all of a sudden the machines started screaming.

Bleep! Bleep! Bleep!

Half a dozen nurses appeared, building a human wall around Amber's incubator. Tracy didn't know what to do.

"What's happening?" she pleaded, scrambling to put Hope down.

There was another mum in the room, staring at Tracy with sheer horror, as if it were her own daughter.

Luckily, as quickly as the alarm sounded, it stopped. A registrar from Romania, called Irena, explained the drama away.

"Amber tugged the ventilator out of her mouth; babies do it all the time," Irena reassured Tracy. It transpired that Amber had pulled her tubes out several times before. For some reason it was difficult to get the ventilator back into Amber's airway, but luckily Irena seemed to have mastered the knack of it.

"It's like living on tenterhooks," Tracy told Julian later that day. "As soon as you think you're out of the woods ..."

"... A storm appears." Julian finished Tracy's sentence. They always did that; finish off what the other was thinking.

Tracy found it harder than usual to sleep that night – she felt a storm brewing. She tossed and turned. The neon glow of the alarm clock next to her bed was feeding her anxiety.

Ring ring. The phone bellowed. It was 2 a.m.

Tracy nearly jumped out of her skin. Julian sat bolt upright in bed.

They recognised the number – the same number they called first thing in the morning to check if the girls were okay.

"Hello?" Julian asked tentatively.

"Hi, it's Jess from neonatal."

Julian's heart dropped through his stomach. He'd gone from asleep to wide awake in a nanosecond. *This can only be bad news*.

"Amber's pulled out her ventilator again and we're struggling to put it back in," Jess said. He could hear the concern in her voice. "We're trying to get Irena to come in to help."

Then there was a long pause.

"But it's not looking good. Do you both want to come down to the hospital?"

"Come down to the hospital," Julian repeated. He knew what that really meant – it was a nice way of saying it was all over.

"Oh God, *no*." Tracy clasped her hand over her mouth.

Julian put the phone down and they both rushed around the bedroom throwing on the first clothes that came to hand.

Every day that they'd endured over the past six weeks had been a mixture of highs and lows, but generally they'd been thinking, *The twins are doing well, there's a chance*. This moment put it all into perspective. It knocked their legs from underneath them.

They practically skied down the staircase in the rush to get to Amber's bedside. Not a word was spoken, as they both knew talking about it would make it worse. The reality was, if the Romanian registrar couldn't get to Amber in time, their baby would die.

They were just pulling out of the driveway when Julian's mobile went off, breaking the deathly silence.

"Hiya, it's Jess again."

Julian's foot was frozen to the brake as he waited for the bad news.

"Just want to let you know that Irena has put Amber's ventilator back in."

He heaved a sigh of relief.

"Panic over, do you still want to come in?" she asked.

Tracy could hear every word of the conversation through the silence of the night. She nodded her head fiercely, indicating to Julian that she desperately wanted to see her baby.

Amber was fast asleep when they arrived, as if she didn't have a care in the world.

"You gave us quite a fright," Julian whispered. He glanced across the incubator at Tracy, whose hands were still shaking. Her body was racing with adrenaline.

"Is Irena here?" Julian asked after the registrar who had saved their girl's life. They wanted to thank her with all of their hearts, but she'd gone straight back to bed. The couple felt humbled by the human touch, how invested the staff were in saving those babies.

Although everything was back to normal, Julian and Tracy were fearful of leaving both Amber and Hope in case something else happened. The scare had knocked the wind out of their sails.

So much so, they couldn't find it in themselves to celebrate when Hope moved into the next room along. It was *her* turn to leave her sister behind and they couldn't stop thinking about the 'what if?'s.

"Why's this happening to us?" Tracy kept asking Julian.

Julian hadn't questioned anything, until now, because, as far as he was concerned, bad things just happened – he'd simply been grateful for every day the twins were alive.

He found it easier not to talk about the serious things, and tried to keep the mood light-hearted. If Tracy had a concern, Julian would always put a positive spin on it. If there had been an app for optimism, Julian would have been going up by a percentage each day.

But the scare with Amber's ventilator had left a chink in Julian's armour. He just didn't know it – until one afternoon when he was working on a job in Rugby.

Julian had finished for the day and was packing his tools into the back of the van. His mobile started going off – it was Tracy.

"What's happening?" he asked. Any phone call immediately made him think there could be an emergency.

"Everything's fine," she reassured him. They chatted for a bit and then Tracy broke the news.

"We all had to leave the room today …" she started.

Julian knew that something terrible must have happened because the nurses only asked the other parents to leave when it was serious.

"You know that man who's always praying …"

"Yes." Julian's stomach clenched; he instantly knew who she was talking about: the dad who had been with them since the start.

"His baby died."

Julian felt a tidal wave of sadness roll over him. Julian and this man hadn't said as much as one word to each other over the past two months, but they'd shared so much together.

For whatever reason, the news set him off. All that emotion, which had built up over the past weeks, came crashing down.

Julian broke down in tears by the side of the road.

He felt so sorry for the father and his child.

It could have been us, was the only thing he could think.

It could have been us.

Julian sobbed.

CHAPTER 5

Joy and Despair

Birmingham, September 2010

"What's that?" Julian pointed at a tiny glass figurine on Tracy's bedside table. It was only the size of a thumb; blink and you would have missed it.

"It's an angel." Tracy explained how her friend, Claire, had given it to her, to protect and watch over the family.

Neither Julian nor Tracy was religious. However, when bad things happen, it's human nature to want to believe in something. Often people become a little superstitious, adopting rituals that might bring about a change in luck.

Julian was cautious not to knock it off its perch from then on in. If he happened to be on Tracy's side of the room, he would always keep one eye on the angel.

Silly, really, he ticked himself off. But ever since it had arrived a month ago, things had being going okay with the girls, who were now – miraculously, it seemed – three months old. Hope had almost reached the final room and there had been no more scares with Amber.

Claire was one of many friends who had been checking up on them. They felt a bit bad for neglecting their friends but all their time had been devoted to the girls since the birth. As far as family went, both Julian and Tracy's mum, dad, brothers and sisters didn't live close by. Tracy's mum and dad were all the way out in Spain's Costa Brava. Debs lived down the road, though, and she had been visiting the twins whenever she could.

Debs was there when Tracy first tried Kangaroo Care – a technique used to strengthen the bond between a mum and her baby.

"That's adorable," Debbie giggled, as Hope was strapped to Tracy's naked chest – just like a joey in his mum's pouch.

Tracy felt like she had been wrapped in a warm cosy blanket. Hope's mouth opened and shut as the heat and purr of her mum's heartbeat sent her to sleep.

Pang.

There it was again – that feeling of guilt that kept poking her. Tracy felt guilty that she couldn't share these moments with Amber; that her other daughter was four rooms away, still strapped to a ventilator.

"Yes, she looks peaceful." Tracy smiled through her anxiety. The guilt was a secret she couldn't bring herself to share.

Debbie had played the role of 'Mum' for Tracy for the best part of their lives, partly because their parents lived abroad, but mostly for the support she gave Tracy while they were growing up. Their mum often left the sisters to their own devices. The experience had given Tracy a tough exterior. She found it difficult to show her emotions. She found it impossible to share her fears with Debs.

At first glance, you wouldn't have been able to tell they were sisters, as Debbie had long dark hair and Mediterranean skin, whereas Tracy was pale and freckly with red hair. Their height gave it away though, for they were both on the shorter side – Tracy was 4 foot 11 and that all-important half-inch, while Debs was not much taller at 5 foot 1.

Debbie gently stroked Hope's cheek. Hope was three months old now and almost double the size of Amber.

"Do the doctors know why Amber is struggling to breathe without the ventilator?" Debbie asked. Debs was much more direct than Tracy.

The conversation made Tracy nervous. Amber's difficulty breathing had been the elephant in the room ever since she had pulled her ventilator out in the middle of the night. They didn't have to wait long for an answer to Debs's question though. A couple of days later, Amber was sent in an ambulance to the Children's Hospital on the other side of Birmingham.

"She has a stridor, which means she's wheezing when she's breathing. Something is obstructing her airway so we need to investigate," the doctor explained.

They were going to insert a balloon into Amber's windpipe to see if they could stretch the airway.

It was more tests; more medical terms; more procedures for Julian and Tracy to absorb.

They waited nervously at Heartlands for the return of their baby. Julian was like a frog leaping between lily pads – he couldn't sit still. Every 20 minutes he would step outside the main entrance, watching the ambulances zip in and out.

"Come on, Amber, be on that ambulance," he muttered under his breath. The not knowing was killing them.

Four hours later, Amber returned to the neonatal unit. Julian and Tracy were guided into the family room next door. The walls were a pasty colour, decorated with wishy-washy pictures of seascapes. There were scuffmarks around the sides where the chairs had been moved about. It all looked a bit tired, a lot like how Julian and Tracy were feeling.

Julian leaned forward in his seat to get closer to the information the doctor had for them, as though doing so might help him to understand the unfamiliar terms.

"We dilated her airway," the doctor explained.

Tracy took Julian's hand.

"But I'm afraid it wasn't successful," he sighed.

Amber's airway had retracted almost as soon as it was expanded. Suddenly it was all making sense – the reason the nurses had struggled to get her ventilator back in was because her airway was tiny.

She's still alive though, Julian thought. However callous that sounded, it was the first thing that went through his mind – *she's still alive, that's the main thing.*

"So what now?" Tracy asked.

They were going to have to monitor Amber's breathing and go from there. Julian and Tracy had no idea where 'go from there' might lead. The past three months had been a blizzard of medical terminology that had largely gone over their heads.

What they did know was that Hope was almost ready to go home, and Amber was still in intensive care. Tracy had breast-fed one child but had barely been able to hold the other.

But whatever had happened in the past was nothing in comparison to what was to come. Their lives changed forever on the night of 13 September 2010.

Julian and Tracy were at home when they received the call – Amber had been rushed over to the Children's Hospital because the doctors were very concerned about her breathing.

It was back in the car, foot on the pedal, hearts racing at a million miles an hour as they rushed to be by Amber's side.

On arrival, Julian and Tracy were ushered into another white-washed, sterile-smelling room.

"Help yourself to a cup of tea or coffee." The nurse pointed to the tower of cups and saucers in the corner. Tracy poured a cup from the filter jug, which looked like it had been cooking for hours. It jolted her awake – not that she needed it.

It was stop, start, stop, start again.

A surgeon with thick, black-rimmed glasses glided into the room. He looked like he'd been on his feet all day; you could almost see *stress* etched into his forehead. He spoke quietly but with authority.

"We have to take Amber into surgery," he explained.

Julian and Tracy listened intently.

"I see Amber has had an Airway Balloon Dilation," he said, looking through his notes. He licked his thumb and turned the page.

"Uh huh, that's right," they said in chorus, in their gentle Brummie accents.

"We'll try that once more – but if that doesn't work she will probably come back with a tracheostomy," the surgeon went on.

"'Tracheostomy'? What's that?" they asked, baffled by the medical jargon.

"It's an artificial airway."

Which, again, meant absolutely nothing to the Austwicks.

"Ah, okay." They nodded quietly.

It was all so quick, so confusing. The doctor slipped out and Julian and Tracy were left trying to decipher what was going on.

"Well, as long as Amber is alive then that's all that matters," Julian stated.

Tracy nodded; she just wanted her girl back safely.

It was a long night for Julian and Tracy. Julian held his head in his hands while Tracy kept getting up to refill her cup of coffee. The hard chairs dug into their backs, reminding them of their uncomfortable situation.

Tick tick tick sounded the hands of the clock mounted above the door.

Tracy wanted to scream at it to shut up. Instead, she bottled up her anger, her frustration and her guilt.

By 9 p.m. there was still no news. There was no place for the couple to sleep, so the nurse insisted they go home.

"There's nothing you can do here, we will call you when we know a bit more." She guided them out of the family room.

They went home as she directed, but neither of them could get a wink of sleep – how could they? Julian sat up in bed, flicking through his vast collection of comics, while Tracy lay on her side curled tightly in a ball. She stared at the little angel looking down on her.

"Please let Amber be okay," she quietly prayed.

The warm glow of the streetlamps outside eventually changed into an autumn sunrise. Tracy sprang out of bed, raring to get going. She'd been like that all night, like a racehorse waiting for the starting gun. They decided to split themselves up – Julian would take a taxi to Heartlands to check on Hope, while Tracy would drive to the other side of Birmingham to see Amber. They hadn't heard any news; Tracy was stepping into the unknown, again.

Debbie was already at the Children's Hospital when Tracy arrived at the intensive care unit.

"Are you okay?" her sister asked tentatively.

"Yes, I'm fine," Tracy lied.

Debs arched an eyebrow as if to say "Really?", but thought it best to leave her sister for now.

It wasn't long before the doctors came to see them – and they had terrible news. Amber had been rushed into surgery for an emergency tracheotomy. They knew it was on the cards, but Tracy had been praying all night that her daughter wouldn't need an operation.

Tracy had no idea what to expect when they went to see her little girl. As they walked along the corridor, Tracy gripped Debbie's arm, as if she knew something awful was coming.

"It's going to be okay, isn't it?" Tracy begged her sister for reassurance. She had a swarm of butterflies in her stomach.

"Yes, everything is going to be alright." It was Debs's turn to lie.

They both steeled themselves for what was to come. The nurses guided them through the double doors into the ICU.

It was horrific – a jungle of machinery, wires, bleeping and nurses rushing around. Tracy had to block it all out and tunnel her vision to Amber's bed; it was the only way she could cope. As she walked up to her baby, she let out a gasp of horror.

Tracy turned away, shielding her eyes with her hands.

"It's okay." Debbie pulled her back.

Tracy slowly inched her head around. Peeled her fingers away one by one. Gradually adjusted herself to the heart-breaking sight.

Amber was barely recognisable. Her face was swollen and bruised and engulfed by a big tube sticking out of her neck. There was pus and blood oozing around it, spilling out from the hole that had been carved in her windpipe.

"What on earth have they done to you?"

Tracy burst into tears.

"It will be okay, it will be okay." Debbie tried to calm her sister, but Tracy was inconsolable.

She messaged Julian to come to the Children's Hospital immediately.

Is she okay? Julian texted.

Yes. She's had the operation. She's doing okay, Tracy replied.

Short sharp answers. She needed her husband by her side more than ever.

There was a rule of only two by the bedside in intensive care, so Debbie left to meet Julian in the family room next door. Her face said a thousand words.

"Don't be too alarmed," she said, as she gave Julian a hug.

Don't be alarmed. Her words had the opposite effect; Julian was feeling highly alarmed now.

"I think Tracy is a bit ..." She paused for a moment, as if carefully choosing her words. "... Tracy is a bit shocked." She tailed off.

Julian knew that was code for 'utterly distressed'. He had to throw on his battle armour and be ready for what was to come.

It was Julian's turn to have butterflies as he walked the long corridor to ICU.

Brrrrrr. There was the familiar grinding sound of the hand sanitiser. He rubbed the liquid through his palms and then pushed through the double doors.

The first thing that hit Julian was the size of the ward. He'd been used to the cosiness of the neonatal unit with its six incubators and staff that had become like family. Tracy had blocked out everyone around her when she'd arrived, but Julian was looking for answers from his surroundings. There was so much going on, however, that not a single answer came.

It was heart-breaking to see all these sick children in one room, and a lot of them were older kids, lying helplessly with tubes coming out of them in every direction. He couldn't see tiny Amber for the sea of sick kids.

Julian eventually spotted Tracy crouched over Amber's bed. Tracy spotted him coming, too, and pressed her lips together, forcing a small smile.

"Hi, lovie." He squeezed her shoulder.

It was a good thing Julian was standing over Tracy – because that way he could hide the tears rolling down his cheeks.

Oh Jesus, he thought.

The noise was almost worse than the sight of the wound. It was an awful rasping sound, like an old man who'd smoked cigarettes all his life struggling for breath – but this was the sound of his baby breathing. Combined with the thump of the ventilator pumping air into her neck, it was just horrific.

Her eyes were closed and looked like they'd been folded into her swollen face.

Although Julian was indebted to the doctors for saving Amber's life, it broke his heart to see her that way.

"Is she okay?" he asked the nurse hovering close by.

"Yes, the operation was successful. It's just a case of waiting for the swelling to go down," she explained, checking Amber's readings.

Julian was trying to be strong for Tracy, however much he wanted to burst out crying. But the tears came anyway. While the nurse was talking, helpless tears quietly slipped down his face.

He had no idea where they went from here. Would Amber be like this forever? Would she even be able to leave the hospital? Julian felt so overwhelmed; he had to step out for some air.

Debbie caught him on the way through. She grabbed his arm – he was in a world of his own.

"Are you alright?" she asked, sharing his pain.

"I … I … can't stand seeing her like that," he said, scratching the teardrops away with his sleeve.

There had been so much drama that morning; Julian hadn't even had the chance to tell Tracy the news that Hope was finally allowed to leave the hospital. It was a joy and despair at the same time – to have one of their babies coming home and the other in that horrific state. Julian couldn't get his head around it.

He ran his hands over his face, trying to rinse the stress out.

"There's so much we need to prepare before Hope comes home." He shook his head, as he counted up the items on the checklist in his head.

"I can stay here with Amber while you get on with it." Debbie stepped in.

It was a relief that Debs would be there to keep an eye on Amber. It was a horrible thing to admit, but Julian couldn't bear the thought of walking back into that room, not just yet. Seeing Amber like that had really affected him.

For Hope to come home, it was necessary for Tracy to spend the whole night with her in hospital, breast-feeding and looking after her under the watchful eye of the nurses. Debbie was across town with Amber, while Julian was at home, frantically preparing the nursery and zipping backwards and forwards to the supermarket to pick up nappies and anything else he'd forgotten on the last shop run.

The Austwicks had bought two cots for the spare room not long after they'd found out they were having twins, but had never got around to decorating with everything that had happened. The room was now a graveyard of unopened boxes and flat packs.

Julian crouched down on the blue carpet and began tearing off the Cellophane holding the chest of drawers together. It was strangely satisfying to immerse himself in the project. It took his thoughts away from what was really preying on his mind: *will Amber ever be able to come home?*

By the time he'd finished, it had just gone midnight. Julian rubbed his bleary eyes and rose to his feet to admire his handiwork. It was now looking much more like a room, but it was very sterile, just like the hospital wards he'd lived on for the past three months. He went through to their bedroom and unplugged a lamp from the wall.

That looks a bit more welcoming, he thought, after placing the lamp on the drawers and turning it on. The warm glow made it look a lot more like a nursery. Julian then clambered into bed and tried to switch off his brain until morning, when all his energy would be needed for the 'big day': Hope's homecoming.

Julian met Tracy at Heartlands the next morning. Apart from looking exhausted – Tracy had been up all night breast-feeding, after all – she seemed nervous.

"How are you doing?" he asked cautiously. He knew his wife didn't like being hugged or fussed over.

"Yes, I'm fine," she said, through a strained smile.

They had spoken to the nurses at the Children's Hospital already that morning, and Amber was recovering well.

"We'll check up on Amber later," Julian promised, hoping that might soothe Tracy's worries.

Tracy carefully threaded Hope's arms and legs into the white Baby-gro, and then rolled pink socks and pink slippers with embroidered butterflies over her tiny feet.

"Trace?" Julian tried to break Tracy's intense stare.

"Yes, I'm fine, that sounds good," Tracy fobbed him off. She didn't want to talk about *it*. She didn't want to address the fact she was leaving one baby behind.

It was an emotional moment lifting Hope out of her cot and strapping her into the car seat. The nurses gathered around, saying their goodbyes to their little friend.

"Bye, Hope, we'll miss you," they cooed.

The nurses had been like a family for Julian and Tracy – a crutch to lean on for support. It was daunting for the couple to think about how they were going to have to fend for themselves; and strange to think how they were only now doing the normal parent thing – three months down the line from the babies' birth. It was also weird to think that Hope shouldn't even be born yet – she was going home a week before her actual due date, which had been 15 September 2010.

Julian added the finishing touch to his little girl's outfit: a white bobble hat with rabbit ears to protect Hope from the brisk autumn air.

It took about three hours in total to prepare her for her departure, before they finally carried Hope to the car. Julian locked the car seat into place, and then gave all the straps a good tug to double check it was safe.

"She looks tiny in that big car seat," Tracy exclaimed, craning her head to look back at her baby.

She suddenly felt jittery – they had announced the homecoming to friends and family, and a mini celebratory gathering had been planned at their house for when they got back.

Apart from Debbie, no one had been able to see Hope yet because they had a strict visitors' rule at the neonatal unit. So everyone was gagging to meet her. Tracy's mum and dad had flown over at the last minute, especially.

"I'm dreading this," Tracy sighed, as she buckled up.

Julian tried to shake her out of her mood.

"Come on, lovie, it will be nice. I know it would be much better if Amber was with us too, but we should just celebrate this moment," he said.

They drove home in silence – not because they'd had a row, but because Tracy had gone into lockdown mode where she didn't want to discuss anything. When she wasn't turning back to check on Hope, she'd stare out of the window.

It was a grim overcast day. All the houses seemed grey and dreary as they snaked their way into the suburbs. Tracy's mood was getting darker and darker.

Her heart was pounding by the time they pulled into their drive. The outside light pinged on, illuminating a 'Welcome Home' sign across the door.

Pang. There it was again. The feeling of guilt was more like a blunt knife than a poke this time.

She spotted shadows milling around inside, getting ready to explode with excitement.

Tracy told herself off for being so grumpy. She threw on a smile, and opened the car door.

"Oh, she's adorable," Tracy's brother's wife, Kate, bubbled, as she peered through the car window.

"Make way, make way," Julian joked, as everyone bottlenecked in the doorway and then spilled onto the driveway.

There was Tracy's brother Lee and his wife, and their three kids – eleven-year-old Liam, Logan, eight, and five-year-old Ellie. There was Debbie, and her husband Lee, and young daughters Natalie and Olivia. Standing back from the throng were Tracy's mum and dad.

Everyone had made a real effort: scattered across the living room were cards, balloons … and nibbles like crispy cakes and sandwiches. It was exciting but, at the same time, a little awkward, because everyone wanted to hold Hope and Julian and Tracy were on high alert.

Julian's initial reaction was to worry about infection, and in particular he worried about the other children touching her. He braced himself, ready to jump in at any moment.

Hope was handed to Tracy's mum, Holly, next. Her mum was little, like Trace and Debs, and had a deep tan, as you would expect from anyone who had been living under the Mediterranean sun.

"Are you sure this is a good idea?" Julian whispered into Tracy's ear.

Holly had had a stroke not too long ago, and she was a bit shaky. Julian was worried she might drop Hope.

"It's fine." Tracy stepped in. She guided her mum over to the sofa and then carefully placed Hope into the crook of her mum's arm. Hope opened and closed her eyes, wriggled a little, and then went back to sleep.

Tracy wished she could be so relaxed.

Jab.

The feeling of guilt that she had left her other baby behind was now razor-sharp.

As lovely as it was to have Hope home, to have her family around her, Tracy couldn't enjoy the moment because Amber was still stuck in hospital.

Only two nights before, Amber had been through this horrific operation. The thought of her lying there helpless, a big green tube sticking out of her neck, was too much to bear.

Tracy put on a show of smiles for everyone, but she felt as if she wasn't even in the room, like she wasn't there. Half of her was still in the hospital at Amber's bedside.

For some reason, everything seemed dark. It was overcast outside but the living room appeared much gloomier than it should. Tracy was feeling all these conflicting emotions but she didn't know how to express them.

Julian glanced across the room at Trace. She was putting on a front that she was fine, but Julian knew his wife well and had an inkling it was time to usher everyone out.

"It's been a very long day, I hope you don't mind but we should really get some rest now." Julian handled the situation.

Everyone took it in turns to give Hope a little 'goodbye'. Tracy's mum and dad were the last to leave; they were staying up the road with Debbie. As soon as the last guest was out the door, Julian slumped back and gave a little sigh of relief.

Tracy was in the living room, laying out a blanket on the carpet for Hope.

However close they were, to get Tracy to open up about how she was feeling was really difficult. Julian suspected Tracy was doing the same thing as he was – trying not to talk about the problems in order not to make them worse.

Julian crouched opposite Tracy on the carpet and gave her a reassuring smile. Then he looked down at the blanket. Hope was wriggling around like a worm on the hook.

It was Julian's turn to feel emotional. It was the first time he'd thought about being an actual parent; they were now in the position 'normal' mums and dads would be in if they'd just had a baby – and it was daunting.

He looked at Tracy as if to say: "What do we do now?"

"She needs her nappy changed." Tracy grimaced a little, knowing she would be taking the honours for that duty, but at the same time it was lovely to be taking responsibility for her daughter in her own home.

Just before bed, Julian called the hospital to check on Amber. He was relieved to hear the swelling had gone down and she was adjusting well to her new airway.

Hope slept in a Moses basket alongside her mum and dad that night. Tracy would get up at regular intervals to breast-feed her and then slip back under the duvet for a few hours' rest.

It was just after 5 a.m. when Tracy found herself wandering into the twins' bedroom on the way back from the bathroom. The sun was threatening to rise, giving off enough light to illuminate the room.

Tracy stared at the two cots through her exhausted eyes. The tears that had been building up all day ran down her cheeks.

"You should both be here," she whispered.

She felt as if a piece of her heart was missing.

CHAPTER 6

Learning the Ropes

Birmingham Children's Hospital, Birmingham, Ten days later

"I've got this," Tracy said confidently.

Tracy carefully turned Amber over so she rested on her other side. The nurses were a little concerned Amber's skull was becoming misshapen because of her always lying in the same position.

Julian stood back and watched with admiration: Tracy was in control of the situation. Every day she'd check to see if Amber had been moved, and carefully do it herself if she hadn't been. Julian wasn't sure what had triggered the change in her mood, but it was clear that Tracy wanted to cope. However much she was struggling inside, outwardly she appeared to be juggling every demand.

They were far from out of the woods, but things did seem to be going better with Amber. It had been ten days since Hope had come home and, in that time, Amber had had her bandages removed and she'd been moved off intensive care, and given her own room on a children's ward.

The whole family – Julian, Tracy and Hope – came to visit her on Sunday, 22 September.

"Look who it is, Amber, it's your sister." Julian beamed as he lifted Hope out of the carrier and cradled her by Amber's side.

It was all going so well – and then Tracy's phone rang, breaking the peaceful mood.

"Hello?" Tracy answered quickly, to silence the ring. She listened intently.

And then her whole face dropped, like a wounded bird.

Julian knew what it was straight away. He could tell immediately from her expression that it was something to do with Tracy's mum.

She stepped out of the room, into the corridor, leaving the nurses and Julian to wonder exactly what had happened. Julian craned his ear to listen.

"When? What happened?" she spluttered.

Julian slowly put the pieces of the jigsaw together – Tracy's mum had died.

What a time for this to happen, he thought. However bad that sounded, all he could think about was Tracy, and how she'd been through enough as it was.

Julian was ready for his wife when she came back into the room. He held his arms out, beckoning her in for a hug. At first she was rigid like a board and then she slowly melted into Julian's warmth.

"My mum had another stroke," Tracy whimpered, still in shock, still coming to terms with the news.

Even though Tracy wasn't that close to her mum, it was still her mum, and it was still a massive thing to happen.

"I'm really sorry," Julian said. He felt so bad for his wife.

Tracy slipped out of the room again to call her sister. Julian kept one eye on the girls and the other on his wife. He picked up on a few keywords like 'feeling helpless', 'feeling guilty'. *That is so typical of Trace to blame herself*, Julian thought. Even though her mum had been a difficult woman to get along with, Tracy was beating herself up that she should have done more for her.

In those days before the funeral, Julian didn't get a lot out of Tracy. She didn't want to talk about her mum. There was never a point where she got upset and let it all out.

As far as Tracy was concerned, she simply didn't have time to grieve. There were so many other things to worry about with Amber and Hope. Julian had gone back to work to deal with the mounting pile of bills so she was left holding the fort. Her mind was one huge checklist, which she ploughed through every moment of the day. Having one daughter at home and the other across the other side of the city was a problem. Tracy turned her frustration into road rage.

"Get a move on!" she yelled at the car in front, as the rush-hour traffic snarled to a halt.

The traffic may have been slow, but her life was moving fast. Now, Tracy can barely remember her own mum's funeral. It was in Coventry, and they took Hope with them. Tracy remembers there being a few hymns and readings but she would struggle to tell you what they were. Julian kept a watchful eye – every so often he would glance across to see if she was okay. Typically, Trace didn't give a thing away.

But in fact, the same thing was happening as on the day they took Hope home – Tracy felt like she wasn't there. Her body was in the crematorium, but her mind was by Amber's bedside.

Tracy picked at a few ham-and-mustard sandwiches at the wake, and then she made her excuses.

"We've got to get back to the hospital," she apologised to Debs, her brother and her dad.

The car journey back to Birmingham was so tense you could have cut the atmosphere with a knife.

"So that was a nice service." Julian broke the ice.

There was no response. Tracy was a million miles away.

"Are you okay?" he checked in.

"Yes!" Tracy snapped back into the car. She pressed her lips together as if contemplating her next answer. "I'm absolutely fine," she lied.

From the second they parked in the hospital, Tracy switched into autopilot, picking up where she had left off. She sort of forgot about her mum dying, because she was concentrating on Amber, hoping her baby would get better.

The next two months were a seriously steep learning curve for Julian and Tracy. The couple studied the nurses' every move, taking mental notes about how to deal with Amber's tracheostomy.

What's that? Julian thought, looking in puzzlement at the long tube the nurses slipped through the hole in Amber's neck. It was a catheter – which was attached to a suctioning machine, which vacuumed out any gunk trapped in Amber's airway. The nurses would do this constantly.

And that? Tracy furrowed her brow at the green balloon-like thing that was attached to Amber's tracheostomy several times a day. That was a nebuliser, which melted the gunk in Amber's airway.

"Is it a bit like sticking your head over a bowl of hot water with Olbas oil in?" Tracy asked the nurse.

"Yes, I guess you could say that." The nurse smiled kindly at her naivety.

And that was just the start of it. There was the tube that snaked its way through Amber's nostril and down into her tummy. That was called a gastro nasal, or 'feed', through which artificial milk with extra vitamins and minerals would be dripped. And then there was the mountain of painkillers and antibiotics poor Amber had to take in order to stop her feeling the pain of the tracheostomy or catching an infection from the wound.

There was a time to do this, and a time to do that. It was all very confusing.

Julian and Tracy had only just got their brains around how things were done at the neonatal unit and now there was a whole new process for everything – even getting to know the different machines was a challenge in itself. It was like being rebooted and reprogrammed.

It was only a matter of days before Amber was coming home and they were going to have to take over from the nurses, and Julian and Tracy were petrified at the thought of all that responsibility on their shoulders.

After all, the way it was explained to them made it sound like the scariest thing in the world. The warnings were piled thick and high:

"You *must* make sure you wash your hands before you use the catheter. You *must* only put the catheter exactly six centimetres into Amber's windpipe, because if you insert it a millimetre deeper, it could close her lungs. You *must not* apply suctioning when you insert the catheter, only when you pull it out. You *must* suction for no more than fifteen seconds."

And then there was the Golden Rule:

"Don't *ever* go back into her windpipe with the same catheter," the nurse, demonstrating, stressed. Her eyebrow was arched fiercely, as she checked they were both listening.

"If you need to suction some more, put the catheter in the bin and use a new one."

"Okay, yes, got that." They nodded obediently.

"And how many times will we have to suction a day?" Julian asked the obvious question.

"It could be a hundred times a day, it could be five times, depending on if there are any blockages," the nurse replied.

"A hundred times," Julian and Tracy mouthed to each other in disbelief.

Julian and Tracy found the whole thing very serious and very frightening.

There was one rule they couldn't shake from their minds, very much like when the sonographer had told Tracy that her babies would be placed on her chest if they couldn't save them.

"You only have a 20 minute window to change the tracheostomy before the hole will grow over," the nurse warned.

Julian and Tracy looked at each other, gobsmacked.

They would have to change the trachy tube once a week, and if they somehow couldn't manage to do it in time, that was it: game over. Amber wouldn't be able to breathe. The stakes were sky high.

Just when they thought things couldn't get any tougher, they were called into the surgeon's office to discuss Amber's future.

Mr Kuo, the ear, nose and throat consultant, greeted the Austwicks with a firm handshake and signalled at them to take a seat. Julian did his usual thing of eyeing up his surroundings.

Not surprisingly, the office was as sterile as the hospital. The shelves were bare except for a collection of medical books, leaning against each other like dominoes. His desk was clear except for a neat pile of manila folders and a silver picture frame angled in such a way that only the doctor got to see who was special to him. Julian surmised that Mr Kuo spent next to no time in his office, except when snatching a much-needed cup of coffee. The deeply ingrained caffeine tidemarks on his mug and coaster gave the game away.

Though they'd had to navigate the hospital corridors to get there, the office couldn't have been far from Amber's room as the view through the blinds was the same – the Ronald McDonald House across the road.

Mr Kuo, who was Chinese, lifted his glasses onto his forehead and rubbed the tiredness from under his eyes. The conversation began with the paediatrician saying how pleased he was with Amber's recovery. Tracy felt herself tensing into a tight ball as she braced herself for the 'But …'

Up until now, all the Austwicks had known was that Amber was breathing out of this tube in her neck, which was under her voice box. They had been living from day to day, not looking towards the future.

"We just don't know if she will ever be able to speak," Mr Kuo delivered the heart-wrenching prognosis.

"What do you mean?" Tracy erupted.

The doctor explained there was a chance Amber's voice box might be damaged and, if that was the case, not even a speaking valve attached to her trachy tube would help.

"Will she need to have the trachy for the rest of her life?" Tracy pushed for more answers.

Mr Kuo leaned forward in his chair, sensing the rising tension. He cleared his throat and said: "We just don't know."

Little Amber would have to weigh at least 10 kilos before they considered her for another operation on her airway so, being barely a kilo and a half, it was simply out of the question for now. Plus, the chances of reversing the tracheotomy working were slim. Tracy had zoned out by this point.

"Will she be able to taste?" Julian stepped in.

The doctor clasped his hands together, his fingers knotted as if in prayer.

"I'm sorry, we don't know."

Tracy's stomach clenched like a fist. The thought of her baby girl growing up mute and with this 'thing' sticking out of her neck was unbearable. Julian was much more of the other school of thought – *Well, at least she's alive* – but for Tracy, it was a mother's worst nightmare.

Pang. There it was again, that nauseating feeling of guilt.

This is all my fault. Unfairly, she blamed herself for giving Amber 'a bad start to life'. Tracy swore there and then she would do everything in her power to 'fix' her baby; she made a promise to Amber she would look after her. The pressure she had just put on her shoulders would eventually show itself, of course, but for now, Tracy wanted to be Supermum.

She insisted on taking everything on her plate. In the final hours before Amber left the hospital, Tracy wanted to learn everything – even how to put the 'nasogastric tube' in.

"Oh God, I just don't fancy that." Julian hid behind his hands as he watched Tracy thread the tube through Amber's nose and down into her tummy. Before she could attach the milk, Tracy had to check the tube was in the right place by syringing some of the contents of the stomach out and checking its PH level on litmus paper. Julian scrunched up his nose in horror. It was fiddly, and almost worse than the trachy tube to cope with. It was a blessing that Tracy had pushed to get the hang of it, though, otherwise they would be driving back and forth to the hospital throughout the day and night.

There was one final test they both had to pass before they could take Amber home – changing the tracheostomy tube, twice. Julian could handle that because there was no 'gunky' stuff involved. The hole in her airway had healed into a tiny dark dot. Julian carefully slipped the curved plastic tube down the dark hole, the whole time watching Amber's facial expressions. If she squirmed a bit, he'd freeze.

"Keep going, it's fine." The nurse hurried him on.

It was a strange feeling, but Julian almost had to forget that Amber was his daughter for a moment, just to get the job done. He strapped the trachy in place and then gave her a kiss on her forehead.

"That wasn't so bad." Julian grinned proudly.

The nurse flashed him an awkward smile, as if she knew something he didn't.

Little did he know that his lesson was a summer's breeze compared to what was in store.

Amber was discharged from the Children's Hospital on 12 November 2010, six months after being born. Tracy couldn't wait to get her home, to finally have her girls together under the same roof. Poor Trace hadn't even been able to hold Amber in her arms since she'd had the tracheotomy because of all the tubes, drips and wires. The past three months had felt like a lifetime.

Preparing for the car journey home was a bit like doing a big supermarket shop. They had to do half a dozen runs, as they filled the boot with boxes full of catheters and medicines and tracheostomy tubes. They had enough to start a pharmacy.

"Oh my God," Tracy groaned, as she lifted the suctioning machine. Appearances can be deceptive, and the bright-yellow rectangular box weighed a heavy 8 kilos. They were going to have to carry that everywhere Amber went from now on.

"Come on, lovie." Julian took it out of her hands and placed it on the back seat of the car. From now on, one of them would always have to sit in the back with Amber, armed with the suctioning machine and catheters, just in case there was a blockage in her airway. Tracy sandwiched herself between the two seats – Amber on her right, Hope on her left.

"Look, Hope, your sister's coming home," Tracy said, smiling with happiness.

It was nearly dinnertime when they finally pulled into their driveway. After the drama of Hope's homecoming, they'd decided to keep Amber's under the radar. A quiet house awaited them and a nice cup of tea.

Julian set up camp in the lounge. He laid out a blanket and pillows for the girls and built a fortress of equipment and medicines around them. The Austwicks wanted to enjoy their first moment all together, but it quickly became apparent it was impossible to relax.

All they could think about was Amber's breathing.

If they heard even the slightest change, the smallest crackling noise, they unwrapped a catheter and suctioned. They must have been jumping to their feet at least every five minutes, terrified Amber might suffocate otherwise.

God only knows how many times Julian and Tracy had suctioned Amber's airway by bedtime. Julian was sitting on the floor with his back propped up against the sofa while Tracy lay by his side, guarding her babies. They were too scared to move upstairs in case anything got trapped in Amber's airway.

"Let's just sleep down here tonight," Julian said decisively.

Sleep was the magic word, of course, because they didn't get a wink of it. Every time their eyelids started to become heavy and roll down like shutters, they'd be shaken awake by Amber making a tiny noise. They spent the night in a bit of a daze, somewhere between being awake and dozing.

That night was a massive wake-up call for the Austwicks – how were they going to cope? They'd been taking so many notes in the hospital they hadn't actually realised the practicalities of caring for their baby, or the enormous responsibility involved.

Normal everyday things that they had taken for granted had now become a problem.

"When can you take a shower? When can you go to the toilet?" Julian questioned the next day. If Julian or Tracy was on their own with Amber, they literally couldn't leave the room. You couldn't go up and brush your teeth, you couldn't go out and make a cup of tea because you only had to turn your back for a moment and she could suffocate.

"How about we try putting Amber in her cot in our room tonight and have Hope next door linked up to the baby monitor?" Tracy suggested.

Julian nodded; he would have agreed with anything Tracy suggested by teatime, because the pair were utterly exhausted after a night and day of constant suctioning and zero sleep.

They both climbed into bed early but, within ten minutes, the process started all over again.

"I'll do it." Tracy jumped out of bed. Amber was closest to her side anyway.

"Maybe we are being overcautious about the suctioning?" Julian questioned.

Tracy tutted, loudly enough for Julian to hear.

"Well, it's better to be safe than sorry," she snapped. The tiredness and tension were getting the better of them.

"Here, I'll do it." Julian tried to appease the situation.

Tracy waved him off. She wanted to be Supermum.

They agreed to have 'shifts' throughout the night, whereby Julian would get a few hours' shut-eye, and then Tracy. Of course that didn't work, because the sound of the suctioning machine was so loud that even the soundest sleeper would have been kept awake.

By 6 a.m. the next morning, when Hope started to stir, Julian and Tracy were on the edge of reason. They felt hungover with tiredness and drama. It was obvious having Amber in their bedroom wasn't going to work. How could they function on no sleep? They wouldn't be able to look after Hope, let alone Amber, that way. Something needed to change.

"Okay, I'll be back in an hour," Julian announced.

"Where are you going?" Tracy panicked.

"The bed shop," he said, throwing on his jacket and snatching the car keys off the kitchen counter. Desperate times called for desperate measures.

It was the only thing Julian could think of doing – buying a single mattress for the twins' bedroom. Julian and Tracy were going to have to work alternate night shifts. He hated the thought of sleeping apart from his wife but it had come down to basic survival.

As money was becoming an increasing worry, Julian bought the cheapest thing from the local bed shop. Luckily it was delivered later that day and Julian volunteered to do the first night. He was going to need a lot of coffee and matchsticks to keep his eyes open as it was coming up to 72 hours without sleep.

"Stop worrying, lovie, I've got this." Julian gave Tracy a hug and a kiss. He then patted her in the direction of their bedroom, as he wanted her to rest.

"I know what I'll do," he muttered to himself. Julian dug up a mountain of his old comics and placed the pile next to the girls' cots. He switched on the side lamp and buried himself under a blanket. It was like being a kid again in a way, staying up late reading comics in a single bed.

Luckily for Julian, the cheap mattress worked a treat to keep him awake. Any time he rolled over, *boing*, another spring would eject into his side; *boing*, or into his bum. Also, being alone made him feel less panicky about Amber's suctioning. Perhaps they had been winding each other up a bit?

Luckily for the Austwicks, they had the dream baby in Hope: she slept through the engine-like noise of the suctioning machine.

Things weren't quite as peaceful next door. Tracy had been handed this gift of a night's sleep but, however she tried, she couldn't fall asleep. The faint grind of the machine made her panic. *Is Amber okay? Will Julian cope without me?*

She couldn't let go of the control. She needed to be there, managing the situation, being Supermum. She'd made a promise to her daughter.

As her eyes blinked in and out of consciousness, Tracy thought about moving the little angel to the girls' room.

"I don't need looking after," she whispered to the figurine. "You need to watch over them."

If you'd asked Julian and Tracy how they coped with the lack of sleep and with the responsibility of caring for Amber, suctioning her sometimes a hundred times a night, they would have both shrugged their shoulders and said: "We just did. We had no choice but to get on with it.

"When it's your child, you do anything for them."

They each discovered their own rhythm and routine. Tracy found it easy to stay awake through her shifts because she was so wired with adrenaline.

Her biggest fear was Amber pulling out her nasogastric tube when she was having a feed. Being a baby beginning to explore the world around her, Amber loved to tug on it, and the tube was particularly irresistible as it ran across her cheek – within perfect tugging reach. Amber would only have to pull on it the slightest amount – and it would be out of her tummy and onto her lungs. If it went unnoticed, she would drown in milk.

If she ever felt herself drifting off, Tracy rose to her feet and carried out little tasks, like folding clothes or tidying the room.

She would check there were enough catheters; she would make sure all the medicines were lined up. She'd always been a woman who did a little of everything, all of the time.

Tracy would of course peer into Hope's cot, to make sure her other baby was sleeping soundly, before returning to the badly sprung mattress.

One night, when she couldn't muster the energy to stand, Tracy sat beside Amber's cot and threaded her hand through the bars. She softly placed her fingers on Amber's tiny chest so she could feel it moving up and down.

Relief – her baby was still alive.

Tracy had never really understood what people meant by the phrase 'the sound of silence', until she experienced what it was like to be awake in the dead of night while all her neighbours, including her husband, slept soundly in their beds.

She felt so alone she could hear her own heartbeat.

Tears collected in Tracy's eyes. She had never thought being a mum would feel so lonely.

CHAPTER 7

Can't Hide the Scars

Sutton Park, Birmingham, July 2011

The sky exploded with an enormous thunderclap.

No one at the Donkey Sanctuary Riding Therapy Centre in Birmingham had foreseen the storm. It had been a beautiful summer's day in July 2011 but, within the space of half an hour, dark clouds had swept overhead and the air had turned thick and muggy.

"The rain is on its way," Andy Perry, whose job it was to look after the donkeys, shouted across the yard.

He was desperately trying to round up all 21 donkeys and get them into the stables before the heavens opened.

Worse still, they were expecting the arrival of Shocks at any moment.

"He couldn't be coming at a worse time," Andy panicked.

Another thunderclap rolled overhead.

The donkeys were jumpy, and the few staff who had stayed behind later than usual for Shocks had a job getting them to do what they were told. Zebedee, the only white donkey there, the leader of the pack, was dancing around the courtyard.

"Come here, you." Andy lunged at Zebedee's head collar. "I'm trying to keep you dry," he said, leading his stubborn friend into the stables.

The last lock was bolted just in the nick of time. The sky started to spit, and then *whoosh*, all of a sudden it was like someone had tipped a massive bucket of water over them all. The raindrops were firing down like gun pellets.

Andy threw his fleece jacket over his head and ran for cover inside the riding arena. The force of the storm was deafening as it hammered on the roof.

"That new donkey is going to be petrified," another Sanctuary worker, Nick, said to him, as he wiped his face dry with a hand towel. Nick had worked as a general handyman for the riding school for just over ten years. He was one of the 16 members of staff and 30 volunteers who made up the team in Birmingham. He'd spent the day fixing one of the broken fences, until the rain put paid to that.

Andy nodded, all too aware that not only did he have a thunderstorm to contend with, but also a much-mistreated donkey, who was arriving in terrifying conditions. Amber Brennan had filled him in on Shocks's heart-breaking story. She'd described what he was like when she'd visited him in Devon a year ago. She'd warned them they had a challenge on their hands.

Amber was there now to oversee Shocks's moving day. "We're going to have to get him inside as quickly as possible," she said.

Everyone nodded, as if they were SAS officers being given their brief before heading into a warzone. It *was* like a battlefield out there, though – the thunder and lightning was exploding; the rain was horizontal.

Ring ring. The shrill noise of the office telephone cut through the heavy air. Amber ducked into the office to pick it up. Everyone else craned their ears.

"Where are you?" Amber asked. It was the lorry driver transporting Shocks on the line. "Be careful coming down the drive because it's narrow. It will be treacherous in this rain." Amber reeled off instructions.

She reappeared in the office doorway, looking a little worried.

"He's just entered the park, won't be long now," she said, biting her fingernails nervously.

It was almost time for action. The team pressed their noses against the windows, looking for a sign through the torrential rain.

Then it appeared: two beams of light slicing through the storm. Andy, Amber, Nick and a couple of volunteers who'd been working that day braced themselves – and then they headed out into the storm.

The weather was vile. Andy thrust his hands into his pockets and hunched his shoulders around his neck, trying to protect himself from the rain. Everyone else's coats, which they'd used to cover their heads, flew into the air, like sails catching the wind on a stormy sea. Andy, along with Amber, waved wildly with both arms, trying to guide the driver down the narrow lane. The branches of the trees battered noisily against the top of the lorry, no doubt scaring poor Shocks even more.

"Stop! Stop!" Andy shouted, holding his hands up. The driver needed to reverse into the yard so they could let Shocks out.

Another lightning bolt lit up the sky, and then they were thrown back into darkness.

"I can't see a bloody thing!" the lorry driver yelled, craning his head out of the window.

Amber and Andy rolled their hands in a tumble-dry motion.

"Keep coming," they said, beckoning. The driver's hair was flapping in every direction as he tried to steer the huge lorry with half his body hanging out of the window.

The lorry finally screeched to a halt and the team ran to lower the ramp. They knew Shocks would be tethered, but they didn't know what state he would be in. Andy prepared for the worst.

The ramp crashed down onto the concrete. Another huge thunderclap rolled overhead. Shocks was pinned to the back of the lorry, hidden in the shadows.

"I'll go!" Andy shouted over the noise, cautiously making his way up the ramp.

Andy knew everything there was to know about donkeys. He'd been working with them on farms since he was twelve years old, and he was now in his late twenties.

"Easy, boy." He inched forward.

Shocks was shivering with fear; thrashing his tail; thumping his hind legs.

"That's it, easy, boy." Andy edged closer, and closer.

It was like a dance – Andy took one step forward and Shocks took one clop back. Luckily he was tethered so he couldn't go far.

Andy took a leap of faith and lunged to grab his head collar. Shocks tried to rear onto his hind legs, but Andy held on tightly.

"Steady, steady." He spoke in his calm and soothing way.

Everyone else was poised at the end of the ramp, ready to jump in if needed.

Andy clipped the lead rope onto the collar and started to coax Shocks out of the lorry. The ramp was now soaked with rain and treacherously slippery.

"Be careful," Amber shouted.

Shocks's hooves were slipping in all directions. Another lightning bolt exploded. Shocks dug his heels in. He tried reversing up the ramp but his legs fell away from under him.

"Where do you think you're going?" Nick grabbed hold of the rope. Together, Nick and Andy pulled Shocks off the ramp and into the yard.

"Oh thank God," Amber said, guiding them to safety.

Once out of the lorry, Shocks gave up the fight, and followed Andy into the riding arena. His big purple rug was soaked through and needed to be taken off immediately.

Now, Andy knew from experience that the first thing most donkeys would do after having their coat taken off was to roll around in the sand. They'd have had a good scratch to celebrate their freedom.

But Shocks didn't want to know. The poor thing was trembling. He was frozen to the spot.

"I think he's gone into shock," Andy panicked.

Amber joined Andy in the arena and they stood back against the wall, assessing the situation.

They could have a good look at Shocks now he was under the bright strip lights.

"God, he's massive," Andy exclaimed in his Dudley accent.

Shocks was the biggest donkey the riding sanctuary had ever seen. He was almost the size of a horse. Andy was concerned about his hooves – for they too were massive and could do a lot of damage if he became scared and started kicking.

"What do you think we should do?" Andy looked to Amber.

"Can we get him another rug?" Amber called out to the others, who were waiting behind the gate. A volunteer scurried off to get one.

"The first thing we need to do is get him dry and warm," she said, even as she shook the water from her own hair.

That was typical behaviour from the riding team – always putting the donkeys and the children they helped before themselves.

Andy slowly approached Shocks with the new rug. Shocks wasn't putting up a fight this time; he was glued to the spot, shivering with cold and fear. His eyes were wide like saucers. His big ears were pricked and facing Andy – listening to every footstep.

"Good boy," Andy purred, as he slowly teased the rug over Shocks so as not to scare him.

"We'll keep him in here tonight," Amber announced, after watching this performance. She'd usually pair up a 'new arrival' with another donkey, down in the stables, but it was clear that Shocks was in no fit state to move anywhere.

"I don't mind staying with him." Andy volunteered to take the night shift. He was really worried about the poor animal.

After the others had left, Andy wrapped a blanket around his own shoulders and bedded down for the night in the arena.

He could tell Shocks appreciated the company – because he stayed close by. Donkeys do sleep lying down, but Shocks was far too nervous for that. It must have been incredibly disorientating for the animal to board the lorry in sunny Devon and then appear, 170 miles later, in stormy Birmingham. It must have been scary to be around all these new smells too.

As if Shocks was reading Andy's mind, he rolled his top lip back, which is a donkey's way of taking in the scents.

"You can smell all the other boys, can't you?" Andy chatted to him in a soft tone.

Shocks let out a giant sneeze, which shook his whole head.

Andy grinned. He took that as a 'yes'.

Now they were out of the rain, he could see his new friend had a lot of distinct features. The fur on his face was very fluffy, and he had a soft white muzzle that curved in a heart shape around his nose. Andy found his 'Mohican' – which was where his mane tufted out between his ears – particularly endearing. Shocks had this way of looking up through his long lashes, making his eyes very soulful.

As he lowered his head to the ground, Andy sensed that Shocks carried the weight of the world on his shoulders. He could see the scars of his past peeping out from under his blanket.

"Why have they sent you here?" Andy shook his head, bewildered at headquarters' decision to send their worst-ever case of neglect to their therapy centre.

Every week, 200 children with special needs come to the Assisted Therapy Centre in Birmingham to ride the 15 donkeys that have been cherry-picked for their gentle nature. The healing qualities of the animals have been proven time and again. However, rescue donkeys are not usually good with visitors or children, because they are too timid, too damaged – so Andy didn't know what he was going to do with Shocks.

"You've had a tough life, haven't you, fella?" Andy whispered. He had this special way of connecting with donkeys; he could almost feel their pain.

Andy must have drifted off – he was woken by the light streaming through the big glass windows and the raucous whistling of the birds. Shocks was standing in exactly the same spot. He'd been watching over Andy while he slept.

"Morning, Shocks." Andy smiled, lifting his thick black-rimmed spectacles and rubbing the sleep from his eyes. Andy always chatted to the donkeys. He'd have long – one-way – conversations with them sometimes. It was reassuring for the donkeys to hear a softly spoken voice as they were being groomed. When Andy was in a silly mood, he liked to impersonate accents – such as speaking to the Irish donkeys in an Irish accent. He'd never do that to Shocks, though, because he didn't want to bring back bad memories of his terrible life in Ireland.

"Did you have a good night's sleep?" Amber breezed into the arena.

"I've had better," Andy said, dusting himself down and getting ready for the day ahead.

You have to be an early riser to work at the Sanctuary – the donkeys are let out into the paddock not long after sunrise. Breakfast is a net full of hay, which they pull to pieces within minutes. You'd think they'd never been fed in their lives the way they ravage it.

The Sanctuary in Birmingham is one of six riding therapy centres in the UK. However, it is the only one to have all male donkeys. This was a decision made by the manager, Sue Brennan – Amber's mum – when they first opened in 1994. Even though all the boys are gelded, introducing female donkeys would have been too much of a 'distraction' and encouraged the boys to misbehave. Why all boys instead of all girls? Sue felt male donkeys were more up to the job, but that was a personal preference and not scientifically proven!

Having all boys meant that the paddock turned into a school playground – with the most popular boys, the naughty ones, the cheeky ones, the ones who get egged on by others, and the quiet ones.

But Shocks wasn't any of the above. He was a loner from Day One.

The first thing the team always did when a new donkey arrived was to immediately introduce him to the whole herd. To everyone, that is, except for the 'bosses'.

The three bosses were King, Mackenzie and Zebedee. You knew they were top of the pecking order because they were always the first to the hay nets in the morning, and the first ones to go into their stables at night.

If Andy were to scatter apples and carrots across the yard, you could be sure the Three Musketeers would be first on the scene. They also wouldn't be shy about telling the others to back off. "This is my food," they would say, with a kick here or a nip there.

They were the most confident and assertive donkeys and would have been sure to intimidate Shocks. That was the last thing he needed after his years of suffering. Shocks would eventually meet the leaders of the pack, but slowly, one by one.

As soon as Andy let Shocks out into the paddock, he kicked up his heels and ran for the furthest possible corner. And that's where he stood for the rest of the day – tucked away on his own, leaning against the wooden pillar of the field shelter, as if it was his crutch.

"Let's bring him into the ménage with some of the other donkeys," Sara Gee, the riding instructor, suggested.

"No," Amber said, looking out across the field. Shocks's head was down, his eyes were half closed; he clearly just wanted to disappear into the background.

"Let's leave him. Let him get his head around where he is," Amber insisted.

Of course, there was the little problem of bedtime. Shocks didn't want to be around any of the other donkeys, but there wasn't enough space to offer him a stable to himself.

"I think we should put him in with Jacko," Andy suggested. His reasoning being that Jacko was a quiet sweet donkey, who wouldn't say boo to a goose. The perfect stablemate for a donkey as fragile as Shocks.

They never had to worry about remembering it was bedtime at the Sanctuary – the donkeys let the staff know. Come 5 p.m., the more noisy boys, like Tony, always started braying as if to say: "Hurry up, I want my hay and bed!"

The sound of Andy sliding the paddock gate open was enough to cause a stampede. The cheeky boys galloped towards the stables, playfully nipping each other's necks and tops of legs on their way through.

What's more, they all knew where they needed to go without any prompting. The well-behaved ones, like Jacko and Rambo, would quietly make their way to bed. Whereas the naughty boys, like Zebedee and Bob and Lob, would always try it on.

"Out of there, Zebedee," Andy scolded the white donkey for sneaking into Mackenzie's stable. He was just being greedy – trying to get a few extra mouthfuls of hay somewhere else first. It was the same drama every night, but the place wouldn't be the same without the little terrors.

Andy looked back across the paddock. Shocks was still there, pressed against the fence.

"I'll get him," Amber volunteered. Although Andy had spent the night with Shocks, he'd quickly noticed how Shocks was more nervous around him and the other male staff than the women. Amber was right to go and fetch him; she'd probably have more luck attaching the lead rope to his collar.

Shocks didn't resist Amber, but he trailed behind her, much like a beaten dog with its tail between its legs. Shocks had his ears pricked but his head was down. It was like he didn't want anyone to notice him – he wanted to slip away quietly into nothingness.

"Well, I'm afraid you're not going to be alone tonight, we've found you a friend, my boy," Andy said, holding Jacko's stable door open for him.

Jacko, who was brown all over, and petite in comparison to big old Shocks, looked up from 'his side' of the stable. He had white eye rings which made him look like he was wearing glasses.

Jacko cocked his head as if to say: "Hello there."

Shocks gingerly slipped through the stable door, and positioned himself as far away from Jacko as he could get.

"He won't hurt you, he's as soft as anything," Andy reassured.

Jacko didn't bat an eyelid at his new friend. Instead, he stretched out his long tongue and took a lick of the mineral bar hanging from the back wall. The bar is the equivalent of a lollipop to a donkey; only it doesn't contain sugar, but is packed full of nutrients.

Jacko was six years old when he came to the riding centre in 2009. He had lived with goats on a farm in Kent, but sadly had to leave when his owner became too poorly to look after him. He was one of the 'quiet' lads, and you'd always find him grazing with Rambo – his best friend.

Shocks rolled his lip back to take in the smell of his new stablemate, and then bashfully turned his head the other way, to face the corner.

"I think he's just shy." Amber leaned over the stable door.

I hope you're right. Andy kept his thoughts to himself. He'd never seen a donkey be so standoffish, so damaged by his past.

Andy's concerns were cemented the following morning, while carrying out the simplest of tasks.

He let the donkeys out into the paddock as usual, leaving Shocks and Jacko until last.

"So you've managed not to kill each other overnight," Andy joked, peering over the stable door. Jacko was already under Andy's nose, raring to get out and have a good roll and a scratch. Shocks looked as if he hadn't moved. He was still facing the corner, like a naughty schoolchild who'd been punished for misbehaving.

"Time to get some fresh air, my boy." He opened the sturdy wooden door. It was another beautiful summer's day out there. The dew was shimmering across the grassy paddock. *It must look very juicy to a hungry donkey*, Andy thought.

Shocks was in no rush to have his breakfast though. He hung back while Bob, Lob, Jacko, Christopher and all the other boys raced towards the hay and carrots.

Meanwhile, Andy grabbed the hose to fill up the water trough – the donkeys always liked a good slurp to wash their food down.

But as soon as Andy raised the hose – Shocks bolted.

"I'm not going to hurt you," Andy cried after him. It was too late; Shocks had sprinted across the paddock. He could see the poor donkey was trembling with fear.

"What did they do to you?" Andy shook his head with frustration and sadness.

He heard the crunching of boots on gravel as Amber came up behind him.

"Just let him be, he'll come around," she said confidently. The pair rested on the gate, their chins tucked into their arms as they stared across the field.

"The kids are arriving, time to get the donkeys saddled up," Amber instructed. The donkeys take it in turns to have their day in the arena. They love being around the children so it's a real treat for them to be called up for duty. It was Moses and Oscar's turn to take the reins that morning.

Andy and the rest of the team did as Amber suggested – they left Shocks alone. It seemed to work; after several weeks of putting him through the same routine, day in, day out, he became a little less frightened.

Instead of bolting when he saw the hose, he ran for a bit, stopped, looked back, ran a bit more.

"See, it's not going to hurt you." Andy held the hosepipe openly in his hands. The worst thing he could have done was hide the hose behind his back, because Shocks would then think there was a good reason for him to be scared of it.

It was a form of 'breaking him in', you could say. Andy was slowly, but surely, getting Shocks to come around to the idea that Andy wasn't going to hurt him.

The next time Andy filled up the trough, Shocks simply walked away, swishing his tail. He looked over his shoulder and cocked his head. *Maybe you aren't going to hurt me?*

"That's it, boy, it's just a hose." He held it out again, as an offering.

Shocks did a half turn so he was now facing Andy. His long furry ears were pricked up, twitching to every sound. He lifted his left hoof to make a move, and then thought better of it.

"Come on, Shocks, it's not going to bite," Andy egged him on.

Shocks took a few steps towards Andy. Then he stopped – he didn't want to come all the way. They could have been playing Grandma's Footsteps. It was a painstakingly slow process, but at least they were making headway.

"You're coming a bit closer today, you are getting used to it," Andy murmured with a smile. "I told you it would be alright: we are not going to hurt you here."

Shocks stared back at Andy, as if to say: "You're not that scary after all."

It was an incredibly rewarding feeling to see these changes. It made all their hard work at the Sanctuary worth it.

Andy had been a keeper at Dudley Zoo before he joined the Sanctuary. Although he loved caring for the wild and exotic animals there, nothing quite compared to the donkeys. They were so cute and lovable – and yes, they could be stubborn at times, but that just made them even more endearing.

He arrived for work the next day with a spring in his step. He greeted the boys with a cheery "Good morning!" as usual, before letting them out for breakfast. He then grabbed the broom as it was time to sweep out the poo from the field shelter – a covered area in the paddock where the donkeys could get some respite from the scorching sun. It was also Shocks's favourite leaning post – where he could watch the others from afar.

Andy marched out without a second thought. Shocks took one look at the broom – and bolted like lightning. There was no stopping, no turning back; the poor thing was utterly terrified.

"Oh, Shocks," Andy sighed helplessly.

Shocks couldn't even look at Andy. His eyes were lowered as if he was preparing for a beating.

Andy could almost feel his pain. Amber had shown him the pictures of Shocks's injuries and they were now flashing through his mind. *How could anyone be so blind to an animal's suffering? Does Shocks think his life will always be that painful?*

The staff had learned to cut off their feelings about the donkeys' pasts in a way; they had to, or else they'd be in tears most of the time. However, Andy was finding it very difficult to detach himself this time. He felt overwhelmed with sadness.

If he's this scared of a broom, how is he ever going to cope when we ask him to walk over massive poles in the riding arena, or allow children close to his neck injuries?

"Oh, Shocks, why have they brought you here? Why are we putting you through all this when you have already been through so much?" Andy shook his head in despair.

CHAPTER 8

Worlds Apart

Sutton Coldfield, Birmingham,
Spring 2011

"I'm going to have to give up my job." As he said the words, Julian shook his head in despair.

There was no way Julian could carry on looking after Amber through the night and do a full day's work. There was not a chance in hell that he would allow Tracy to pick up his slack, so he was going to have to do the unthinkable in his eyes – ask for help.

Julian hated the idea of not being able to provide for his family; it went against every fibre in his body, every principle he was raised by: You're the man, you work hard and you provide for your family. The thought of claiming benefits made his toes curl.

He slumped back into the sofa and closed his eyes for a moment, letting the sea of tiredness wash over him.

"We'll be fine, we'll manage," Tracy said. Always the practical one, forever optimistic, no matter how much she was struggling inside.

He felt the warmth of her hand cup over his as she gave him a reassuring squeeze. It wasn't like her to reach out to him. There was more.

"I feel bad for saying this …" she started.

"What's up, Trace?" Julian tried to make it easier for her to open up.

She looked at Amber and Hope, who were on the mat. Both the girls were on their backs in their matching pink-and-white Baby-gros. They were dressed the same but, at eight months old, they couldn't have been more different. Hope was wriggling around like a fish, reaching her arms out for something to hold onto. Her eyes were bright and searching. Amber, on the other hand, was completely still. Her pretty blue eyes were like glaciers – cold and distant. It was like the lights were on but nobody was home.

"It feels like we don't have twins, but two completely different children," she explained. "It feels like I'm a mother to one, and a carer to the other."

Tracy looked away to plug her rising tears.

Julian nodded understandingly, and admitted he felt exactly the same.

There was something else plaguing Tracy, but the words were caught in her throat. She felt so mean even for thinking it.

I feel closer to Hope than Amber, she thought.

"Trace?" Julian tried to break into her reverie.

Tracy smiled tensely. It was her guilty secret she could never share.

The uncomfortable moment was broken by the familiar crackling noise of Amber's clogged airway. Tracy dived to her baby's side, unwrapped the catheter, and suctioned Amber back to safety.

That was the problem – whenever Tracy touched Amber, it wasn't to hold her or cuddle her, it was to do something medical, be it suctioning her, changing the trachy tube, putting on a feed, giving her a nebuliser, wiping sick away. It was like being a nurse in a hospital tending to a sick patient.

It was relentless.

And then there was Hope, who didn't need any medical attention.

What made the gap even larger was the fact that Tracy had never been able to do the normal motherly bonding things with Amber. She hadn't breast-fed her, she hadn't held her over her shoulder and patted her back to gently 'burp' her. She rarely cradled Amber in her arms and cuddled her, for all the tubes and wires.

In many ways, Tracy just didn't have time to cuddle Amber because she was too busy caring for her. But what broke Tracy's heart more was the fact that it was becoming startlingly obvious that Amber didn't even *want* a cuddle; she just wanted to be left alone.

"You can see it in her eyes," Tracy said to Julian one morning after coming off the 'night shift'. "She just doesn't want to know. I think she's had so many people prodding her, sticking needles and tubes into her, that she just wants to be left in her cot."

Julian tried to reassure his wife, but he had noticed the same thing himself. It seemed more important than ever that he support both Tracy and the girls by giving them more of his time. Even though he found it difficult, he took himself off to investigate what he needed to do in order to claim the benefits to which the family was now entitled.

In the end, Julian was pleased to find that receiving some financial help from the government wasn't quite the mission he thought it might be. The Citizens Advice Bureau in town had pointed him in the right direction, and they were now in the system, being processed. That was one huge problem on the way to being solved, but it didn't help the other problem of how they both desperately needed a break from 'caring'. Tracy's words – coming from a woman who found it so difficult to express her worries and fears – were a deafening sign that things were starting to get too much.

Julian thought back to Amber's discharge meeting at the hospital six months earlier. Mr Kuo had warned them the aftercare would be challenging. He'd offered them help in the form of 'Complex Care' – whereby a nurse would look after Amber for 15 hours a week.

"Nah, we'll be fine." Julian and Tracy had shrugged him off at the time.

The thought of it now was like a slice of heaven. Julian grabbed the phone and called the hospital. *There is nothing wrong with admitting you can't cope, that you need a bit of help*, he reassured himself.

The carer had to change Amber's trachy tube twice before she was allowed to look after her – the same test Julian and Tracy had had to pass all those months ago. The respite was to be divided in two parts – one 12-hour night shift and three hours rolling over for another day in the week.

Karen arrived at their house at 8 p.m. on the dot and gave them a big friendly smile. She must have been in her early twenties, Julian guessed, noting her young age with concern. He hated himself for judging her, but it was the first time they were letting Amber out of their sight – and with, essentially, a stranger. Tracy shot him a glance to tick him off. She knew him too well.

They showed Karen upstairs to the girls' room and ran through where everything was kept. Karen nodded sweetly, like she was used to placating nervous parents. She tucked a strand of her short dyed-black hair behind her ear as she peered into the box of medicines they showed her.

"And we've written a list of everything you need to do." Julian pointed to an A4 sheet of paper which was scrawled with notes from top to bottom.

Karen smiled sweetly. "Don't worry, everything is under control." She herded them towards the door.

Julian and Tracy made their way down to the kitchen, doing their best to let go. Sandwiched between the fridge and the microwave, they looked at each other as if to say: "Well, what now?"

It was a night off; the first time they would be sharing a bed together after months apart. They both felt the uncomfortable pressure to perform.

"I guess we should be doing something special?" Julian said sheepishly.

They both desperately wanted to enjoy their respite, but it was almost impossible for them to surrender Amber's care to a stranger. Plus, they still had Hope to look after – Karen wasn't legally allowed to keep an eye on Hope, even if she was in the same room as her sister.

"Shall we order a takeaway and watch a film?" Julian suggested.

"Good idea," Tracy said, pulling the menus from the pinboard.

They nestled into the sofa as they waited for the delivery from the local Chinese. Tracy cuddled into Julian and buried her head into his chest. Just as her tired body started to relax, she felt Julian's brace. He'd caught the faint sound of the suctioning machine.

"She'll be fine." Tracy pinned his body back into the soft sofa.

Tracy may have been cautious with her feelings, but it was Julian who'd become overcautious when it came to the girls. He was up and down the stairs like a jack-in-the-box over the next couple of hours, peering his head around the door.

"Everything okay?" he asked Karen for the umpteenth time.

Julian was relieved when they finally got to bed, as they were much closer to Amber that way. He admitted it was nice to have

Tracy back in his arms after all those nights alone. They locked eyes and then burst into giggles.

"I know; I'm tired too," Julian chuckled. They couldn't muster the energy for anything more than a cuddle.

They slept in each other's arms, turning and tossing whenever they heard the vacuuming noise. If Tracy strayed too far across the bed, Julian would pull her back into him.

It was a huge relief for the couple to wake up knowing they had an extra three hours' respite in the week. They chose to use it a couple of days later – but not on themselves. Both Julian and Tracy were starting to worry they were neglecting Hope for all the medical attention they needed to give Amber.

"I think we should use the time to focus on Hope," Tracy said, her guilt rising again.

She lifted Hope into her arms and carried her to the car. They were going on a family trip to the local supermarket. It was far from exciting, but life had become like a circus act – juggling a million and one things at a time – and the normality of the shopping trip was just what they needed.

Hope loved her ride in the shopping trolley. Her head rolled from left to right as she took in the bright colours of the fruit and vegetable aisle. She stretched out her little arms to try to touch them, even though they were far out of reach.

They were only small things, but the differences between the twins were becoming obvious. Hope wanted to see the world, whereas Amber didn't want to know. Hope wanted to reach out and touch things, unlike Amber, who wanted to crawl into her shell. Julian shrugged it off as symptomatic of the difficult birth. Tracy wasn't convinced; she had a terrible inkling something else was wrong.

She locked her worries in a box for a while as the next few months whooshed past in a blur of trips to the hospital, night shifts, mini panics about blockages, more to-ing and fro-ing to the hospital for check-ups. They barely saw any family or friends because their life caring for the girls was all-consuming. Even if Debs, or Tracy's friend, Claire, suggested popping over, Julian would have to grill them about their wellbeing.

"You've got a bit of a cold, did you say? Maybe we should just leave it for now," he'd tactfully decline. A cold would spell disaster for Amber's airways; they couldn't risk it.

It was only when Tracy's nan, Irene, offered to pay for them to go to Pontin's for a beach holiday in Brean in July 2011 that they considered breaking their rigid routine. The girls were now eleven months old.

Up until now, the only time they had left their quiet cul-de-sac in the past seven months was to go to either the hospital or the supermarket. They'd become like prisoners in their own home.

Tracy jumped at the chance to get away.

"We need this break," she pushed.

Tracy desperately wanted them to do the 'normal' things other families did. She wanted them to try at least; she fiercely wanted to 'cope', however hard things were. She had her Supermum cape on again.

Julian clenched his jaw as he weighed up the situation in the cautious manner he'd adopted of late.

"I just don't know," he hesitated, thinking about what a mission it would be to pack and unpack all the medical equipment. How scary it would be not to have the hospital nearby.

"I'm booking it." Trace had the final word.

It was a brave thing to do, especially considering the four-hour car journey there was a minefield of danger in itself. If Amber were to have a serious blockage when they were stuck in a motorway jam, what would they do? Tracy pushed through. She sat in the back seat with all the suctioning equipment while Hope slept in the front in her car seat.

Luckily, Amber's airways ran clear for most of the way. Both Julian and Tracy felt a huge sense of achievement when they pulled into the resort car park. *Yes, we've made it.*

The room was basic, but it was away from home, and that was all that mattered right then, particularly for Tracy. It took several runs to unload the boot, which was brimming with machines; and extra machines in case the first lot failed. Julian laid them out across the bedroom with military precision.

Going to the beach was an even bigger military operation because they had to carry the 8-kilo suctioning machine over their shoulder, plus all the extras. Julian wished he were wearing some actual army trousers as they pushed the buggy along the promenade, so that he might have somewhere to clip and hang all the catheters and machinery.

There was no turning back, though; Tracy was determined to have a day on the beach with her family. She bought a red plastic castle-shaped bucket on the way.

"Here: something else to add to the load," she laughed, handing it to Julian.

It was a scorching hot day and the beach was jam-packed with tourists. You couldn't see the sand for all the garish beach towels and stripy windbreaks. But the noisy crowds didn't spoil it for the Austwicks.

"It's good to be out of the house." Tracy gulped the sea air like a cool iced drink.

The family chose a spot not too far from the main concourse. They parked the buggy and set up a little camp on the sand, much like they always did on their living-room floor.

"Have a look at this, Hope, it's the sea," Julian chirped. He pretended to fly Hope like an airplane, landing her on the blue-and-green tartan rug.

Julian and Tracy both looked back at Amber, who was still in the buggy.

"She looks sad," Tracy said glumly.

"We can't get her out, lovie, because the sand might get in her trachy," Julian reasoned.

It was yet another double-pronged moment of happiness and despair at the same time – happy that they were all together on the beach, but sad because Amber couldn't join in.

Julian unfolded a towel and draped it over the buggy like a veil. Just in case a gust of wind swept some sand in Amber's direction.

"Let's make some sandcastles." Julian tried to lift the mood.

As Tracy watched Julian dig around in the sand like a big kid, and Hope trying to crawl over to him, she was hit with that gnawing feeling – something wasn't right.

Why isn't Amber behaving like her sister? All she wants to do is lie on her back and stare into space. The twins were now thirteen months old, but they may as well have been six months apart in development.

However hard she tried, Tracy couldn't kick the feeling over the next few days. The differences between the girls became even more obvious to their mum now they were away from their safe house.

Julian was fighting his own demons on that holiday. It was a huge struggle looking after Amber in their own home, let alone in a strange environment. They were also back to square one with their insomnia. Sharing the same room meant both Julian and Tracy were awake throughout the night. He couldn't wait to get back to his tried-and-tested routine.

They were a little bit ratty with each other as they packed the mountain of things back into the car, but that soon passed as they whizzed down the motorway. It had been their first big test to see if they could be a normal family. Had they passed or failed?

"I am happy to be going home," Julian sighed wearily from behind the steering wheel.

Tracy had been grateful for the break, and the sunshine, but she too was struggling to cope after four nights' bad sleep. It was as if every avenue they tried had some huge obstacle in the way. Tracy was also battling with the realisation that something might be wrong with Amber.

It's like when you spot a scratch on your car; you suddenly notice all the other scratches. Your car isn't quite as perfect anymore. Only Amber wasn't a 'thing', she was a beautiful baby whom Tracy needed to fix. She wanted Amber to be happy and healthy, but she felt helpless to know what to do.

The sun was setting as they turned into the familiar roads that took them home. The five-minute last leg of the route brought them around the edge of Sutton Park – a 2,400-acre oasis of woodland within a suburban desert, the seventh largest urban park in Europe. Neither Julian nor Tracy had taken much notice of it since they'd moved to the area, but Tracy caught herself staring into the wilderness, wondering what it would be like to go for family walks.

Maybe one day, she thought, feeling slightly defeated.

Julian let out a big sigh of relief as they pulled into the driveway – things could now get back to normal.

"Why don't you stick the kettle on, love, and I'll unpack this lot?" Julian grinned. Tea was the cure for all things as far as he was concerned.

Unpacking done and tea in hand, the pair fell back into their cushiony sofa – their imprints still there from when they'd left. Hope and Amber were back on the baby mat, at their feet.

"Be careful, Hope," Tracy suddenly snapped.

Hope was clambering over Amber like she was part of the furniture.

Tracy folded to her knees and pulled the girls apart. She couldn't risk Hope knocking Amber's trachy tube out.

She watched Hope climbing over something else, in much the same manner as she had her sister. "Hope doesn't even notice Amber," Tracy said, shocked by Hope's behaviour.

But the truth was that Amber must have seemed like another piece of furniture to her sister. Amber barely moved; she didn't make any noise; she didn't cry.

They were worlds apart. Tracy had a horrible feeling the distance was only going to get greater.

CHAPTER 9

Breaking Him In

Sutton Park, Birmingham, Spring 2012

"We're not sending Shocks back to Devon," Amber Brennan announced.

No one at the riding school in Birmingham would have wanted that, but Amber needed to put it out there – to settle her own doubts, if nothing else.

They'd left Shocks alone for almost a year, but sadly there had been no changes. He spent all his time alone, afraid to make friends with the other donkeys. It was like he didn't even know how to play and have fun.

"If he can't make it as a DAT donkey [donkey assisted therapy], we will have him as a petting donkey for the children," Amber suggested. She was desperate to find a place for Shocks at the centre.

Amber knew she shouldn't let herself get so emotionally involved, but how could she help it? Because there were only 21 donkeys in Birmingham, Amber and the rest of the staff automatically 'mothered' them all. To send Shocks back would be like losing a child.

"Shocks is too delicate and he lacks too much confidence to move him again. He's made it home." Amber drew a line under the matter.

Andy and the rest of the team lowered their eyes and nodded. They could tell Shocks's lack of progress was getting her down.

They all desperately wanted to see Shocks blossom, but they felt helpless to know how to bring him out of his shell.

"I know what." Riding instructor Sara Gee stepped forward. "I'll start introducing him to the riding arena, break him in gently," the fifty-four-year-old suggested. Amber Brennan and Sara were the two qualified riding instructors at the Sanctuary.

What was the worst that could happen? Shocks couldn't become any more reclusive. It might even be the key to his healing, as most donkeys find happiness when they have a purpose; when they are helping others.

Shocks was used to wearing a head collar by now, but there was a whole bunch of other equipment that he needed to adjust to before they could begin to think about letting a child ride on him.

The two main bits of tack were the bridle and, of course, the saddle. Both would feel very restricting to an animal who'd never worn them before. Shocks was nowhere near ready for either, especially with his fear of anyone going near his neck injuries.

They would need to lead him through it slowly, show him there was nothing to be afraid of. The team had to show Shocks no one was ever going to hurt him again.

Sara went to fetch Shocks from the paddock after the last riding class had finished. They'd had a busy morning – 60 children had been and gone. The arena would have been full of scents, which is exactly what Sara wanted to introduce Shocks to.

"Come on, boy, I've got something to show you ..." Sara chatted away as she clipped the lead rope onto his collar. Like Amber, she was also on the tall side, which gave her the edge when she had to control a big donkey like Shocks.

Shocks followed behind her obediently. He always did what they asked of him, but reluctantly. Some of the other donkeys would push forward, practically volunteering themselves for duties. None of the other donkeys had been mistreated like Shocks though. Sara suspected Shocks might have been forced to do things he didn't like before he was rescued.

The riding team spent most of their time scrambling around in the dark for clues as to what happened to their donkeys in their previous lives but, by carefully watching the animals' behaviour, it was possible to fit the pieces of the jigsaw together.

Shocks hadn't stepped foot in the arena since he'd arrived on that unforgettable stormy night almost a year ago. His body tensed as he inhaled the new scents and surroundings.

"It's okay, come on, Shocks."

Sara gently walked him around the rink. The whole time she kept chatting to him, prattling on about how her morning had been with the children. It wasn't important what she said, but the tone she said it in. Her soft voice was soothing, just like that of a nurse by a patient's bedside.

"Your coat's looking a bit untidy, how about we give you a clean?" Sara reached for the bristly brush.

Shocks's body tensed again as Sara gently ran the brush over his back, belly and legs, taking care not to touch his old wounds. His eyes were fixed to the ground, like he was too afraid to look up.

"Oh look, you have a bit of gunk in your eyes," Sara observed. Donkeys get 'sleep' in their eyes in the morning, just like people do.

She wrung out a cloth with warm water, and then dabbed it around his big sad eyes. Sara believed donkeys' eyes were the windows to their soul; particularly in Shocks's case as they held so much emotion.

"How's he doing?" Andy checked up on the pair.

"I think he's a little bit gobsmacked," Sara laughed.

"He's never been made such a fuss over before," Andy said. "He's probably wondering what the hell's going on!"

It may only have been baby steps, but progress had been made nonetheless. Sara left Shocks to graze alone for a few days and then she brought him back in the arena for some more fussing and grooming. The plan was to build up his confidence so he'd be comfortable trying out wearing the tack.

Back in the paddock, Shocks was cornered by the popular boys. He'd been introduced to the Three Musketeers one by one, and they'd made it known who was boss. Now, they came over to suss out what he'd been up to. Shocks froze as Zebedee, Mackenzie and King circled him like sharks. Zebedee sniffed his neck and gave him a little nip to remind the newcomer who was boss. Shocks stood still and let them do what they wanted.

You could compare it to bullying in the school playground. The boys didn't mean any harm, though; they just wanted to test how strong the new boy was, to see if Shocks posed any threat to their pecking order.

Because – while Shocks did not – some donkeys did. They'd seriously disliked Junior, for example, from the moment he'd arrived. Junior was a six-year-old dark-grey donkey who looked like a mini version of one of the other boys, Donk, hence the staff naming him 'Junior'.

He was strong and bolshie, and had no respect for anyone's personal space, so the Three Musketeers took an instant disliking to him. One day, King had just about enough and actually booted Junior with his hind legs. Not surprisingly, they now stayed well away from each other.

It was pretty clear, though, that Shocks posed absolutely no threat. They sensed how scared and downtrodden he was, so they let him be.

Shocks gazed after them as they finished their interrogation and wandered off. He looked sad, as if he wished he could be one of the 'cool crowd'.

Andy had watched the whole interaction from the field shelter, where he'd been sweeping.

"You don't need to worry about Zebedee; at least you don't have to wear sun cream," Andy joked, trying to boost Shocks's morale.

Because Zebedee had a white coat, he suffered from sunburn, just like fair-skinned people do. Andy had to rub sun cream into his skin every morning during the summer months.

Also, as Andy reminded Shocks in a soothing voice, Zebedee and the rest of the boys weren't getting extra fussing-over from Sara and the rest of the riding team – it was Shocks's time to shine, to be turned into a DAT donkey.

After a few weeks of Sara grooming Shocks in the arena, it was time to try the saddle on him. There are a few things donkeys can take a disliking to when it comes to wearing a saddle. Firstly, the girth strap that wraps under their belly to hold the saddle in place. A donkey's belly is his vulnerable spot, so they don't like being touched there, let alone having a big strap all around it, which must feel a bit like wearing a corset. Then there is the crupper, the long strap that runs down their spine and loops underneath their tail, to stop the saddle sliding forwards. The stirrups can also freak a donkey out when the metal bounces against their sides.

Because Shocks was the biggest donkey they'd ever had, the Sanctuary had to order in a larger breech to accommodate his long body!

Sara didn't have any problems placing the saddle on his back. As usual, Shocks did exactly what was asked of him. He just didn't do it with any enthusiasm. There was no joy for life. There was no happiness in his eyes.

He simply went through the motions, one by one. Next came the bridle, which involved a metal bar being slotted into the back of his mouth behind his teeth. The instructors use the bridle to steer the donkeys around the activities course.

Shocks chomped down on the bit, but he was very well behaved compared to some donkeys, who slide their tongue underneath the bar and end up getting it stuck there.

Something Shocks didn't like, though, was having his ears touched. It's not uncommon for cruel owners to tweak and pull on donkeys' ears as a punishment for not doing what they've been told. Rescue donkeys like Shocks often bear the scars of such torture.

"Okay, Shocks, I'm not going to hurt you," Sara promised, as she carefully threaded his long ears, one by one, through the bridle straps. She then gave him a good scratch behind them – something they all love!

Aside from all the riding tack, Shocks also had to get used to the activities that he'd be taking part in. The therapy centre wasn't just special for the donkey rides, but also for the clever selection of games they got the children to join in with, which helped develop their core muscles and cognitive skills.

Games such as: throwing beanbags into a bucket; reaching out of the saddle to grab hold of the dangling streamers; picking up cards and posting them through various letterboxes. Each time the child reached, or stretched, or bent down, their strength would be tested.

So it was essential that Shocks wouldn't be scared by the sound of a flapping card in his ear, or a beanbag being tossed across his path. It must have looked very strange to an outsider, watching Sara wobbling a piece of card next to Shocks as she walked him around the arena.

Although Shocks was a good donkey to work with in terms of being obliging, he was easily spooked.

The noise of a beanbag whistling past his ear – he froze.

The wobble-board sound of the card – he froze.

Getting him to walk up to the poles – he froze.

But it was imperative that Sara never ended the session on a bad note. If Shocks had been spooked, she would show him there was nothing to be afraid of. The last thing she wanted was for Shocks to leave the arena feeling terrified.

Although Sara took her job very seriously, she couldn't help but laugh at Shocks's phobia of the shaft of light that streamed across the arena floor. Shocks stopped dead in his tracks.

Do I jump over it? Run away from it? You could see the cogs turning in his brain as he tried to work out what this strange beam of light was.

"You are a silly boy," Sara teased, pulling him across to the other side.

And that's how breaking him in worked. Sara would literally break those fears down until there was nothing standing in the way of him being ready for riding.

Well, there was one thing left: testing how Shocks coped with actually having someone on his back.

"Why don't we let Eeyore ride him?" Andy chuckled.

The Sanctuary had a massive cuddly toy of the donkey from Winnie the Pooh. He looked like one of those bears you'd win at the funfair. Eeyore was a gift from one of the parents and had pride of place overlooking the arena.

The children have to be less than 7 stone to ride donkeys at the Sanctuary. Eeyore wasn't anywhere near that kind of weight, but he was big and squishy and gave the right idea. Plus, it was quite fun to place a toy donkey in the saddle.

Andy pulled out his camera; it was one of those moments that would have to be pinned up on the Sanctuary noticeboard to show all the parents and kids.

"Smile, Shocks." Andy grinned.

Shocks looked at him innocently through his long black lashes.

It was a fun and celebratory moment at the same time. It had taken Sara and the team months of hard work and positivity to get Shocks to this point, where he was ready to be a riding donkey.

"Well done, boy," Sara made a fuss of Shocks for completing a faultless ride with Eeyore. She gave him a ginger nut biscuit. He ate it, but as usual there seemed to be no joy in him, either at the treat or his achievement.

The whole team just wished he could be as happy as they were. They knew he had it in him; it was just a question of finding the right key to open the lock to his heart.

CHAPTER 10

Losing Battle

Sutton Coldfield, Birmingham, Spring 2012

"That's it, Amber, you can do it," Tracy cheered her baby on.

But they weren't filming her first steps, far from it; they only managed to capture a minute of footage of Amber sitting up before she flopped forward.

The twins were just over a year and a half old and Amber still couldn't sit up by herself, whereas Hope was on the cusp of walking. It had become a serious worry that Amber wasn't going in the same direction as Hope.

Amber liked to sit between her mum's legs, but if Tracy didn't have a hold on her, she'd flop backwards and forwards like a rag doll. It was distressing for the Austwicks to watch, especially because they didn't know what was wrong.

Tracy didn't want to talk about it, because she never liked to discuss what was on her mind. In turn, Julian didn't want to broach the conversation, in case he worried her. If Julian had the answers, he'd be happy to chat about the problem, but without the magical cure, he'd rather be silent. It was like those days in neonatal, when the elephant was lurking in the room.

What made things even more upsetting was Hope's indifference to her sister.

They never played together; they hadn't so much as looked at each other. The only time they interacted was when Hope wanted to pinch a toy off Amber.

"No, Hope, that's not for you." Julian told Hope off as she tried to pull Amber's dummy out of her mouth.

The hospital had given Amber some special dummies to suck on to try to improve her oral strength. Because it was special, Hope wanted it for herself.

Poor Amber was no match for her sister, and had to give it up unless her mum or dad stepped in.

If it wasn't a dummy, though, it would be a Lego building brick, or a cuddly toy. Hope wasn't taking any prisoners, and Amber didn't have the strength to stick up for herself.

Of course it made sense that Hope and Amber didn't behave like sisters because they'd led separate lives since the day they were born – separate incubators, separate hospitals, separate everything. Tracy had held them together only once in the first six months. How would they have known they were sisters?

It was heart-breaking to watch though.

When Tracy was really upset, she would either bury herself in household chores or go to bed early. That afternoon, Tracy headed to the kitchen to tackle the dirty dishes.

She tried to wash her worries away in the soapy suds, but all it did was turn her hands pink and prune-like. It was no good – she had to tell Julian.

"I think there's something really wrong with Amber." There, she'd said it.

"What's that, love?" Julian shouted from the lounge.

She repeated the words, this time with more force, more conviction.

"I just don't know what to say, love." Julian appeared at the kitchen door. He still had one eye on Amber, the other on Hope, who was crawling at rocket speed towards the stairs – her new favourite thing.

"I think it's time we asked someone for a second opinion," Tracy pushed.

Julian lunged for Hope, scooping her up into his arms before she could cause an injury to herself. The difference in development between the girls was also making it tricky to keep an eye on both of them.

Tracy's word was final, and the next day they asked the community nurse Michelle Snipe – who checked up on them weekly – what to do. The nurse told the early learning support worker about their concerns, and she got in touch with a physiotherapist based in one of the local schools.

It didn't take long before their concern was taken seriously and Lucy, the physio, was scheduled to work with Amber every other week.

"Can you see what we mean?" Tracy grimaced, as she watched Amber flop on her side again.

Lucy crouched down beside Amber and gently took hold of her hands, pulling her up into a sitting position.

"Hello, Amber, I'm Lucy," she said in a baby voice. Amber gazed up at her with a blank expression. Lucy had worked with lots of children with various assisted needs over the years. She had that kind, but firm manner about her.

She only had to let Amber's hand go a little, like slack on a rope, for her to fall backwards onto the cushion.

"Yes, there are some problems with her core stability," Lucy diagnosed, wedging Amber back into the 'V' pillow that helped her sit up.

'Core stability' was about to become one of those keywords in the Austwick household that would be bounced around on a daily basis.

"But I'm sure we can improve it," Lucy said optimistically.

She pressed her hands into her thighs, levering herself to her feet. Lucy had a face that you could trust, with her full cheeks that turned into apples when she smiled. She had mousey-brown hair trimmed into a short bob that skimmed her earlobes. She couldn't have been much older than Tracy, possibly in her late thirties.

Julian and Tracy both liked her, but Amber wasn't so sure, especially when the physiotherapy became a little more demanding.

Lucy would try to improve Amber's core strength by placing her belly over a big inflatable beach ball-type thing. Or she'd pull Amber onto her feet and try to get her to hold onto the sofa.

Julian would have the camera ready to film any progress.

"Nope, she doesn't want to do it." Julian stopped the record button.

Amber had scrunched up her face, her cheeks bunching into her eyes, her skin turning pink, as she cried silent tears.

The fact that Amber couldn't even make a noise when she cried was even more distressing for Julian and Tracy to watch.

Lucy felt bad that the physiotherapy was hurting her. Julian acknowledged it must be a tough job at times because, even though you're trying to help, you're the 'bad guy' as far as the kids are concerned.

"We've got to keep going, though," Tracy pushed again. It was difficult for her to see Amber so upset, but she was determined to have her girl up and walking like her sister.

As the weeks rolled past, Lucy managed to get Amber almost sitting up. Amber liked to lean on her left side and use her right leg to move around, like a paddle. Only she pushed herself in circles, not towards her mum and dad.

Tracy was relieved they were making progress though.

Amber was even using her newfound strength to get away from Lucy. She hated her physiotherapy so much that she would bum-shuffle behind the sofa when she heard Lucy's voice at the door.

"Come on, Amber." Julian picked her up and placed her back on the mat. Two seconds later, she was paddling her way to safety again.

It was a constant struggle to get her to sit still when Lucy was around.

They had now installed four baby gates all around the downstairs of the house to stop the girls from scampering off. You'd just have to turn your head for a second and Hope would be toddling into the garden or climbing the stairs.

The girls were getting close to their second birthday in June and, although the gap between them had grown smaller, Lucy had become concerned about a few things.

"She's still not using her left side," Lucy scowled.

Amber could sit up by herself, and 'paddle crawl' across the room but, if you pulled her onto her feet, she would lean all her weight into her right side and flap her little arm in the air like a wing.

Lucy tried some new exercises like bending and straightening her left knee, wiggling her left ankle and toes. Poor Amber hated it; she'd look to her mum for help, tears streaming down her face.

Trace would often give Amber a paracetamol when Lucy left to take some of the pain away. It must have been horrible for Amber to always have someone prodding and stretching her, suctioning her airway, sticking tubes through her nose. Amber would spend the next few hours hiding behind the sofa, hiding from the world.

"What's wrong with her?" Tracy searched for answers again.

"If I knew the answers, love, I'd say," Julian snapped, equally frustrated by the situation.

Tracy tried to stay positive. Amber was making progress at the end of the day. Tracy found it hard to accept there might be something seriously wrong with Amber – what mum wouldn't? It was better to lock her worries away in a box for now. Bury them in housework, in caring for her girls.

It was Lucy who eventually dared to open Pandora's box.

"I need to speak to someone at my school about Amber. I don't know what's going on." Lucy scratched her head.

Lucy eased the Austwicks' worries by explaining she was just looking for a bit of advice on how to improve Amber's core stability. There, that word again, it was always about the core strength with Amber.

Lucy booked an appointment with the 'spasticity lady' at Wilson Stuart School, which was only up the road. Pauline Christmas was a physiotherapist who worked with children with mobility problems, and was very experienced in dealing with assisted needs. Julian was pretty relaxed about going to see her; it was just words to him, yet another specialist. Tracy was more apprehensive, but not to the point that she was walking into the office expecting to hear bad news.

They brought Hope along, who immediately tried to wriggle free from Julian's grasp when she spotted the play kitchen in the corner of Ms Christmas's office.

She scooted past Ms Christmas, just as the consultant was reaching out her hand to greet Julian and Tracy.

Ms Christmas raised her eyebrow as if to say: "Manners, dear child." She cleared her throat and signalled to the Austwicks to take a seat, pointing to the two hard school-like chairs in front of the old-fashioned desk. She returned to her wooden chair behind the desk; it creaked as she nestled into the well-worn seat.

Ms Christmas was in her late fifties; her hair was short and brown, flecked with grey.

She's quite prim and proper, Julian thought, bemused.

But she is clearly very experienced at what she does – he ticked himself off for being judgemental again.

The chair let out another sigh as Ms Christmas leaned forward and rested her elbows on the desk.

"So what seems to be the problem?" she asked, twizzling a pen between her forefinger and thumb, poised to take notes.

Julian recounted all they had been through. It had been an emotional rollercoaster and he felt quite sad at certain moments. Tears prickled behind his eyes. He blinked them off – he didn't want to get upset in front of a stranger. Tracy sat quietly with Amber in her lap, her face not giving a thing away.

Ms Christmas listened patiently and then she rose to her feet.

"I'll have a look at Amber walking," she instructed, moving to the spongy rubber mats.

Amber could sort of walk, if someone was holding her hand. Tracy lifted her off her knees and took Amber's shoes and socks off.

"Come on, Amber." Tracy took her tiny hand in hers.

She pulled Amber to her feet and slowly they walked across the rubber mats towards Hope. Amber was walking on her tippy-toes and flapping her left arm in the air for balance.

Ms Christmas was making a 'hmmming' noise as she looked at Amber from every angle. She had that same mechanic-checking-under-the-bonnet-of-a-car way about her that the sonographer had had.

"What can we do?" Julian asked. He was waiting at the finishing line, armed with the suctioning machine and catheters in case the walking caused some mucus to get stuck.

"Hmmm." Ms Christmas hummed to herself again, digesting the information. She then turned to the Austwicks.

"I think she's got cerebral palsy."

It was so matter of fact.

Tracy looked at Julian in disbelief.

"What?" she spluttered. "I don't think so. What do you mean?" Tracy said this more aggressively, protectively.

Ms Christmas returned to her desk and drew a breath before calmly addressing the Austwicks.

"I've been doing this for many years and, in my experience, the way Amber is walking, and the way she is holding her left side, indicates she has cerebral palsy," she reiterated.

How can you look at my Amber for a few seconds and give a massive diagnosis? Tracy thought, fuming.

When Tracy thought of cerebral palsy, she imagined people in wheelchairs, people who couldn't eat properly, who couldn't move their arms and legs.

Julian was much more relaxed about the whole thing. He wanted to give Pauline Christmas a chance to explain.

"Did she have a bleed on the brain when she was born?" Ms Christmas asked.

Oh my God.

Julian and Tracy locked eyes.

There had been so many dramas around the birth – the twins had even suffered two bleeds on their lungs in the first week – that Julian and Tracy had forgotten all about what their doctor had said to them two years ago.

Amber *had* had a bleed on the brain when she was born. Was it now causing the left side of her body not to work properly?

No, she can't have cerebral palsy. Tracy couldn't believe it. She was in denial.

Tracy cut short their meeting. They politely said their goodbyes to Ms Christmas. The whole while, Tracy was secretly fuming. As soon as she got in the car, she exploded with anger.

"Why are you so upset, love?" Julian tried to calm his wife down.

"It's ridiculous. Who's Pauline Christmas to tell me that my daughter has cerebral palsy?"

She leaned over to Amber and gave her a protective kiss on the forehead.

"Hang on a minute, this lady knows her stuff," Julian reasoned. He was much more willing to accept things. He could see Tracy's point, to a degree, but he felt she needed to be open-minded.

"I'm sure she wouldn't just turn around and say 'cerebral palsy' unless she had faith in her ability to diagnose it."

If she can walk, then does it matter if she's got a little bit of cerebral palsy? She's alive at the end of the day was Julian's school of thought.

Tracy was having none of it.

"Aren't there tests that need to be done? We need a second opinion," she snapped. "I want her to have a brain scan. I want to know how big the bleed is, and what it looks like."

Julian was overprotective about the girls in a different way.

"A brain scan won't make things better. Why do you want to put Amber through that?" He fought his corner.

"Because I need to know for sure." Tracy crossed her arms defiantly.

The not knowing was the worst thing.

Julian didn't think he did a very good job of appeasing Tracy, or even calming her down for that matter. He felt frustrated that he couldn't comfort her or, rather, that she wouldn't let him be there for her.

Tracy announced that she would do the night shift, and took herself and the girls off to bed early.

Julian felt sad and defeated as he watched the TV downstairs, alone. He had a little cry as it had all got a bit much.

Little did he know, Tracy was doing the exact same thing in the room above him. All those emotions she'd stored up came pouring out.

Deep in her heart, Tracy knew there was truth in what Pauline Christmas had said. Amber did have a bleed on the brain when she was born, and there was something wrong with one side of her body.

As she lay on the single mattress next to Amber, she imagined all these painful thoughts, such as Amber ending up in a wheelchair.

She hated Pauline Christmas for what she'd revealed, but not as much as she blamed herself for what Amber was going through.

Hasn't she been through enough? she thought to herself, as she sobbed. Tracy's body was shaking as she let it all out. All her hurt, guilt and sorrow seeped into the pillow. She wished she could reach out to Julian for comfort, but she just didn't know how to.

Julian hoped Tracy would have calmed down by the morning, but his wife was more determined than ever to get a second opinion from a medic. She'd already arranged an appointment with the paediatrician, Dr Diwakar, before he'd even made his breakfast.

Tracy wouldn't let it drop. She was fuming on the phone to her sister Debbie. Julian caught fragments of the conversation, and could tell Debs was also having little luck calming her down.

I guess her anger is Tracy's way of coping with her fear that the diagnosis is true, Julian reasoned. It was difficult for Julian to cope with, though. He was relieved when it was time to see the doctor at the hospital.

Walking through the corridors of the Birmingham Children's Hospital brought back unpleasant memories for the Austwicks. They'd been back and forth lots over the past year and a half, but for routine check-ups, not for something serious like this.

Dr Diwakar welcomed the Austwicks with a warm smile. He was a very nice man with a gentle calm way about him. He was also at the top of his game; the paediatrician revealed that he would soon be moving to work at Great Ormond Street Hospital in London.

Tracy had a hundred words on the tip of her tongue, ready to spew at him. She sat with her legs and arms crossed, knotted like a big pretzel.

Julian started to explain the situation, and about the cerebral palsy diagnosis, but then Tracy cut in. Julian shook his head, astounded by his wife's aggressiveness.

"Pauline Christmas asked if Amber had a bleed on the brain when she was a baby, and said that might have been the cause." Tracy looked at Dr Diwakar for answers.

The consultant peeled open Amber's file and leafed through the pages. His eyes flickered behind his frameless oval glasses. His eyebrows bounced up and down as he absorbed the information. Julian shot Tracy a look as if to say: "Listen to what the man has to say." He hadn't ever seen his wife behave like this before.

Dr Diwakar cleared his throat before delivering his findings.

"Yes, there was a bleed on the brain," he confirmed.

Julian and Tracy listened intently as the doctor explained he was 95 per cent sure Amber had mild cerebral palsy. To be 100 per cent sure, they would need to send Amber for an MRI scan.

"I want you to do a brain scan," Tracy leapt in.

Dr Diwakar nodded gently as if he understood their pain. He was clearly experienced at placating upset parents. And he had a job on his hands now, because in his opinion it was too dangerous to give Amber the scan Tracy so desperately wanted.

The problem with an MRI scan was that Amber would have to be put under a general anaesthetic. She would also not be allowed anyone in the room with her, so who would suction her airway in the case of an emergency?

"The risks are too high, I'm afraid," the doctor apologised.

Tracy was still 'if'ing and 'but'ing. The doctor pushed his glasses up his nose. He spoke calmly and slowly so she could absorb what he was saying.

"It would be more harmful to send her for a brain scan than to leave with the diagnosis,' he rationalised.

Tracy looked to her husband for back-up, but Julian agreed entirely with Dr Diwakar.

"At the end of the day, it's not going to make any difference; sending her for a scan won't change things."

Tracy sighed deeply as she realised she was outnumbered.

"Okay," she mumbled, drumming her fingers on the wooden armrest.

Julian had made her see sense; he had this way of calming Tracy down. That's why they worked so well together as a couple.

As soon as they got home, Julian held out his arms for Tracy.

"Come here, love." He hugged her. "We are still going to love her just as much, if not more," Julian whispered into her ear.

"Yes, it's fine, it's all going to be okay," she lied. What she really wanted to say was how terrified she was of what was to come. It was constantly two steps forward and one step back.

Tracy felt like she was fighting a losing battle.

CHAPTER 11

Silver Lining

Birmingham Children's Hospital,
Birmingham, Summer 2012

Tracy did a double take.

"Liz, is that you?" she asked, calling after the woman walking down the hospital corridor.

It was definitely Liz, as she was with her daughter Abbie, who was unmistakable with her platinum blonde hair. 'Baby Boris Johnson' they had nicknamed her in the neonatal.

"Liz!" she called again.

"Oh, hi, Tracy!" Liz turned around, her long dark hair swooshing after her, like in a shampoo advert.

Tracy had met Liz in the breast-pumping room at Heartlands Hospital, of all places. They had crossed paths every now and again as their daughter also had a tracheotomy.

"How are you?" Tracy asked. She had Amber with her in the buggy; the suctioning machine slung over her shoulder. Tracy felt tired and drained and wondered how she must be coming across.

"We're okay, aren't we, Abbie?" Liz beamed at her daughter. Poor Abbie had more complications than Amber. She was half a year older but wasn't developing the way she should. She couldn't interact at all with her parents. She was the cutest girl, with her button nose and white hair – she looked elf-like.

Whenever Tracy met Liz, she was always bubbly and incredibly positive about life. Tracy didn't know how she did it. She admired her strength.

I wish I could be as brave as you, Tracy thought, downtrodden by Amber's diagnosis.

"So how are things with you? How is Julian?" Liz asked after her family. She spoke with a posh voice, even though she wasn't really that posh.

"Not too good, actually. Amber's been diagnosed with cerebral palsy." Tracy's face dropped. She couldn't fake the smile any longer.

Liz tilted her head in a sympathetic way, as if to say, "There, there." She squeezed Tracy's arm and told her everything would be fine. Tracy knew she meant it, because Liz seemed to believe everything would be okay in the end. Tracy wished she could bottle her friend's optimism.

"I've got an idea," Liz said, as if a light bulb had switched on in her head. "Why don't you, Julian and the girls come for a walk with me, Sam and Abbie in Sutton Park?" she suggested.

Liz was married to a handsome PE teacher eight years her junior. Julian had met Sam a few times but they hadn't spoken much.

"That would be lovely," Tracy said with a smile, appreciating Liz's thoughtfulness.

"Sutton Park is beautiful, you know," Liz said as they parted ways.

"I've never been, look forward to it." Tracy had only driven around the perimeter. She remembered taking note of it on the way back from their beach holiday though, how she'd wondered what it would be like to walk through it. It wouldn't be long until she found out.

It was a beautiful hot June day when the Austwicks pulled into the car park at the south entrance to Sutton Park. They were a little early and Julian used those extra minutes to check out the noticeboard that had walking routes mapped out in red.

"This place is massive," he called back to Tracy. "It's 2,400 acres." He squinted in the sunlight. He'd had no idea what had lain on his doorstep for all those years.

They were just unfolding the double buggy out of the boot when Liz and Sam parked up beside them.

It was comforting for Julian and Tracy to know other parents who were going through the same strife – other mums and dads who could sympathise with them when they had to carry all the machinery just to walk ten feet.

"I'll take that, love." Julian heaved the bright-yellow suctioning machine over his shoulder. Sam grinned at him, as if to say, "I know what you mean, mate."

They started off down the dusty track, which was well trodden except for the odd big stone jutting out of the compacted earth. The conversation was light and friendly; what you'd expect from four people who didn't know each other that well. It was strange seeing Liz and Sam away from the hospital; it was as if they had to start over on new terms.

"We couldn't have hoped for a better day," Liz bubbled in her usual positive way.

"Yes, it's wonderful here," Tracy said. It was hard for her to take in the beauty around her though. She was so immersed in worrying about Amber's future; she couldn't see the wood for the trees.

"So, what sort of things can you find in the park?" Julian feigned interest.

Hope, on the other hand, didn't have to feign interest at all. She was so excited by the new sights and sounds that she was making squawking noises and reaching her arms out to try to touch the wild flowers. In contrast, Amber sat quietly beside her, as did poor Abbie in the buggy next to them.

"Well, there's a donkey sanctuary over there." Liz waved into the distance.

"A what …?" Julian exclaimed.

"A donkey sanctuary," Liz and Sam repeated in chorus.

"You know, where they look after donkeys," Liz went on.

Julian imagined a stable and a few donkeys dotted around a paddock.

"Oh, nice." He shrugged, with disinterest.

But Liz revealed more. She explained the sanctuary was a riding school for children with assisted needs. That it didn't cost a penny. That they had taken Abbie there a few times and she'd had a whale of a time.

"It's meant to help the kids improve their core strength." Liz illustrated her statement by running her hand across her tummy.

There it was again, those words: 'core strength'. Suddenly Tracy was listening. Could this be the answer they were searching for?

"Is it safe? How would Amber and Hope stay in the saddle? How much does it cost? Have you seen any changes with Abbie?" Tracy asked a stream of questions.

Liz admitted she didn't know much about the running of the place but she'd heard many life-changing stories.

"You don't have to worry about the girls, there is someone holding them throughout the ride," Liz reassured.

Tracy saw a glimmer of hope. She felt better already having something to believe in. Without hope, there was nothing.

"Let's go," Tracy told Julian.

Julian rolled his eyes; donkeys weren't really his thing. But still he said, "Okay, love." He liked an easy life.

They arranged there and then to take all the girls later that week. The riding took place in the morning, Liz told them; you just needed to show up and wait for a turn.

When the day arrived to take the girls to the Donkey Sanctuary, Julian found he wasn't quite as laid-back as he had been in the park, despite his desire for an easy life.

"What if someone knocks Amber's trachy? What if she gets some dust in her airway? How can we get to her to suction if she's riding? What if she catches a cold from one of the other kids?" He fretted long and hard.

"Let's just see what it's like, we can always go home," Tracy reasoned.

However overprotective Julian had become, he knew, if it wasn't for Trace pushing for more, the girls would be wrapped up in cotton wool for the rest of their lives.

Julian tapped the Sanctuary address in the sat nav, while Tracy strapped the girls into the car. It was only a stone's throw from their house, but Julian envisaged them taking a wrong turn and getting lost for hours in the woods. He couldn't dream up any more worst-case scenarios if he tried.

"We're off to see some donkeys," Tracy said excitedly to the girls.

Amber looked at her blankly. Hope screeched, reaching out to her mum.

"Mumma!" She smiled, her eyes twinkling. Tracy grinned back at her daughter. Hope's speech was really coming along.

But there was another reason, too, for Tracy's broad smile. Tracy had built their day out into being some sort of miracle cure for Amber. All her hopes were riding on those donkeys.

She had to do quite a lot of suctioning in the ten minutes it took to drive to the Sanctuary. Trace barely got to take in the picturesque surroundings, except for feeling the car shudder as it went over the cattle grids.

"I wasn't expecting this." Julian cheered up as they approached the Sanctuary. There were two pristine horseboxes in the car park, emblazoned with the Sanctuary's logo. There were paddocks as far as the eye could see and a large outbuilding. *That must be where they do the riding*, Julian concluded.

Hope squealed as she spotted a couple of donkeys grazing in the field.

"Oh look!" Tracy pointed. "They are so cute." She had a really good feeling about what was to come.

Liz was waiting for them in the car park with her usual TV-presenter smile. She waved enthusiastically as they backed in next to her.

"Oh, yuk, what's that smell?" Julian fanned his nose.

"Nice to see you too," Liz laughed. "I should have warned you," she continued, giggling, "the donkeys are quite smelly. But you get used to it."

Hope looked like she had got a whiff of it too as she scrunched her button nose in disgust. Amber didn't seem to notice it; further confirming Tracy and Julian's fears that she might not be able to taste and smell.

Wherever they went, they were reminded of the differences between the twins. It was painful.

The girls were lifted into the buggy and they all followed Liz as she walked them through the formalities.

"You have to sign in here." She pointed. "And you have to get a number for your ride here."

Julian was struck by how friendly everyone was. The lady at reception made a fuss over all three girls as she scribbled their numbers with a thick felt-tip pen.

"Lucky number nine." She patted the sticker on Amber's jumper.

Amber pinned herself into the back of the buggy. Her experiences with the physiotherapist, and at the hospital, had left her fearful of everyone except her mum, dad and sister.

"It's alright, Amber." Julian ruffled her blonde curly mop of hair as they moved on from the reception hall. It opened up into a much, much bigger hall.

"Oh my," Julian gasped.

He wasn't expecting the vision before him. There must have been at least 20 children of all ages, and all disabilities. There were kids in wheelchairs, kids with feeding tubes, kids with oxygen masks. They were camped around tables with their parents.

It was like stepping into another world. Until this moment, the Austwicks had led a very sheltered life. They knew what a tracheostomy was, of course, but they were still getting to grips with understanding cerebral palsy. They didn't have a clue about other assisted needs, like autism and Down's syndrome.

Julian felt very much out of his comfort zone.

Tracy, meanwhile, was fighting her own internal battle. Being around children with assisted needs suddenly made her uncomfortably aware that her own child had a disability. Although she'd accepted Amber's diagnosis, she hadn't really come to terms with it until that very moment.

They locked eyes. *What do we do now?* they said, without uttering a word.

Tracy spotted the canteen hatch.

"Let's have a cup of tea and some snacks." She followed the salty smell of freshly cooked chips.

Julian handed a bag of crisps to Hope, while the adults tucked into a piping hot bowl of chips. They were just chatting amongst themselves when a girl walking past their table suddenly reached across and pinched one of their chips.

Tracy and Julian were so taken aback they didn't know what to say.

The girl, who couldn't have been much older than seven, turned on her heels, and did the same thing again. What was even more odd was the way she did it – looking in the other direction the whole time.

"Mind out, it's hot," Tracy said, worried.

Meanwhile, Julian was concerned that the girl might bump into Amber's trachy tube. He hated all the potential hazards that were closing in on them.

Suddenly, the girl's mum appeared.

"I'm ever so sorry," she spluttered apologetically, pulling her daughter away.

Tracy felt for the mum.

"Oh, I really don't mind if she wants a chip, I just don't want her to burn herself," Tracy said.

"She is autistic," the mum mouthed.

Tracy smiled sympathetically.

How awful to feel like you had to make excuses for your child, Tracy thought.

Tracy looked down at Amber protectively. She felt a twinge of sadness as she worried that one day she would have to explain why her beautiful girl had a plastic tube sticking out of her neck, or why she couldn't walk, or why she couldn't talk.

"I wonder how long we have to wait until the ride." Tracy suddenly felt impatient to get to work on helping Amber.

"Oh, that's us!" Liz piped up, as Abbie's number was called.

"Let's go and have a look," Julian said, jumping at the chance to get the girls back safely in their arms and away from the other kids. He'd been fretting the whole time about whether one of them might knock into Amber. The twins were by far the tiniest of all the children there.

Julian and Tracy carried the girls as they followed Liz and Abbie into another hall, four times as big as the last one.

Julian got another huge whiff of donkey as they emerged into the riding arena. And then he caught sight of the wood chippings, and the dust, and the animal hair, and the dirt ...

He panicked. It was all too much like hard work.

"Stop fussing!" Tracy playfully punched his arm.

Tracy was more interested in the two donkeys in the arena. One was brown and the other was dappled grey. They were standing side by side. The brown one seemed a bit cheekier – he kept nibbling at his friend's neck like he was trying to get a rise out of him.

"That's Oscar," Andy said, approaching the Austwicks. He'd read Tracy's thoughts. "Hiya, I'm Andy." The groom introduced himself.

"They're lovely," Tracy said, mesmerised by the donkeys. She'd always been an animal person; unlike Julian, who was never that fussed about pets or nature.

"Oscar is infamous for being the naughtiest donkey here," Andy explained.

"How'd ya mean?" Julian asked.

"He is partial to the odd nibble. So look after your bags and scarves!" Andy chuckled.

Julian pulled all their belongings closer.

"Don't be silly, he's miles away," Tracy teased Julian. She turned back to Andy. "And what about that one?" She pointed to the grey donkey.

"That's Moses. He's a real 'steady Eddy'. We use him for riding as well as pulling the cart and we take him to shows." Andy was enjoying revealing his friends' profiles. "Moses came to us in 2002 when his stablemate died."

Tracy pulled a sad face.

"Yeah, a lot of donkeys are kept on farms to keep horses company so, when the horse dies, the farmer or horse breeder has no further use for them," Andy explained.

Tracy's concern must still have been apparent.

"But these two are the best of friends now, they are always together," Andy consoled Tracy.

The whole time they were chatting, Abbie was getting ready for her ride.

"Oh, I'm needed." Andy dashed off to return to his post of leading Oscar around the arena.

Julian studied Andy as the groom carefully weaved the riding-hat strap around Abbie's tracheostomy.

"Aren't you worried about it getting knocked out?" Julian asked Liz, who was busy waving at her baby girl from behind the gate.

"Oh no, they know what they are doing here." Liz brushed him off.

Julian wasn't convinced. As far as he was concerned, all animals were unpredictable.

A very tall woman with a boyish haircut lifted Abbie into Moses' saddle. She whispered some friendly words into Abbie's ear and fastened her arm around her tightly.

"This is the best bit!" Liz squealed with excitement.

Andy made a clucking noise and gently tugged on Moses' rein while the tall lady pinned Abbie into the saddle. Moses let out a giant sneeze that made his whole head shake up and down. He put one hoof in front of the other, slowly gathering speed like a steam engine chugging away from a station.

Watching Abbie bob up and down made Julian's hairs stand up on end. He gripped hold of Amber a bit more tightly. He was going off the whole thing by the second.

Julian was ready to make a run for it just as the twins' numbers were called.

"Come on, it will be fine." Tracy beckoned Julian over to the gate. She was determined to see this through.

The first thing they needed to do was find a riding hat that fitted the girls' tiny heads. The tall lady disappeared for a while into the tack room for a rummage.

"These are the smallest ones we have," she said, as she reappeared waving the littlest hats you've ever seen.

Amber may not have been able to walk unaided, but there was still a lot of power in her legs. She squirmed in Julian's arms as the lady placed the hat over Amber's head.

"She's a bit shy," Julian explained.

The lady crouched a little to meet Amber's eyes.

"Hello, I'm Amber, what's your name?" she cooed.

Julian and Tracy giggled. It broke the ice.

"She's Amber too," Julian replied for his daughter.

"Big Amber and Little Amber," Amber Brennan said playfully, as she opened her arms wide to welcome her new friend.

Julian didn't want to let her go. A million and one worries were racing through his mind.

"Don't worry, it will be really good for her," Big Amber said, practically prising Amber out of his grip.

She slung Amber onto her hip and shimmied her way over to Oscar.

"Will the hat bump her trachy?" Julian called after her.

"Stop worrying," she laughed.

"Do we give you the suctioning machine?" Julian pulled it off his shoulder, ready to hand it over.

"No, it's all fine." Big Amber waved him back.

The staff were so relaxed about the whole process. They clearly knew what they were doing, though, which did help to ease Julian's nerves.

Amber was so tiny her feet didn't even meet the stirrups. She looked so small and vulnerable in the giant saddle. Big Amber held her tightly while she waited for the other riding instructor to get Hope saddled into Moses.

Hope didn't seem worried at all about the whole thing. In fact, she scarcely took interest in the donkeys. Amber, however, wasn't looking so happy. Her eyes became big and watery as she searched for her mum and dad.

"Oh God, she doesn't like it." Tracy suddenly panicked. *What have I done?*

Amber's face turned bright pink as she started to cry.

"She doesn't like it, shall we get her off?" Tracy shouted out.

Big Amber whispered some soothing words into Little Amber's ear, which seemed to help a bit.

"Don't worry, it will be good for her," Amber tried to reassure Tracy and Julian.

Meanwhile, Oscar and Moses were patiently waiting for their cue. Andy swapped over to Oscar this time to make sure he kept the cheeky chappy in check while Amber rode him. Andy clucked twice, and they were off.

Tracy's stomach fluttered as she watched the girls bob up and down, their helmets rocking from side to side. Her hands were gripped so tightly around the gate her white knuckles were showing.

"Well done girls," she called out through a forced smile. She couldn't let on to the twins how worried she was.

Over on the other side of the arena, Julian was wound up like a spring. He'd positioned himself at the top of a ramp, squatting like a rugby player about to make a tackle. He'd chosen the location deliberately.

This way, I can jump into the arena if Amber needs to be suctioned, he thought.

It must have looked a funny sight to the staff: both parents ready to pole-vault their way in to rescue their kids.

Julian and Tracy had made some sort of silent agreement whereby they wouldn't speak to each other in case one alarmed the other. They were trying to be as strong as they could.

Julian had a conversation with himself instead.

Hope is doing okay, she's fine. The girls look secure; the instructors are holding onto them really tightly. Hang on, the donkey is making some strange noises, what happens if he bolts?

"Shall we go round again?" Big Amber said enthusiastically.

Oh God, no, Julian thought.

Tracy couldn't watch any longer. She prised her fingers from the gate and turned her back on the arena. In the corner there was a small pen where a single donkey was grazing on hay.

Tracy thought he must be very old, as all his hair was white. His back dipped like a hammock.

Pascoe was the Sanctuary's oldest donkey at the grand age of thirty-four. He was too frail now to be ridden by the kids, but that didn't stop him being one of the most popular donkeys there. He was so relaxed about life; the staff often let him wander around the buildings and grounds. Children loved to pet him because he was so friendly – and cute, with his big white ears.

Pascoe spotted Tracy hovering by his pen. He looked at her through his grey eyelashes, and clopped forwards. He was looking for attention as much as Tracy was.

"Hello." Tracy stroked the tip of his long nose.

Pascoe rolled his tongue over his snout as if he was wiping his nose. It made Tracy laugh and forget her worries for a moment.

Julian was still poised for action at the top of the ramp. Every second that passed felt like an eternity to him.

He breathed a massive sigh of relief when the donkeys finally came to a stop. Hope was smiling, but Amber was pointing at Julian, wanting her dad back. Of course, the Austwicks didn't want to appear *too* eager to burst through the gate and grab their kids back.

"It's fine, take your time," Julian fibbed.

Big Amber turned to Little Amber.

"Did you enjoy that?"

Little Amber forced a smile, but Tracy could tell she hadn't really enjoyed herself. Amber was desperate to get back to her mum and dad.

"Did you enjoy that, Hope?" Julian asked as he strapped the girls safely back in the buggy. Hope giggled and high-fived him.

Julian, Tracy and Liz thanked all the staff as they had been so welcoming and kind. Big Amber had fallen in love with Little Amber and gave her a cuddle goodbye.

"Thank God that's over," Julian mumbled, as soon as they were out of earshot.

Liz told them there were many more donkeys to meet in the paddock behind the arena.

"Think we'll leave that for another day," Julian muttered, as he pushed the twins back to the car.

Liz didn't pick up on Julian's mood.

"Did you like it? Would you go back?" She beamed.

"Hmmm, maybe not," he said.

Tracy was lost in her own thoughts. She'd desperately hoped Amber would have reacted better to the riding. She felt guilty for making her baby cry. She felt like another hope had been dashed. Another roadblock had been set up in the way of Amber's recovery. She was taking it far too much to heart. And, of course, she was bottling it all up inside.

"Don't give up. They'll enjoy it more the more times they come," Liz said confidently as they parted ways.

But Julian had already made up his mind they wouldn't be going back, and Tracy thought there was little point in putting Amber through any more upset. As far as the Austwicks were concerned, that was the last time they would be coming to see the donkeys.

A poorly Shocks with severe neck wounds.

Getting better with the help of Andy
and the staff at the Sanctuary.

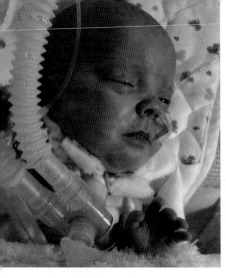
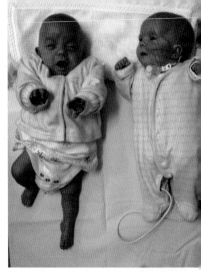

Amber and her twin sister, Hope, as babies.

Cuddles with Mum and Dad.

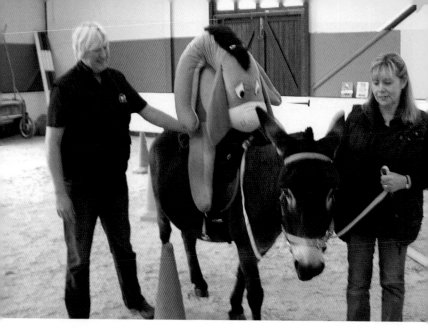

Thanks to months of hard work, the team finally had Shocks practising carrying Eeyore on his back.

Amber smiling with her new playmate.

Shocks and Amber sharing some special moments and
helping each other on the road to their recovery.

A healthy, happy Shocks has lots of friends
at the Sanctuary – donkey and human!

But best friend Amber is a regular visitor.

Happy Amber
and Hope, and
hero Shocks.

CHAPTER 12

Breaking Point

Sutton Coldfield, Birmingham, Late Summer 2012

"I think the girls could benefit from some interaction with other children," Barbara, the early learning support worker, announced.

She'd been visiting Amber weekly for the past year and had seen how Amber had struggled.

Tracy and Julian knew Barbara was making sense. The girls didn't mix with any other children except Abbie. They lived a castaway life, much like their parents. Julian and Tracy had become so overwhelmed with caring for Amber they never met with friends or family; they didn't have time to.

"Have you thought about sending them to nursery?" Barbara suggested.

Julian and Tracy looked at each other blankly. The thought had never crossed their minds, especially with Amber having a tracheostomy.

"You're entitled to 15 free hours a week when your child turns two, thanks to government funding."

"We had no idea." Julian raised his eyebrows in a surprised way.

Barbara's face dropped as if a sad thought had drifted into her head. She tilted her head sympathetically.

"Are you feeling a bit lonely and isolated?" she asked tentatively.

Julian and Tracy were a little taken aback. The past two years had been all about caring for, and worrying about, their girls; no one had ever checked to see how *they* were doing.

Julian stared down at his hands awkwardly. "We have a few people that we see, like your sister." Julian nodded at Tracy.

Tracy smiled back. "We have each other." She looked at Julian lovingly, and explained to Barbara: "It's always been that way because we've moved around quite a bit, and most of our family live far away."

Barbara was touched by the love and care that was radiating from the couple. They were clearly devoted to each other and their girls.

"Well, I have no problem trying to help you find a nursery," she offered.

Tracy felt relieved by the offer. She'd been feeling down in the dumps since their day out at the Donkey Sanctuary, since meeting Pauline Christmas. She felt permanently tired and had this overwhelming desire to be on her own.

It's just a phase, it will pass. Tracy tried to shrug off her mood.

She pulled on her last reserves of energy to get her through the next couple of weeks. It was a busy time that summer, as the Austwicks dipped in and out of all the local nurseries. It wasn't as easy to find a place as they thought it would be, though, despite Barbara's help. They faced rejection, after rejection, after rejection. No one wanted to have the responsibility of looking after a girl with a tracheostomy.

Julian handled the news in his usual pragmatic way. Tracy, on the other hand, took it personally. It was a slight on *her* daughter. She felt more tired, more deflated, more helpless. And of course there was that gnawing feeling of guilt eating her up from the inside.

Tracy wouldn't give up though – she buried her worries and kept knocking on doors.

There was one nursery school that caught both Tracy and Julian's eye – Smart Start Day Nursery. It was one of those places where you just step inside, and it feels right – the staff, the facilities, the smiles on the children's faces.

"Oh, look at this garden!" Tracy beamed as they were given a tour.

The building was a converted terrace house so it had a real homely feel. The garden was one big playpen – they had covered the yard with fake grass, which was littered with toys like pedal cars and tricycles. There were plenty of things for the kids to clamber over, like a pirate ship and miniature slides. Tracy was particularly taken by the big sunflowers painted on the garden sheds.

She set her heart on the place.

"I love it!" Tracy twizzled around to face Julian and Barbara. "And the girls love it too," she said, reading the twins' mood.

Hope was trying to free herself from her dad's grip so she could play in the garden. Amber's face was buried in her mum's armpit, but every now and then, she would raise her eyes to look around. She was like a tortoise cautiously peeping her head out of her shell.

Whenever there was a glimmer of hope, Tracy clung onto it like it was the last Coca-Cola in a desert. It made Julian nervous because he worried what the fallout would be.

"Let's have a chat with the nursery lady." Julian made a 'calm down' motion with his hands, and then they followed the nursery manager into her office.

The Austwicks had lost count of how many offices they had been ushered into over the past two and a bit years. This one was much more colourful than usual, though, as it was wallpapered with pictures drawn by the kids. Tracy cradled Amber in her arms, while Hope had a nosey around.

"Stay close, Hope," Julian said, keeping one eye on his mischievous daughter.

Tracy and Julian warmed to the nursery manager, Sue, as much as to the actual place.

She handed them both a cup of tea and a Rich Tea biscuit. Sue looked like she had just stepped off a plane with her mahogany holiday tan. Tracy had a good feeling about the meeting as Julian explained their situation.

Sue took a slurp from her mug to lubricate her words.

"You have two beautiful daughters," she started.

Julian knew there was a 'but' coming.

"But it's going to be difficult to have Amber here with us ..."

Julian could feel Tracy's anger and disappointment being exhaled next to him. He couldn't look at her, as he didn't want to set her off.

Sue pressed her hands together in a businesslike way. She explained she didn't mind someone from Complex Care shadowing Amber, but it wasn't fair on the other children to have a different helper coming into the nursery every week.

"We can't guarantee it will be the same carer," Julian admitted. They were still receiving their 15 hours' respite a week, but they could never predict who would be taking care of Amber.

There were other complications. Hope was eating finger foods and baby meals like other children her age. But Amber was unable to do that. She had recently undergone a mini operation whereby an incision was made in her stomach so she could do away with the nasal gastric tube. The incision was called a Gastronomy Button, or 'G-Button' for short, and it came as a massive relief for her parents: no more scares and sleepless nights worrying the milk might fill her lungs. However, Amber still needed to be linked up to the feeding machine throughout the day. She still couldn't swallow food normally. Brutal as it sounded, all these were problems Sue and her staff at the nursery could do without. The nursery manager came to a conclusion and revealed it to the Austwicks.

"We would be more than happy to have Hope, but I'm sorry ..."

Sue didn't need to finish her sentence.

"Okay, thank you," Tracy said bluntly, then realised she was being a little rude and corrected herself. "Sorry, it's just not been easy," she sighed.

Sue smiled sympathetically. It was the same smile so many doctors and nurses and professionals had used before her. Julian knew he had a tsunami of rage heading his way.

As soon as they were in the car, Tracy unleashed.

"Hope's not going to go to nursery if they won't allow Amber to go," she snapped, distressed at the school's refusal to take on both their twin daughters.

"Calm down, Trace," Julian said, as he drove them home.

"They are treating Amber differently from Hope. I know Amber has her difficulties, but it's a private nursery so we would pay them to look after her," she raged.

Julian shook his head – he knew what Tracy was like when she got an idea in her head.

"Let's look at it from their side," Julian tried to reason. He reminded her of the nursery's position. The nursery argued that, because Amber had a tracheostomy, because Amber couldn't speak, because she would need a helper with her, all of that would be upsetting and disorientating for the other children.

"Hope's not going if Amber can't go." Tracy crossed her arms defiantly.

Julian sighed deeply as he pulled into their driveway. He switched off the ignition and turned to look his wife in the eye.

"Look, we have to think about separating them. It's going to be good for Hope to go," he insisted.

The heart-breaking truth was that Amber was holding Hope back. The twins were two years old, and Hope would have been speaking much more by now if it weren't for the fact that her sister, her only playmate, couldn't talk. But admitting that the twins needed to be separated forced Tracy to confront her worst fear: that Amber might never be able to lead a normal life like her sister.

Once Tracy had calmed down, she went to find Julian. He was busy having a clear-out of the garage. Tracy knew Julian was equally upset because he always threw himself into a project when he felt unhappy. She cleared her throat to get his attention and Julian looked up from behind a bunch of boxes he was sorting through.

"You're right. We are going to have to separate the girls," Tracy announced.

Julian stood up and dusted off the knees of his jeans. He held out his arms, beckoning Tracy in for a hug.

"It's going to be okay," he reassured her, giving her a tender squeeze.

That was the magic of their relationship – teamwork. It all stemmed from how they met all those years ago, working behind a bar in a pub: they were used to working together as a team.

However, when the day finally came to take Hope to nursery for the first time, in October 2012, it was Julian who was the one worrying. His heart raced as he carried Hope in his arms to the nursery gates. He looked back at Tracy, who was waiting in the car with Amber.

"Go on," she mouthed through the window.

Julian couldn't help his worries; it was a natural instinct to be overprotective of the girls – to want to wrap them up in cotton wool because of how close they had come to losing them at birth.

Julian and Tracy had trained themselves not to be *too* protective, but every inch of Julian was screaming as he handed Hope over to the teacher at the gate.

Hope was wearing her best outfit: purple leggings, a pink-and-white top and her green fleece-lined coat. She also had on her first pair of shoes – a pair of trainers that had flashing lights in the sole. She grinned through her long blonde fringe as the nursery teacher greeted them.

The teacher quickly picked up on Julian's nerves and flashed him a warm smile.

"It's fine, it's all good, you get going and we'll see you later," she reassured.

Julian took a deep breath and gave Hope a kiss goodbye. The teacher took hold of Hope's hand and guided her over to where all the other kids had gathered.

Oh God, they look massive compared to Hope, Julian thought, as he watched her toddle over.

Hope turned back to look at Julian with big watery eyes. Julian panicked: his daughter looked like a little lost puppy.

"It's fine, go," the nursery teacher signalled.

It was almost impossible for Julian to let go, though. He was suffering two emotions in one. On the one hand, it was great that Hope was doing something normal, but at the same time, there was the sadness of letting her go.

"She did really well," Julian said to Tracy when he got back in the car. "She didn't cry once," he said, wiping his own tears away.

But within minutes of getting home, Amber started showing signs of distress.

"Hope, Hope." She kept silently mouthing her sister's name. Tracy looked at Julian in despair. She had dreaded this would happen.

"Hope's at nursery, and you're here at home with Mummy and Daddy," Julian said, trying to calm Amber down.

Amber seemed lost and confused. Amber wanted to search for her sister, but she didn't have the strength to walk. Instead, Amber turned circles on herself on the living-room rug, using her arm as a pivot. It was heart-breaking for Tracy to watch, and she blamed herself for causing Amber's distress.

Hope spent only half a day at the nursery, but even that was enough time to leave an imprint. The teacher had reported back to Julian how Hope had made friends with some of the other children, and it was clear when she got home that Amber had missed Hope more than Hope had missed Amber.

Amber reached out her arms for Hope, but her sister ignored her. Hope was more interested in showing off her new plastic pinny, which she'd been wearing in the finger-painting class.

"This is the first time Hope has seen children that can talk and run around, she's just excited by it all," Julian said, trying to explain Hope's behaviour to Tracy.

But it was just the start. Every time Hope went to nursery, she would return more confident – and less interested in her sister. Hope was developing on a day-by-day basis, whereas Amber was regressing. Hope was blossoming, but Amber was becoming even shyer, even more reclusive.

Hope would come home proudly carrying pictures she'd painted that day. Tracy and Julian tried to do the same with Amber, but it was really hard.

"I'm too scared the paint or the glitter will go down her trachy," Tracy snapped, and eventually gave up.

The reality was, Tracy and Julian couldn't do normal things with Amber. All they could think about was suctioning Amber's trachy, and giving Amber her medicine on time. They couldn't leave her alone in a room for even a moment. Tracy and Julian felt more like her carers than her parents, which in turn made the guilty feeling worsen.

Julian bottled up his emotions because he was afraid if he let them go, he too would feel the guilt that Tracy was suffering. Julian had to remind Tracy it was the best thing for Hope. It fell on deaf ears, though. For weeks, Tracy tortured herself.

She was haunted with the same thoughts day in, day out – that she had done something wrong, that she was to blame for Amber's health problems.

One night, it all got a bit much. Tracy was folding the clothes in the girls' room when her legs turned to jelly. She slumped into a heap next to Amber's cot, staring at her baby as tears streamed down her face.

How is anything going to make her better? She's going to be like this forever, Tracy cried.

The self-hatred kept coming. Her thoughts turned darker and darker.

I'm a rubbish mother. Julian would be better off finding someone else.

She wrapped her hands over her head to try to suffocate the nasty thoughts, but it was no good, things had gone too far.

After that, Tracy lost count of how many nights she lay beside her girls, somewhere between asleep and awake. Often she'd move her face on the pillow and feel all the tears that had seeped out without her noticing.

Things finally came to a head when Tracy was dealt yet another hand of bad luck a few months later, in January 2013, when her nan Irene, who lived in Burnham-on-Sea, was diagnosed with bowel cancer.

Tracy was devastated. It had been one thing after another since the girls had been born. She hadn't even had time to grieve her mother's death. The pain had been building up, layer upon layer.

She was in the car with her sister, driving down to see her nan, when the wall finally collapsed.

Debbie was chatting about something unrelated. Tracy's head was pressed against the window, watching the cars whoosh past.

Suddenly, she burst into tears. All of the grief, the worry and the guilt came pouring out of her.

"Trace, are you okay?" Debbie shrieked in panic. She'd never seen her sister cry like this.

Tracy held her head in her hands.

"I can't cope anymore, I just can't cope," she sobbed.

Debbie careered off the motorway and into the layby. She smacked the warning lights on and then turned her full attention to her weeping sister.

"Tracy, you're scaring me, are you okay?" She tried to cuddle her.

Tracy recoiled into the car seat.

"Stop being so bloody silly, come here." Debs pulled her back.

Tracy's whole body was shaking.

"You're not Superwoman," Debbie said, looking her straight in the eye.

But that was the whole problem: Tracy had tried to be Supermum, Superwife, Super-in-control for the past two and a half years, and it had all got a bit much.

"Everything is horrible. I've made a complete hash of things." Tracy didn't want to hear anything to the contrary.

Debbie lovingly tucked a strand of Tracy's tear-drenched hair behind her ear.

"You've not been right for a while," Debs told her. "All these terrible things have happened to you, one after the other, and I think you need to go to the doctor and speak to someone about it."

Tracy nodded.

"You can't cope, and you'll get worse if you don't do something about it," she went on.

Tracy kept nodding. She knew her sister was right. It was hard for her to ask for help though. She couldn't bear the thought of Julian knowing things had got too much.

"You won't tell Julian I got upset?" Tracy begged.

"That's the whole problem right there, isn't it?" Debs sighed, a little impatiently.

"Promise you won't?" Tracy grabbed her sister's arm.

Debbie looked the other way for a moment, sighing noisily in protest. In the end, Debbie made her sister a deal.

"I won't tell Julian, as long as you promise to get yourself to the doctors."

"Okay." Tracy nodded.

And so Tracy didn't let on to Julian the real reason she was seeing the doctor, when she went to the surgery later that week. He kept an eye on the girls while she went to face her fears, head on.

It wasn't as hard as she'd imagined telling the woman doctor about her struggles; perhaps it was because she was a stranger who wouldn't judge her.

The doctor passed Tracy a clipboard with a form to fill in. There were about twenty questions asking her about her feelings.

How often do you feel in a low mood? Occasionally? Once a week? Once a day? All the time?

Tracy ticked the box that said 'all the time'.

How often do you find it difficult to concentrate? All the time. Tick.

Tracy hadn't got to the stage where she was having suicidal thoughts, but she did think everyone else's life was better than hers – that they must be having fun, and doing fun things, while she was stuck at home, suctioning all the time.

Tracy's eyes welled up. She felt terrible for ticking all the 'yes' options; all the 'all the time' boxes. She was also scared – she didn't know what was going to happen to her, to the kids. She couldn't see the writing on the form for all the tears – all the letters swelled into one giant watery splodge.

Tracy passed the form back to the doctor, who studied it closely. She pushed her glasses back up her nose with her forefinger. The diagnosis was quick. Tracy braced herself.

"You're not very well," the doctor said.

Tracy worried what that meant.

"You have a poorly mood."

Tracy looked at her wide-eyed, innocent to the world of 'analysing your feelings'.

The doctor diagnosed Tracy with depression, and prescribed her a course of antidepressants called Citalopram, as well as booking her onto a course of therapy.

"Don't worry, we will sort you out," the doctor reassured Tracy.

Tracy dabbed her tears away with her sleeve.

"You will get better, it will just take a bit of time."

At that, Tracy felt even more disheartened.

I don't want to be feeling this way in a few months' time. I need to feel better instantly, for the sake of my family. I have so much to do … And so she piled the pressure back on.

Tracy left the surgery a little shaken up. She dreaded confiding in Julian, but she knew she had to.

The whole car journey home, Tracy played with the words – 'depression', 'tablets' – and how to tell her husband. Her anxiety was rocket high by the time she pulled into the driveway. She sat in the car for a good five to ten minutes, trying to calm her nerves.

"What are you doing, lovie?" Julian eventually appeared at the door with Amber in his arms. Aged two and four months, her daughter still looked tiny against Julian's familiar frame.

"Oh, nothing," Tracy lied. Her chest tightened at the thought of telling him everything.

"Come on, I've just brewed you a cup of tea." He hastened her inside, out of the January cold.

Tracy followed Julian into the kitchen and hovered by the table, quietly watching as he drained the teabag against the rim of the mug. Julian could sense something was wrong.

"What is it, love?"

"I n-n-need to talk to you about s-something." Tracy tripped over her words.

"Okay, let's sit down." He guided her over to the sofa. Tracy could feel her chest getting even tighter; her breath was straining.

"Oh God, I can't breathe," she gasped.

Her heart was racing. Her chest was pounding. The room was spinning.

Tracy was having a panic attack.

"Take deep breaths." Julian jumped to her side. He massaged her back as she drank the air.

She put her head between her knees. Slowly and steadily, Tracy managed to regain control of her breathing.

Julian crouched in front of her and held both her hands in his.

"What's going on?" He was totally confused. Tracy had been a magician at hiding everything from him.

Tracy rummaged around in her handbag.

"I have to take these pills, and I'm panicking about taking them." She held out the packet.

Tracy felt embarrassed and ashamed to tell Julian she needed antidepressants. Of course, Julian wasn't judgemental in the slightest. He was more bothered about the fact he hadn't been able to spot how depressed his wife had become.

"I'm letting you down, I'm letting the girls down," she wept.

"Rubbish, you've had so much to cope with." Julian jumped to her defence.

"I'm only thirty-four; I shouldn't be taking tablets at my age."

"Nonsense," Julian cut in again. "If they make you feel better then there is nothing wrong with taking them," he rationalised.

Julian disappeared into the kitchen and came back clutching a glass of water.

"Get it down ya." He tried to lighten the mood.

Tracy pushed the tiny pill out of the foil and onto the palm of her hand. She counted backwards from three and then washed it down.

"See, that wasn't so bad!" Julian said. "I'm proud of you, lovie. You're a brilliant mother, and a brilliant wife, and I don't want you ever to feel like you can't talk to me anymore, you hear?"

Tracy nodded.

"I mean it." He wagged his finger playfully.

And, finally, Tracy cracked a smile.

CHAPTER 13

Breaking Free

Sutton Coldfield, Birmingham,
February 2013

"Are you excited about seeing your friends today?" Julian asked Hope as they set off for nursery.

"Daisy," she said excitedly, clapping her hands.

Daisy was Hope's new best friend. The teacher had reported back how the girls were inseparable, eating lunch together and holding hands in the playground.

Hope breezed past Amber on her way out. It was like her sister was invisible. Amber's blue eyes narrowed, as if she was giving her twin a dirty look.

As soon as Julian and Hope were gone, Amber looked lost. She was back to turning circles on herself on the living-room carpet. It was a similar sight to what you sometimes see with animals in captivity – they rock backwards and forwards to soothe their pain of being behind bars.

That's exactly how Tracy felt – trapped.

She switched on the TV to try to distract Amber, but Amber wasn't bothered. Round and round she went, trying to claw her way onto her feet but not quite managing it. Tracy felt edgy and anxious. She couldn't keep still; she needed Julian to come home and calm her down.

Tracy turned her face away so Amber couldn't see the tears in her eyes.

Julian had walked Hope to nursery; it was *their* new thing that they did together. It was great for Hope's development, but Tracy felt guilty that Amber was missing out, again.

The room was closing in on her – she needed to get out.

GO NOW, a voice shouted in her head.

Tracy had never taken Amber in the car on her own before. She had been too terrified in case Amber needed to be suctioned and there was nowhere to pull over. But desperate times called for desperate measures. She was sick of her fears controlling her.

"Come on, Amber, we're going for a walk." Tracy sniffed, putting on a brave face.

She placed the car seat next to her in the front this time. As she was strapping Amber in, Tracy remembered the Donkey Sanctuary's therapy centre, where they had taken the girls eight months ago. Amber hadn't enjoyed her donkey ride much, but it was a really pretty place to visit as it was out in the countryside.

I know the route, I know where to pull over in case of emergency, Tracy reassured herself. It was a brave thing to do, and she was going to see it through.

She left a note for Julian on the kitchen counter telling him where she was going, that she wouldn't be long, and that she loved him.

She closed the car door and they were off – Tracy and Amber on their own little adventure, for the very first time.

It only took ten minutes for Tracy to leave the suburbs of Sutton Coldfield, Birmingham, behind. As soon as she turned off the busy bypass and through the gates of the Sanctuary, Tracy gasped and took in a massive breath of air. She hadn't realised she'd been holding onto her breath for so long. It was like stepping into an oasis, as the long drive up to the stables snaked its way through fields and forests. Tracy glanced across to check on Amber and saw that Amber was transfixed by her new green surroundings.

Of course, the first thing that hit Tracy when she parked was the smell of those donkeys!

"Pooey." Tracy waved her hand across her nose to Amber as she lifted her out of the car and into the pram. Amber's tracheostomy meant she couldn't smell or have any sense of taste, but that didn't stop her giggling at her mum's impressions.

It took a few minutes for Tracy to get ready to leave the car park; she needed to load about five bags onto the back of Amber's pram, including the suctioning machine. It was like a military operation but Tracy had the strength for it; she was a fighter, like her daughter.

They hadn't seen where all the donkeys were kept on their last visit, so Tracy was curious to find out more. As they made their way down to the stables, they were greeted by Andy. He had a broom in his hand as he had just been cleaning out one of the stables.

"I remember you," Andy said, grinning, as he crouched down beside Amber.

Amber pinned herself into the back of the pram. She looked like a rabbit caught in headlights.

"She's very shy," Tracy explained. "She doesn't like people because she thinks everyone wants to stick a tube or a needle into her." She told Andy how Amber's condition had made her become reclusive.

Andy did his best to change the subject. He told Tracy and Amber how, apart from his wife, the donkeys were the love of his life. Andy had left the Sanctuary to work at a zoo for a couple of years, but he'd had severe withdrawal symptoms and was now happy to be back. Andy guided Tracy and Amber over to the paddock, where the donkeys were milling around and grazing on hay.

The gate was far too high for Amber to see over, so Tracy lifted her daughter out of the pram and cradled her in the nook of her arm. Amber was mesmerised by the animals, who were a hotchpotch of all sizes and colours. Some were brown all over; some were black with splodges of white. One donkey had white feet, which made him look like he was wearing socks. Their heads bobbed up and down as they sniffed and grazed on food. One of the donkeys caught Tracy's attention.

"Why is he standing alone?" Tracy pointed to the big brown donkey standing in the corner of the paddock. His head was down as he stared into the dirt. His big tufty ears were droopy. Tracy could almost feel his sadness.

"That's Shocks," Andy sighed.

Andy recounted the horrific story of what had happened to Shocks. Tracy sensed it was a hard story for Andy to tell as his voice quivered at certain points.

"How could anyone be so cruel?" Tracy shook her head in disbelief.

Andy didn't have an answer. It was beyond his comprehension to understand how anyone could inflict such pain and misery.

"He's had a bit of a hard life, like yourself," he said, turning to Amber.

Amber couldn't take her eyes away from Shocks. They were big and watery, as if she had understood everything Andy had said. She then buried her face into Tracy for comfort.

"Well, the good news is, Shocks is almost ready for riding." Andy changed the subject as they made their way back to the car park. Amber listened intently. As they walked away, she couldn't stop craning her neck to look back at Shocks.

Julian had a very surprised look on his face when they arrived home.

"I can't believe you drove on your own!" He grinned. He felt very proud of his wife, especially after everything that had happened recently. He was worried the depression might hold her back, make Tracy fearful to do things, but she was as determined as ever not to let anything get in the way of helping Amber.

He also noticed a subtle change in Tracy. She seemed to have a new lease of life; a bit more energy. Maybe seeing the donkeys had been good for her too?

Tracy couldn't stop thinking about the story of Shocks for the rest of the day – and neither could Amber. Amber was much more excited than usual, and kept putting her hands on the top of her head to mimic donkey ears. Tracy decided that another trip back to the Sanctuary would do some good – for both of them.

CHAPTER 14

Little and Large

Sutton Park, Birmingham, the next day, February 2013

The following morning, Tracy bundled both the girls into the back of the car. She dropped Hope off at nursery and then took a little detour from the usual route home.

"Would you like to see the donkeys?" Tracy asked Amber, who was still wiping the sleep from her eyes.

In response, Amber nodded her head excitedly. It was the first time Amber had shown any sort of enthusiasm. She was looking out of the window, inquisitive – she was engaged with her surroundings.

Tracy had that same feeling of relief when she turned off into the Sanctuary driveway. It was as if all her problems, all her worries, were left at the gate. All that lay ahead were green fields and very cute donkeys.

Shocks was in the courtyard being groomed when Amber and Tracy arrived. He was huge – the size of a small horse. Shocks was the biggest donkey at the therapy centre. Amber, who was only two feet tall, didn't seem fazed at all. She became mesmerised watching Andy brush Shocks's belly. Amber wriggled like a worm in her mum's arms so Tracy lowered her to the ground and took her hand instead.

"God, he is massive ..." Tracy started, but before she had time to finish her sentence, Amber had tugged free of her mum's grasp, and fearlessly crawled into the path of Shocks.

"Nooooo!" Tracy shrieked as, inevitably, Amber fell over at Shocks's feet.

Andy lurched forward to grab Amber, but it was too late. Something magical had happened.

Andy and Tracy watched in awe as Shocks looked down at Amber through his long eyelashes. He then tilted his head as if to say, "What do we have here?" The whole time, Amber gazed up at the giant. Shocks gently bowed his head as if he understood what Amber wanted. Amber stretched her little arms as far as they would go and wrapped them around Shocks's nose. She then gave him a kiss and pressed her cheek into his face.

Tracy clasped her hand over her mouth to stop herself crying. The atmosphere was electric as Tracy and Andy could see there was an instant connection blossoming before their eyes. It was like they were old friends, giving each other a hug.

Tracy thought this could be the cure she had been searching for.

It was the first time she'd seen her daughter show affection. Instead of hiding in her shell, Amber was reaching out for the warmth and connection she'd clearly been longing for. Her eyes were bright and alert. The corners of her mouth were curled up with happiness.

"Can Amber ride Shocks?" Tracy asked, with urgency. *If this was the reaction Amber had from hugging Shocks, imagine what changes could happen if she rides him!* Tracy thought.

In turn, Andy believed Amber could be the remedy he'd been looking for to fix Shocks, as it was the first time Andy had witnessed his friend show affection or a desire to be hugged and stroked. Maybe he'd found the key to unlock Shocks's heart. He quickly got the donkey saddled up for his very first ride.

"Are you ready to ride Shocks?" Andy crouched by Amber's side to ask her. She nodded her head and held out her hand as if she knew what she needed to do.

Amber was given the smallest size hat to wear, but even that was too big. Andy had an idea – he fetched a woollen bobble hat to fill the gap.

"That should do the trick," he chuckled, gently pulling it down over Amber's head.

Shocks saw her coming, and once again lowered his nose to greet her. Amber gave him a few strokes and then Andy lifted her up into the saddle.

Amber was so tiny, her feet wouldn't meet the stirrups, so she had to let them dangle down. Amber couldn't even sit up by herself. Big Amber now joined Andy in the arena as she had done before, so she could hold Little Amber in place so she didn't fall forwards or backwards.

Watching from the sidelines, Tracy now started to panic at seeing her tiny baby in the massive saddle, on a donkey the size of a horse.

What if she bumps her trachy? What if she needs to have her throat suctioned? Tracy found it hard to let go, to let someone else take charge. She gripped onto the suctioning equipment from behind the gate, ready to run out at any moment.

It was as if Shocks could sense Tracy's worry and sense Amber's vulnerability. He patiently waited for Amber to be ready – he stood there perfectly still, not moving an inch. Amber, meanwhile, was grinning from ear to ear. Tracy had never seen a smile on her face quite like it.

"Okay, boy." Andy gave Shocks a pat to say it was time to go.

Shocks walked slowly, hugging the outside of the arena. Meanwhile, Tracy's knuckles turned white, she was gripping onto the gate so tightly. Shocks stopped and started as if he knew he needed to take his time with Amber. Amber couldn't stop smiling for the whole four laps they rode together.

The ride came to an end. Tracy let out the breath she'd been holding. Big Amber loosened her grip on Little Amber and Andy prepared to lift Amber out of the saddle.

But Little Amber didn't want it to be over. With no warning, all of a sudden she lurched forward and wrapped her arms around Shocks's neck. Around the neck where the old, tender scars from his abuse lay hidden under his fur, sensitive to the touch and an always-instant trigger for his fear.

Andy and Big Amber tried to intervene at once. They were terrified that Shocks might bolt from the fear of having his old wounds touched.

But there was no need to jump to the rescue. Shocks looked the picture of happiness. He slowly closed his eyes as Amber nuzzled her face into his tufty fur that had grown over the tender scars.

"He doesn't normally let anyone touch him there." Andy turned to Tracy. He was gobsmacked.

Tracy was deep in thought when a somewhat bemused Andy came over, carrying a very happy Amber. She carefully strapped Amber back into the pram and then revealed her theory to Andy.

"It's as though Amber understands his pain, because she has also been through a lot," Tracy contemplated. "People had been horrible to him, and in Amber's eyes, people have been horrible to her – all those doctors and nurses sticking needles and tubes into her," she went on.

"I think you might be right," Andy said, as he led Shocks out of the arena and back down to his stables.

Amber stared at her new friend clopping off into the distance. She couldn't stop smiling the whole way home. Every time Tracy looked over at Amber, she was grinning and making donkey ears impressions.

Just as Hope had changed after her first day at nursery, Amber also showed a marked difference in her confidence after making friends with Shocks. What was most noticeably different, though, was Amber's change in behaviour towards her sister.

Julian picked Hope up from nursery that day. Amber would normally have been waiting for her sister to get home with an anxious look on her face. She would have reached out her arms to Hope for a cuddle the second her sister walked in.

But, that afternoon, Amber was so relaxed she didn't even turn her head away from the cartoons she was watching when Hope came running into the room.

Tracy chuckled to herself.

"Look – she's not even bothered about Hope, she's got a new playmate now," Tracy said to Julian, filling him on the day's adventure.

It was such a relief for Julian and Tracy to see Amber happy and less needy of her sister.

"I know, look at her!" Julian grinned. "Amber's got a 'my day was better than your day' kind of thing going on," he pointed out.

It was just a small change, but enough to bring some hope to all the family. That horrible feeling of guilt, which had been pressing down on Tracy's shoulders for so long, was finally lifting.

CHAPTER 15

Breakthrough

Sutton Park, Birmingham,
March 2013

"Look, Shocks has made a friend." Andy grinned as he watched the donkey follow his stable pal, Jacko, around the paddock.

When Jacko clopped forward, Shocks followed. When Jacko sniffed the ground for leftover food, Shocks copied him.

It had taken a year and a half for Shocks to bond with another donkey. Andy wondered if it had anything to do with Little Amber's influence. For this blossoming friendship had only come about since Amber had been riding Shocks.

Big Amber and Sara Gee joined Andy – the three of them leaned on the gate as they gazed across the field at Shocks and Jacko. A smile spread across each of their faces, like a Mexican wave.

It's a very good sign if a donkey eats next to another donkey. It shows they are trusting and relaxed. Something Shocks had not been until now.

It was funny to watch them together because they looked like 'Little and Large'. They had almost identical markings. Their white noses bobbed up and down in tandem as they grazed.

Shocks had gravitated towards Jacko because they were stablemates. And then, because he had made friends with Jacko, he was introduced to Jacko's friendship group – who included Rambo.

"It must sound bizarre to outsiders," Andy chuckled.

Within no time, the three of them were hanging out, just like a bunch of lads at school.

Jacko and Rambo had been good friends from the word go. Rambo was a nineteen-year-old donkey from Swansea. His owner had to let him go, along with four other donkeys, when his circumstances had changed. Rambo was brown, and the only way to describe him would be 'scruffy-looking'. His coat was a tufty mess. He sadly suffered from a skin condition called Sweet Itch, which meant he had an allergic reaction to midge bites. As a consequence, Rambo had to wear a special rug that covered him from head to toe during the summer.

The new best friends soon caught the eye of Zebedee, Mackenzie and King. They glared at the new gang, as if to say: "What's going on here?" Mackenzie, who was brazen, especially considering he's one of the smallest donkeys, took a few strides towards Shocks, Jacko and Rambo. King shot him a look.

"Don't bother; we have bigger fish to fry," King said in donkey language.

Andy laughed out loud. It was his favourite pastime, watching the 'field politics'. He was over the moon that Shocks was coming out of his shell. It was just a matter of time before he took on the big boys!

One thing he was yet to see, though, was Shocks bray. A bray is that very loud 'hee-haw' noise donkeys make when they are happy or when they want something.

Andy had heard all of the boys bray – except Shocks. He also knew which bray went with which donkey. They all had a very unique sound; some would be high-pitched, some more whiny, some quick and breathless. The donkeys brayed when they were having fun in the sunshine in the field. They brayed when Andy scattered apples and carrots. Sometimes, even, when the donkeys rolled in the sand, they made a lovely moaning happy noise.

Andy had got to know which donkeys brayed for which activity, too. Charlie and Donk would bray for breakfast, lunch and tea. Junior, Teddy and Dillon would bray out of excitement when they saw Andy walking down to the yard.

None of the donkeys brayed quite like Tony though. You could set your watch by him. To this day, he hollers a loud hee-haw at 11 a.m. and 3 p.m. on the dot; every single day. The reason for this is because he used to be a beach donkey, and those were the times he was fed, just like a dog knows when it's teatime.

Tony is a grey all over, and has a 'distinctive' personality. He had to retire from giving rides to children on the beach in Blackpool because he was afraid of the smoke from the barbeques and the noise of fetes and passing trains. Tony is much happier with his quiet life in the Sanctuary.

Andy was always watching and waiting for Shocks to let out a noise. It would be a breakthrough moment for the team. It would mean Shocks was happy.

In the meantime, there were a few other small changes in Shocks's lifestyle that Andy had picked up on. By the cafeteria, there was an outside play area for the kids – somewhere the children could go while they waited for their number to be called for a ride. There was only a wooden fence separating the play area from the paddock, so the children could be close to the donkeys.

Shocks had started to creep up to the fence to have a nosey at what was going on. He seemed to be drawn to the children. He'd hover there for a while, his big ears twitching to the sound of the children's laughter and squeals. As soon as an adult appeared, though, he'd back off and return to his favourite spot by the field shelter. He'd stick his head down, he'd disengage – it was two steps forward, one step back as usual.

"I think Shocks is intrigued by the innocence of the children." Amber Brennan offered her analysis on the situation. Andy agreed, as he had seen this behaviour before with one of their other boys, who was wild around adults but golden when it came to the kids.

"Because the children are small and unthreatening, Shocks knows they aren't going to cause him any harm," she reasoned.

Her theory also explained why Shocks withdrew when the adults arrived on the scene.

Andy had a thought.

"I think the reason he's formed a bond with Little Amber in particular is because she can't speak," he said.

Noise can alarm donkeys, so there was no doubt Shocks found Amber calming and comforting to be around. Shocks and Amber didn't need words; they had their own language they used to communicate with each other.

Meanwhile, not too far away at the Austwicks' home, Little Amber was also making progress.

She'd had a growth spurt in her legs over the past month and a half she'd been riding Shocks. Her mum and dad suspected it was due to all the exercise she was doing. The only downside was that it meant the tendon at the back of her foot, on her 'bad side', had become tight. Amber had to have a cast fitted, which she would wear for a week at a time to help hold her foot in place, to ease the strain on her muscles. Julian and Tracy chose a pink plaster cast because it was one of Amber's favourite colours and matched a lot of her outfits.

Luckily, she could still ride Shocks with her 'pink boot'. In fact, it actually helped with the riding because Amber's left toes could reach the stirrup now!

The downside was it meant Amber needed more physiotherapy – something she hated with a passion.

The pink plaster didn't slow her down one bit though. As soon as she heard Lucy's voice at the door, Amber rocketed across to the other side of the room on her hands and knees. Tracy could hear her daughter making a run for it, all the way from the hallway.

Tracy rolled her eyes at Lucy the physio, and Lucy burst into giggles. It was the same performance every time.

They walked into the living room to find Julian pulling Amber out from behind the sofa. Her hands and legs were swimming through the air like a turtle being held by its shell. He placed her back on the carpet, and she was off again.

"For goodness' sake, Amber!" Julian snapped.

Tracy had an idea.

"Amber, if you sit still for Lucy, we'll take you down to see Shocks."

The bribe popped out of her mouth before she even had time to think about what she was saying.

It worked though; Amber screeched to a halt and looked back at her mum.

"That's right, we can go and see Shocks," Tracy said enthusiastically.

Amber knew exactly what her mum was saying, as a big smile crept across her face. She put her hands above her head to imitate donkey ears.

Never before had bribery worked. It was her love for her new friend that made her sit still and behave.

To say she was as good as gold with Lucy would be a slight exaggeration, but there was no wriggling, no crying. There was definitely no more scrambling for shelter behind the sofa.

It was a breakthrough moment for Julian and Tracy. They found they could get Amber to do a lot more things with a gentle bribe about Shocks.

"I feel a bit bad using underhand ways to get Amber to do what we want," Tracy said sheepishly.

Julian laughed.

"No you don't," he chuckled. He knew his wife was secretly taking pleasure in the fact she'd found a quick and easy solution. And it wasn't like they didn't stick to their promise. They always took Amber to see Shocks afterwards, even if it was just to say hello to him in the paddock or over the stable door.

They discovered they could also use Shocks as a ruse to get Amber to try eating solid food. Until now, Amber had been fed artificial milk, first through the tube in her nose, and more recently through the 'button' in her tummy. Since Hope had been going to nursery, Julian and Tracy had been spending their days with Amber trying to get her to swallow solids.

Their aim was not only to get Amber to eat normally, they were also desperately keen to find out if she could actually taste food with the air passing through her tracheostomy rather than her nose. Taste and smell are of course closely linked – without being able to smell, the likelihood was Amber would never be able to taste.

In the past, Lucy had tried feeding her pungent fruits, like mango and strawberries, but Amber had always resisted. She had a habit of curling her hands into little fists and pushing Lucy and the spoon away.

If Lucy had managed to get a little bit of fruit into Amber's mouth, the next problem was stopping her from being sick, as poor Amber had terrible acid reflux. Julian and Tracy had given up trying because they were terrified the reflux could go down the wrong tube and into her lungs.

However, things had changed since Amber had been riding Shocks. Not only had the muscles in her legs strengthened, the muscles in her upper body had too. She had become capable of swallowing little morsels of fruit and mashed-up vegetables. The incentive to make her do so? Another little bit of bribery.

"Just one more mouthful and we can then go and see Shocks …" Tracy winked at Julian.

A smile of delight lit up Amber's face. She guided the spoon into her mouth this time, instead of pushing it away.

"This is genius," Julian chuckled.

Tracy couldn't wait to tell her new friends at the Donkey Sanctuary about Amber's progress and how Shocks had made their lives a lot easier. Tracy had only known Andy and Big Amber and the rest of the staff for a short while, but she felt like they had been friends for years. It sounded clichéd to say such a thing, but it was because they were so welcoming, and non-judgemental. It was as if all the barriers you'd usually expect with meeting a new acquaintance were down from Day One. The Donkey Sanctuary had welcomed Tracy with big open arms and it was just the medicine she needed to help with her own recovery from depression.

Julian decided to keep Tracy company this time around. He hadn't been back since their first riding experience, but he thought it was about time considering the positive impact it had made on Amber and Trace. He couldn't help but grumble a little again at the smell and the dust but Tracy told him to put a sock in it.

"It hasn't done Amber any harm." She poked him in the ribs playfully.

Julian lugged all the equipment, while Tracy carried Amber on her hip. Amber was making donkey ears the whole way down to the stables, desperately excited about seeing her friend.

The mood in the yard wasn't quite so happy though. Andy was running around looking stressed. Big Amber was shouting orders. The donkeys seemed jumpy and tense. Shocks had retreated way over the other side of the field again.

"I wonder what's happened," Tracy said, worried.

As they walked closer, they could see that the yard was sprayed with pieces of broken wood and nails.

"Don't come too close!" Andy held out his hand to stop the family in their tracks.

The wood splinters were sharp and he didn't want any children getting hurt.

"What's happened?" Tracy asked, alarmed.

It turned out not everyone was quite as well meaning towards the donkeys. Andy told the Austwicks how some thugs had smashed up a picnic bench.

"Why?" Julian couldn't believe what he was hearing.

Andy pointed to the far corner.

"Every year the fairground sets up in the field next door, and occasionally we get trouble.

"There is a pub directly behind the stables and the landlord told us some drunken yobs smashed up a beer garden bench and threw the bits of wood over the fence into our yard last night."

Amber's eyes were wide and distressed. She seemed to be picking up on the mood, and buried her face into her mum. Tracy stroked her blonde hair and whispered some soothing words in her ear.

"Are the donkeys okay?" Tracy asked, concerned.

"The sound of the wood crashing into the yard startled them, so they are now on edge. It was the worst kind of thing for an already traumatised donkey like Shocks." Andy looked across the field to where he was hiding.

Amber's ears pricked up at the mention of her friend.

"It would have brought back memories of his past," Andy said glumly.

Amber looked at Shocks longingly, willing him to come over and say hi. But the donkey didn't move.

Julian broke the news to her gently. "Shocks is feeling a bit poorly today, Amber, so you can't ride him."

Amber wriggled, pushing and shoving her way out of her mum's grip. Tracy had a job hanging on to her – she'd grown a lot stronger in the past few weeks.

"Shocks will be better tomorrow so you can ride him then," Julian explained. He looked to Tracy, amazed by Amber's fierce reaction.

As for Andy, he threw on a smile for Amber's sake; he could see she was getting upset by the whole thing. But inside he was furious over what had happened. Sometimes it seemed like a never-ending battle to get Shocks back on his feet.

He can't give up now though, Andy told himself. He was still determined he would find a way to save Shocks.

It just might take a little longer than planned.

CHAPTER 16

Best of Friends

Sutton Park, Birmingham, Spring 2013

Amber couldn't wait to show off her new best friend to her sister.

It had been nine months since the twins had been to see the donkeys together, and the tables had completely turned.

Amber was leading the way, rather than crying and cowering behind her parents. It was Hope who was much more apprehensive this time.

Because Hope was at nursery during the week, they were going to ride at a Saturday Club.

Amber banged her fists together the whole car journey there. It was her latest thing to show how happy and excited she felt. Hope shot her a glance. She wasn't used to her sister having all the fun.

Amber wore one of her purple-and-white party dresses. It was her new thing to insist on wearing her best frock when going to see Shocks. Tracy would have to hold up a selection and Amber would point to the one she wanted. Julian joked she was turning into a 'right little madam', although they both secretly thought it was the cutest thing to watch their daughter wanting to dress up for her best friend.

As soon as the girls arrived at the Donkey Sanctuary, Amber was itching to show off. She still couldn't walk by herself, but she insisted her mum held only one of her hands, instead of both.

"It's like she's got a bit of a swagger going on," Julian chuckled, as Amber led the way.

Hope stayed close by her dad's side, unsure of what was going on. She was used to playing with her friends at nursery; this was unknown territory to her.

They reached the reception area and Amber stretched her arm skywards, telling her mum she wanted to be the one to ring the bell to be let in.

"Okay, Amber." Tracy lifted her off the ground so she could reach.

Hope hid behind Julian as Amber confidently waved to the two volunteers behind the reception desk. Because it was Saturday Club, she didn't know who they were, but it didn't seem to matter.

"She's not normally this bold," Tracy whispered to Julian. The pair put it down to the fact Amber was trying to show her sister this was 'her thing'. Hope had nursery, and Amber had her donkey.

The Saturday Club was even more packed than the last time they had all been riding together. But it wasn't just Amber who had changed; Julian felt less apprehensive as they took a seat in the waiting hall. Both Julian and Tracy were finding comfort in being around parents in a similar boat to them, rather than isolation. Tracy recognised a few mums and gave them a wave and a smile.

Julian was contemplating whether to order a plateful of chips when Big Amber breezed into the room. Little Amber's face lit up like a lantern.

"Hello, Amber." Big Amber lifted her into her arms.

It was incredible – just as Shocks was making friends with Jacko and a few of the other boys, so was Amber. She was finally coming out of the shell she'd been hiding in all this time.

Hope didn't like it one bit, though. She held out her arms as if to say: "What about me?"

"This is Amber's sister, Hope." Julian wasn't sure if Big Amber remembered from their last visit.

"Hello again!" Amber crouched to Hope's eye level to greet her. Big Amber never forgot a face.

"So you've both come to ride Shocks today?" she asked the twins.

Amber put her hands on her head and wiggled her fingers around excitedly. Big Amber was pleased that Shocks was going to see what it was like to have another child ride him. Her end goal was still the same – to turn Shocks into a riding donkey for all the children who visited. She wondered how Shocks might react to Hope. Would he realise she was Amber's sister?

Big Amber suggested Hope got into the saddle first.

"Would you like to ride Moses?" Big Amber asked Little Amber.

Amber shook her head violently.

"That's a no then." Big Amber winked at Julian and Tracy.

Hope couldn't wait to leave the other children in the hall behind. Apart from her sister, Hope wasn't used to being around kids with assisted needs. She wasn't sure how to behave and clung to her mum and dad like Velcro.

Amber pulled on Tracy's hand as she confidently led the way into the arena – to see Shocks. She waved her free arm around, almost like she was presenting her best friend to her sister: "Taaa daaa!"

"Hope's not that bothered, is she?" Julian said to Tracy, as the family watched their daughter get saddled up for her ride.

Hope would have been just as happy sitting on another donkey – and it was obvious the feeling was mutual. Shocks didn't greet Hope the same way he did Amber. He didn't lower his nose to say hello. He didn't follow her with his eyes. His big body was there, but his mind was somewhere else. Of course, he behaved himself perfectly when Andy pulled on his reins to get going. Shocks always did what was asked of him, but he just didn't do it with any *heart*. He plodded obediently behind Moses as they took laps of the arena.

Julian and Tracy weren't the only ones to notice. They overheard some of the chatter going on behind them.

"He seems a lot happier when Amber's riding him," one of the regular volunteers whispered.

Julian grinned at Tracy. It was so funny to hear people commenting on their daughters, it was like they were starring in some sort of soap opera.

"Well done, Hopey!" They cheered their daughter on as she picked up a card and posted it through the letterbox.

Meanwhile, Amber was bouncing around by their legs, itching to get on Shocks. She couldn't wait to show her sister how it was really done.

The problem was, Amber was so excited, she was coughing up extra mucus. Tracy had to keep suctioning her, which was making Julian nervous.

"Maybe we should not let her ride today," he fretted.

"You can't do that, Amber would be devastated." Tracy knew how much Shocks meant to her daughter.

"We can't take any risks," Julian argued.

"It will be fine." Tracy cut him dead. It wasn't just Amber who'd grown in confidence over the past few months. Tracy was becoming less fearful of taking risks. Just as Andy, Big Amber and Sara had known they had to push Shocks to get him to come out of his shell, Tracy recognised she had to do the same with Amber.

The children are taught they must always say thank you to the donkey at the end of a ride. Shocks would have normally lowered his nose to make things easy, but he didn't this time. Hope had to make do with patting his leg.

It wasn't as if she minded, though; Hope was more interested in seeing what was happening on the other side of the arena fence. She was a mischievous girl, always looking for the next adventure.

It was now Amber's turn. Never before had Tracy seen her put on such a display of 'look at me'. Andy took her little hand in his, and Amber tried to walk as tall as she could, rocking from her left tiptoe to her right foot.

"There it is again, the swagger," Julian laughed.

Shocks saw her coming a mile off. If donkeys could smile, he would have been grinning from ear to ear. He rotated his big ears in her direction like two satellite dishes, tuning in to her every footstep.

Amber didn't need to hold out her arms; Shocks was already two steps ahead. His nose was to the ground, ready for an Amber hug.

"He looks happy, doesn't he?" Tracy asked Julian.

Julian rolled his eyes. Not being an animal person, reading donkey behaviour didn't come naturally. Having said that, there was no denying Shocks had a special bond with Amber. It was clear as day.

His thoughts were cemented by more chatter from the audience.

"He's taking his time with that Amber," someone commented, observing how Shocks was walking extra slowly. Shocks didn't seem to mind he'd fallen far behind Moses' lead; he was putting Amber first.

Just as Amber had stood tall to show off her donkey, Shocks was showing off too: 'This is my child.'

He plodded through the exercises one by one, giving Amber time to do her thing. The two obstacles Amber struggled with the most were throwing the beanbag into the bucket, and letting go of the saddle to touch the streamers overhead.

Big Amber was a master at pushing the kids to take a leap of faith. Andy, however, was the soft touch, who would always bring the bucket to Amber's side, so all she needed to do was plop it in.

Today, Amber wanted to shine. Before Andy had a chance to pick up the bucket, Amber had hurled the beanbag past Shocks's ear.

"Did you see that? Amber threw it!" Tracy's face lit up.

She'd missed, but only just. Tracy was clapping from the sidelines proudly.

Amber was beaming. If she could talk, she'd be saying: "Hope, look at me, look what I can do!"

Her confidence was skyrocketing and, in turn, so was her balance. It's like walking a tightrope – if you believe you can do it, that's half the battle done. If Amber believed she could walk, then she was halfway there.

Shocks came to a halt underneath the dreaded ribbons.

"Come on, Amber, reach up," Big Amber pushed her.

Amber looked at her mum and dad wearily. She wasn't so sure about this one.

"Come on, Amber, you can do it!" Julian and Tracy egged her on.

There could have been a drum roll for the number of eyes watching her.

Amber leaned forward and rubbed Shocks's neck, as if she was rubbing a genie's lamp, wishing for strength and courage.

She let go of her friend and then let go of the saddle with her right hand, skimming the coloured ribbons with her fingers.

Tracy's eyes welled up with tears of happiness.

"She did it, did you see? She touched them." She turned to Julian.

Julian gave her a hug. To an outsider, it would have seemed such a small thing, but it was a giant step in Amber's journey to recovery.

Happiness radiated off Amber like the fragrance from a flower. Once she'd finished the ride and said goodbye to Shocks and the team, Amber tottered back into the main hall glowing with confidence. She even smiled at a couple of the kids she recognised.

At last, Amber was leading her mum and dad, rather than the other way around.

Her newfound confidence was showing outside the arena too. Back at home, Amber was becoming a little daredevil. She was braving things she'd never tried before, such as using the coffee table as a crutch to help her stand. Julian and Tracy couldn't keep her off the furniture; all she wanted to do was clamber on and off the sofa like it was a climbing frame.

The couple needed eyes in the back of their heads to keep up with the twins – Hope was zipping up and down the stairs and Amber was turning the house into a mini assault course. There was one moment Julian would never forget. He was waiting at the top of the stairs, ready to catch Hope when she reached the final step, and Tracy was at the bottom, holding Amber from climbing after her sister.

"We're like a human train," he burst out laughing.

They were finally feeling like parents rather than carers. Yes, Julian and Tracy still had to alternate nights by Amber's bedside; yes, they still had to suction Amber throughout the day; and yes, they couldn't leave her alone for a second. But something had shifted – they were having fun together.

They started to brave going out more as a family. Until then, the only getaway they'd made was to the beach in Brean. That had turned out to be more of a nightmare than a holiday though.

"How about a day trip?" Tracy suggested.

Being an animal lover, an idea popped into her head.

"What about West Midlands Safari Park?"

Julian chewed it over for a moment, running through all the risks and potential hazards. Tracy raised her eyebrow at him.

"Okay," he agreed. He knew full well, if it weren't for Tracy pushing, they'd live like hermits.

They set off early with a car stuffed three-quarters full with medical equipment and back-up kit and one-quarter picnic. The boot was brimming!

Julian thought he had three kids in the back of the car, not two, when they arrived at the safari park in Bewdley, Worcestershire. Tracy was so excited to see the wildlife she was bouncing around in the back seat. It had been a long time since he'd seen her this happy.

There are 165 species of exotic animals at the park, and Tracy couldn't wait to see them.

"Let's drive through the safari part first," she suggested to Julian.

The only animals the girls had seen up until now were the neighbour's dog, and the donkeys, of course. How were they going to react to giraffes and elephants and hippos?

Tracy agreed to take the driving seat so Julian could capture their adventure on camera. It wasn't something they'd consciously noticed, but they'd been pulling the camera out more and more of late. It signalled things were improving, because they wanted something to remember the moment by.

Hope was strapped into the front seat and Julian was in the back with Amber. The first part of the safari meandered through woodland and fields, where the animals that were not considered to be dangerous roamed.

"Oh, look at the giraffes," Tracy squealed "And the camels over there."

Amber and Hope's faces were swishing from left to right like windscreen wipers. Their eyes were wide, mesmerised by the strange-looking beasts.

The Austwicks were crawling along at a snail's pace behind a train of other cars. They had entered the area where you could wind your window down and feed the animals.

"It's fine, don't be a scaredy-cat." Tracy egged Julian on.

Julian cautiously wound his window down a few centimetres, and Tracy did the same on her side so Hope could get a closer look.

A few oxen ambled past the cars.

"Oh hello," Tracy exclaimed, as one of the shaggy beasts poked his wet nose in the window to have a rummage. Amber pinned herself into the back of the car seat. She wasn't quite sure about him. The ox was a great big hairy thing with horns that curved up like a moustache.

Julian wound his window up a couple of centimetres.

They drove on a little further. Tracy slammed on the brakes for the llama who'd decided to wander into their path.

The llama was white with black ears and had a very grubby coat – as if he'd had a good roll around in the mud. He stood eyeballing them with his black beady eyes.

"What do we do now?" Julian whispered.

Tracy shrugged. She hadn't been in this position before.

The llama drifted to Tracy's side, and then, all of a sudden thrust his head through the window.

He was looking for food, of course, but decided to take a nibble of the steering wheel while he was at it.

Hope burst into tears. She didn't like him one bit.

"It's okay, Hopey, he won't hurt you." Julian reached forward, gently pushed the llama's nose and rolled up the window.

"He was a little scary," Tracy admitted as they drove on. Amber didn't seem to mind, but it was becoming clear she was much more of an animal lover than her sister.

They knew what would cheer Hope up – the yummy fairy cakes they'd packed in the picnic basket.

Julian and Tracy chose a quiet spot in the car park to have their lunch. It was a beautiful spring day so they opened all the car doors wide to catch the breeze.

It was a picture-perfect moment – watching the twins standing side by side on the back seat, munching fairy cakes while watching all the people pass by.

It was hard to work out what Hope was saying a lot of the time – her speech still wasn't brilliant – but whatever she was mumbling, it was directed at Amber.

"Look, she's chatting to her." Tracy nudged Julian.

It was the first time they'd seen the girls interact. Amber had always been invisible to Hope – part of the furniture, something she could crawl over. The gap between the girls was closing by the day and perhaps Hope could sense the change?

Julian and Tracy locked eyes. They didn't have to say a word, they were thinking the same thing: *We've had a family day out. Finally.*

"We should do this again," Tracy murmured to Julian, grinning cheekily.

That was Tracy to a T, always pushing for the next step.

"Well, let's just get home in one piece first," Julian sighed.

That was Julian for you – one step at a time.

CHAPTER 17

First Steps

Sutton Park, Birmingham, June 2013

"She's going to do it, here she goes …" Julian grabbed the video recorder.

But it was another false start. Amber lurched back to the sofa, afraid to take that final leap of faith and walk on her own, without holding on to the coffee table.

She was so close though. Amber's stomach, her back and her legs had become so much stronger thanks to riding Shocks for the past six months that – at the age of three – she was now on the cusp of taking her first steps.

Julian and Tracy were more frightened than they'd ever been to take their eyes off her, in case they missed the magical moment.

"It will probably happen when neither of us is watching," Tracy laughed.

"Yes, the less big a deal we make of it, the more chance it will happen," Julian reasoned.

With that in mind, Julian decided he'd pick Hope up from nursery, and they would walk back together rather than take the car. Julian worried they might be neglecting Hope a bit. It wasn't intentional, of course, but it was hard to keep things balanced when Amber demanded so much of their attention.

The half-hour it will take to walk through the suburbs is the perfect way to give Hope some quality time, he thought.

Julian arrived a little early at the nursery. He heard singing and clapping pouring out from the windows. He couldn't help but take a closer look at what Hope was up to. He peered through the window, and there was his daughter, centre of attention. She was sitting cross-legged on the carpet, next to the music man. Hope was singing and clapping – getting the party started.

That's my girl. Julian grinned proudly.

Hope came toddling out of class brandishing another piece of artwork she'd created that day. The A4 paper had a couple of thumbprints stamped on it, not quite a Monet, but Julian was proud nonetheless. Their fridge was wallpapered almost entirely with her pictures now.

"Have you had a nice day, Hope?" Julian asked.

"Yes!" She nodded cheerily.

Hope's vocabulary was still lagging behind the others in her class, but it was slowly improving. She was talking to Amber more, or rather talking at her. Hope liked to boss her sister around. Amber didn't seem to mind though – since she'd been riding Shocks, Amber had become much more relaxed.

Julian and Hope were peacefully walking the pavements when a leaf cartwheeled across their path.

Hope stopped in her tracks and pointed.

"Leaf." The word bubbled up from nowhere.

Julian was shocked. He'd never heard her say that word before. *Maybe everything will be okay. Hope is learning to speak, Amber is learning to walk.* He felt a flutter of happiness.

Julian couldn't wait to tell Tracy the news about Hope's new word as they walked through the front door. Trace was busy in the kitchen preparing tea. Amber was clinging on to the doorframe, watching her mum's every move.

"I'll have a cup of tea, love," Julian called out, falling back into his favourite spot on the sofa with a smile. Hope came and cuddled next to him. Julian had one eye on the TV and the other on Amber, who was still procrastinating about whether to stay holding the door, or move to the couch.

"Come on, Amber, come and say hi." Julian patted the sofa.

Suddenly, he got a feeling: *This could be it.*

Julian quickly snatched the camera from the coffee table.

"Trace, come look at this!" he yelled. He couldn't have her miss this.

Tracy was sure it was going to be another false start but she humoured her husband anyway. She knelt down by the sofa and waved at Amber.

"Come on, you can do it," Julian and Tracy chimed in chorus.

Amber clung to the doorframe for support.

Her eyes were narrowed on her target. If a toddler could look determined, Amber was showing every sign of it.

"That's it, you're nearly there." Julian smiled. The camera was zoomed in. All eyes were on her.

Amber cautiously lifted one hand off the doorframe, and then the other. She took one step forward, and then another. Tracy covered her mouth with her hand to stop herself from screaming with happiness. Their baby girl was finally walking.

Amber was beaming. You could see the rush in her eyes from the adrenaline.

"It's the same sort of look you'd have if you did a bungee jump," Julian said, drawing the comparison.

"How do you mean?" Tracy giggled at Julian's analogy.

"You know, that adrenaline rush you get from letting go," he explained.

Julian was right. Amber had finally taken that leap of faith and it had left her exhilarated. She couldn't sit still after that. She wanted to try again, and again.

Tracy rang her sister Debs to tell her the good news. Tracy had shied away from family and friends for a good half-year because Trace worried she was burdening everyone with her problems. With the depression hanging over her, Tracy felt she had nothing to offer anyone. Debbie had tried to reach out on many occasions but had been met with a wall of silence. Just like Amber and just like Shocks, Tracy too was finally coming out of her shell to embrace the world.

"Debbie, she's walking, Amber's finally walking!" Tracy choked back the tears.

"I'll be right over," Debbie said, hanging up immediately.

Amber was more than ready to show off her new talent. This was another massive change, as Amber used to be painfully shy.

She took centre stage in the living room, holding on to the coffee table for balance while she steeled herself for the challenged ahead.

"That's it, you can do it for Auntie Debs," Tracy encouraged. The three adults, plus Hope, waited in a semi-circle across the other side of the room. Debbie dropped to her knees and opened her arms wide.

One, two, three, it was lift-off. Nothing was holding this girl back from walking now.

Debbie couldn't contain her giggles.

"She looks a little like she's sleepwalking with her arms stretched out in front like that," Debs joked.

It was true; she did have a zombie-like technique going on.

"I don't care if she walks like that for the rest of her life, as long as she can walk," Julian laughed.

Tracy and he had not anticipated what a ginormous change it would make to their lives to have Amber up and walking. It was as if their babies had bloomed into children overnight. They were zipping all over the place like two bumper cars at the fairground. Forward a bit, bump, fall over, forwards again, and accelerate.

They had to lug the suctioning machine everywhere to keep up with their new racing car.

A couple of weeks later, the couple were slumped onto the sofa, exhausted.

"Do you remember the time when they were lying on the pillows and we were wishing for the day they were up and running about?" Julian sighed.

"Yes." Tracy smirked.

"I'm regretting that wish, the girls are nonstop," he joked.

Tracy patted him on the leg.

"I'll make you a cup of tea," she said. She knew that always made things better.

Amber's walking had not only changed their daughter's life, and injected happiness into the family, but there was another miraculous turnaround. Amber and her sister's relationship had transformed almost overnight.

For starters: they could hold each other's hands. They shuffled back and forth across the living room like two old ladies.

Tracy fell about roaring with laughter. It was the funniest thing to watch.

Hope had also developed a 'schoolteacher' way of speaking to Amber. Because Amber couldn't talk back, Hope liked to boss her around. She would tell her to "Follow me"; to "Sit down"; she'd even wag her finger at her sister.

Amber didn't seem to mind one bit though. She would blissfully go along with whatever her sister asked of her. It was water off a duck's back to Amber. She was developing into a very relaxed, easy-going toddler.

Amber could communicate a bit, mind. Thanks to the speech and learning worker, who visited every week, Amber had learned some sign language. She could say please, which is where you fold your hand away from your chest. She could say thank you and, more importantly, she could say biscuit, which was placing a hand on top of a fist. Of course, she could also say 'Shocks', but that was her own made-up language.

Tracy couldn't wait to show off Amber to the team at the Donkey Sanctuary. She had chatted for hours with the other mums and Andy, Big Amber and Sara about how she'd dreamed of the moment when Amber finally learned to walk. She couldn't have done it without them, without Shocks, and she wanted to express her gratitude.

Amber, on the other hand, was keen to show off her new pair of glasses. Her cerebral palsy was causing her to squint in her left eye, so the optician had fitted her with some nice pink-rimmed spectacles. Tracy made sure she chose a matching pink party dress for the occasion too.

As soon as they arrived in the car park, Amber wriggled like mad in the car seat. She was like a racehorse, waiting for the starting gun. Tracy lifted her to the ground and Amber turned into a show horse prancing around an arena. She lifted one foot high, and then the other.

"Look at me, I can walk!" she would have been shouting if she could.

"Come on you." Tracy took her hand to hurry her along. Amber wasn't having any of it. She was determined to reach reception unaided.

Tracy smiled as she pondered whether Amber had inherited her stubbornness from her mum.

Tracy rang the bell and waited for the grand entrance. Amber toddled past the reception desk, casually waving. Gill, the centre coordinator, peered over the desk as Amber shimmied past; she couldn't believe her eyes.

"She's walking," Gill mouthed in disbelief.

Tracy was beaming. She was the proudest mum on earth.

They could hear Big Amber's voice booming across the reception hall. Little Amber homed in on it like a missile; she wanted to show her friend her new skills.

"Amber, you're walking!" Big Amber shrieked.

Amber giggled with happiness. She reached out her arms to be picked up.

More staff had crowded around now. It was incredibly rewarding for them to see such a transformation. These magical moments made all their hard work worthwhile.

Big Amber spun her around in her arms. She adored Little Amber. It was hard not to; Amber was extremely cute with her blonde hair and now her big geeky glasses.

Little Amber kept on spinning when Amber set her back down to earth – she was enjoying the audience.

Andy spotted the crowd and came over to say hi. Tracy thought she spotted a tear welling in his eye.

"I'm so happy for you both," Andy said, blinking the teardrop away.

Andy was a sensitive guy. He wouldn't be so good at understanding the donkeys otherwise. It was a gift and a curse at the same time – Andy could sometimes feel overwhelmed with emotions.

He'd seen a lot of happy endings at the Donkey Sanctuary. Andy opened up to Tracy about one story that he knew he'd never forget.

"We had an autistic boy come and help out for a while …"

Andy explained how the boy was a bit older than the rest of the children who usually come to ride the donkeys. He was seventeen and hadn't spoken a word his whole life.

Tracy looked at him intently. She found comfort in hearing other children's journeys to recovery.

"He would help me clean out the stables, he worked really hard, and it would be a job trying to get him to stop."

Amber toddled over to listen to Andy's story too.

"He loved the donkeys; his face would light up when he was around them. He was shy when he was around us lot," Andy carried on.

Andy explained how the doctors and his parents weren't sure if he'd ever speak.

"And then, one day, when I was sweeping out the stable, he said something." Andy smiled as he remembered the moment. "'Brush,' the boy said, as he went over to groom Bob's coat.

"I thought I'd misheard it at first, but the teenager said it again, and then again."

Just like Amber learning to walk, Tracy thought. Amber had wanted to try it over and over.

"What happened to him?" Tracy was fascinated by the story.

Andy explained that, as for many of the children who came to the Donkey Sanctuary, the boy's developments there had allowed him to move on to another chapter in his life.

"He gradually started speaking some more. He's gone to college now," said Andy triumphantly.

The story was just one of dozens of happy endings the Donkey Sanctuary had witnessed over the eleven years since opening the centre in Birmingham. When Tracy first came to the Sanctuary a year ago, she would never have believed a donkey could make such a difference to someone's life. Shocks had helped transform Amber, though, and Tracy herself, and now she was a true believer.

The positivity radiating from the Sanctuary was contagious.

But of course there was still a long way for Amber to go. She was only just walking at three years old. There was a question mark over whether she would be able to go to school. And would she ever be able to speak?

Tracy swatted the thoughts to the back of her mind, for today was a celebration.

"Let's go say hello to Shocks, shall we, Amber?" Tracy said.

Amber used her arms like airplane wings to steady her journey over to meet her friend.

All of a sudden, she stopped dead in her tracks.

"What's wrong, Amber?" Tracy said, looking over.

Amber folded her arms and peered over her spectacles grumpily.

Another child was getting ready to ride Shocks, *her* donkey.

Andy instantly sensed what the problem was. He crouched down to meet Amber's glare.

"It's important Shocks rides with the other children because he needs to make friends, just like you." Andy tried to explain to Amber they were both on a road to recovery.

Amber scrunched up her nose and tapped her foot.

"Okay, that's quite enough, madam." Tracy stepped in.

She hadn't seen this side of Amber before, and wasn't quite sure how to deal with it.

"Go on Moses for now, and you can ride Shocks later." Tracy tried to get Amber out of her strop.

Amber shook her head in protest. She wanted to wait for her friend. There was no way she was going to ride another donkey. Tracy rolled her eyes at Andy, who laughed sympathetically.

"Children, eh?" he said.

Amber stood glued to the gate, watching her rival's every move. She really had perfected the disgruntled look of peering over her glasses with her arms crossed.

She waved to Shocks to let him know she had arrived. Shocks noticed her straight away. He turned and tilted his head, as if to say: "I'll be with you in a moment."

It brought a smile back to Amber's face.

Amber couldn't take her jealousy out on a girl she didn't know, so her sister Hope got the brunt of it instead. As soon as Hope was back from nursery, Amber threw her toys out of the pram, literally.

If Hope was playing with a building block, Amber tried to snatch it away.

"No, Amber." Julian told her off, just like he'd scolded Hope all that time ago for doing the same thing.

"And there was me thinking Amber was laid-back ..." Tracy threw her hands up, baffled by the sudden turnaround.

She filled Julian in on what had happened at the Donkey Sanctuary. How Amber had been very possessive over Shocks. On the one hand, it was endearing to see how much she loved her friend, but they could also recognise it was something that needed to be nipped in the bud.

"She's going to have to get used to other children riding Shocks," Julian commented.

Tracy suggested they take both the girls back to Saturday Club. Maybe Amber would be more relaxed about the situation with her sister around?

The morning started off well. There was even a surprise meeting with Liz and Sam and their daughter Abbie.

Liz and Sam couldn't believe how much progress Amber had made.

"I told you, I told you ..." Liz teased the Austwicks about how she had been right about the healing power of the donkeys.

It was a really nice atmosphere, with the adults and the children celebrating together. Amber took Hope's hand; she wanted to show her the outdoor play area. Amber liked to wait there until her number was called because she could see all the other donkeys grazing in the paddock.

Amber pointed at Bob and Lob; the two Irish boys had come to take a closer look at what was going on. The staff called the boys 'twins' because they were rescued from the same farm. They weren't actual twins, although they may as well have been, because they were inseparable. Amber wanted to introduce her twin to the cheeky duo.

But Hope wasn't the slightest bit interested. She was keener on playing with the toys in the yard and watching the other children.

"Hope, Amber, time for your ride!" Tracy beckoned the girls over.

Amber was a little girl on a mission. She practically tripped over her toes trying to overtake Hope on their way to the arena.

"Slow down, Amber." Julian signalled a 'calm down' motion with his hands.

But Amber didn't want to slow down; she needed to get to Shocks.

Tracy spied danger from afar.

"There's another girl getting off Shocks," Tracy reported to Julian. Being grown-ups, they could see that little bit further away to the ménage, where the riders were dismounting.

"Keep her distracted,"' Julian said with a wink.

"Are you looking forward to riding Shocks?" Tracy chirped, pretending everything was hunky-dory.

Amber came to a crashing stop at the gate. She was wheezing and struggling for air.

Tracy knelt down to suction out the gunk from her airway.

"Calm down, Amber." Tracy became more stern. She didn't like to see her baby girl getting so worked up.

As soon as Hope caught up with Amber, Amber turned on her sister.

When Hope wrapped her fingers around the bar on the gate, Amber brushed them off.

When Hope moved closer to where the gate opened from, Amber held her back with her arm, just like children squabbling over the front seat of the car.

"Oh, this is ridiculous," Tracy muttered. "Now, wait your turn, both of you." She wagged her fingers at the girls.

Andy was in his usual post of holding the reins. However, as it was a Saturday, a volunteer they hadn't met before came to greet them at the gate.

She was a very softly spoken woman, whom Tracy suspected might be in a similar boat to herself. A lot of the volunteers had children with assisted needs. They had turned to the Donkey Sanctuary – much in the same vein as Julian and Tracy – as a last-ditch attempt to help their child get better. Of course, once they'd become immersed in the world of the donkeys, it was hard to step away.

The woman, who had ash-coloured hair and very tanned skin, picked Hope up first. She started to carry her over to Shocks, who was waiting patiently behind his friend, Jacko.

Julian sprang into action. This woman didn't know the score.

"Excuse me, excuse me," he called out, waving.

She turned back, a little surprised.

"Sorry, I don't mean to sound picky, but could Hope please go on the other donkey because that's Amber's donkey?" He pointed to Shocks sheepishly.

Julian and Tracy were in a tricky situation. On the one hand, they didn't want to encourage spoilt behaviour but, on the other, Amber wouldn't be getting better if it weren't for Shocks. They couldn't let anything get in the way of her recovery.

"Oh yeah, no worries," the woman said obligingly.

That was the wonderful thing about the Donkey Sanctuary: everyone was friendly and sympathetic – non-judgemental. *To an outsider it would have sounded a ridiculous request,* Julian thought to himself.

Of course, Hope wasn't bothered in the slightest. She could have been riding Bob or Lob for all she cared.

Amber had grown so much in strength the volunteer lady needed only one arm to keep her in the saddle. She waved enthusiastically to her mum and dad every time she passed the gate.

It was interesting for Andy to watch Shocks's behaviour too. He'd been hoping for some time that Shocks might take the lead in the arena. Andy had tried everything, even dangling a ginger biscuit under his nose – they love them more than carrots! – but Shocks had always screeched to a halt behind the donkey in front. It was a confidence thing; he didn't believe in himself enough. It was similar to his stance in the paddock – he would rather hide in the shadows.

Andy thought there was a chance of a turnaround with the help of Jacko. After all, if Shocks could overtake anyone, it would be his laid-back stable buddy.

He gently pulled on the reins to see if Shocks would give it a try this time. No, Shocks was having none of it. He patiently waited for Jacko and Hope to complete their activities and then he followed with Amber.

"That's okay, boy, you don't have to do anything you don't want." Andy gave him a scratch behind his ears.

Shocks twitched his nose and let out a head-shaking sneeze. A good scratch always made him sneeze for some reason.

As the ride came to an end, Amber became anxious about the other children queuing up. She turned to Andy, searching for reassurance.

"It's okay, Amber, no one else is riding Shocks today." He instinctively knew what she was asking.

They were breaking Shocks in gently. Only a few new children were allowed to ride him every week. It was vital the team got the correct balance of pushing him on, but not so hard he regressed.

Amber lurched forward and wrapped her arms around her best friend. She didn't want to let go.

"Come on, Amber, time to say goodbye." Andy tried to loosen her grip.

Amber rubbed her hands over Shocks's scarred neck. Her friend sighed heavily, like he understood she was having a tough day.

Julian and Tracy were waving at the sidelines, reminding Amber it was time to go home.

"Someone's getting heavier," Andy teased Amber, as he lifted her to the ground.

Shocks was waiting for her. His nose was down, his eyes locked onto hers. Amber hugged and kissed him as if it was the last time they would see each other.

"Shocks," she mouthed. Not a sound came out but Shocks understood.

Amber was unusually quiet on the car journey home. Tracy started to worry something wasn't quite right. Everything had been going so well, and now Trace had this ball of anxiety bouncing around in her stomach.

She watched the girls like a hawk at lunchtime.

"Amber seems off her food." Tracy panicked.

It was Julian's turn to tell her not to fret. But Tracy couldn't help it; she had fought so hard to see Amber get better, and she was terrified of going back to the way things were.

She fell back into some familiar routines to calm herself. Doing the washing-up, cleaning the kitchen – burying her feelings.

Amber needed more suctioning than usual that afternoon, which worried Tracy even more. She was a box of nerves, ready to explode.

She hadn't counted on seeing this side of Amber – her jealousy. Her sheer anxiety at the thought of losing her friend.

She remembered what Julian had spoken to her about before she had started going to the Donkey Sanctuary – that she should share her problems with him.

She cleared her throat as she approached her husband. It was hard for Trace to open up.

"What's up, lovie?" Julian read her mood.

She perched on the end of the sofa, like a bird about to fly off at any moment.

"I think we might have to stop Amber from seeing Shocks," Tracy blurted out.

Julian furrowed his brow as his wife continued.

"I just don't want Amber becoming sick again. She's wheezing all day, she's clearly not happy about him riding with other children, I just can't bear to see her …"

Julian cut in.

"It's just a phase, lovie. She'll get over it," he said confidently.

Tracy nodded. But inside her stomach was churning.

Maybe this was the end of Amber and Shocks? she thought. Tracy decided they'd keep their distance from the Sanctuary for a while. Amber's behaviour and her frenzied breathing that day had worried her, and she wasn't prepared to risk her daughter's recovery – for anything.

CHAPTER 18

One of the Lads

Sutton Park, Birmingham,
Summer 2013

The Donkey Sanctuary team should have known better than to put Mackenzie in a stable with Bob and Lob.

There had been an outbreak of Seedy Toe amongst some of the boys – a contagious infection whereby a nasty fungus eats its way up the inside of the hoof, causing cavities. If left untreated, it can cause lameness. Jacko had managed to contract the painful condition and had to be kept in isolation for a little while.

That meant Shocks had to share a stable with the leader of the pack, Mackenzie, and the Irish twins.

"It will be good for him," Andy said to Big Amber and Sara, "to get Shocks to mix with some of the popular boys."

There is always someone who does the 'night watch' at the Sanctuary, to make sure no harm comes to the donkeys. They had recently recruited a mum called Jess. She had moved, with her two-year-old daughter, into the warden's house, which was less than 100 yards from the stables.

The donkeys are quick to cotton on to a new warden. And they know exactly where the warden's house is in relation to the paddock. At around 5 p.m. they bray outside her window, telling her, or rather shouting, that they would like their hay and their bed now.

Shocks was last to come in on that particular night, as usual. He had a habit of hanging back until someone went to fetch him.

"You're sharing with the naughty boys tonight," Andy gently teased, leading him across the paddock.

There was one stable in the yard that had a double lock system – similar to the swinging doors you find in old Western films. If the two locks that bolt the doors together aren't shut firmly enough, a naughty donkey, such as Mackenzie, might be able to break them open with his hoof.

But Andy had no choice but to put Shocks in there because it was the only stable big enough to hold four donkeys.

"Come on, don't be shy," Andy said, guiding him in. Bob and Lob didn't even look up from their chomping. Mackenzie glared at Shocks for a moment as if to say: "Don't even think about eating my hay."

Shocks hid in the corner. He was too timid even to take his share of the hay.

"Oi, you three, be nice to your guest." Andy wagged his finger.

All the other donkeys swung their heads over their stable doors, mesmerised by what Andy was doing. He was just giving the yard one last sweep, but it was much more interesting than what was going on in their stables. Donkeys are nosy creatures.

"Okay, boys, bed," Andy shouted, like a parent to his kids who refused to go to sleep.

Tony let off a whiny bray as Andy walked out of the yard – a 'don't go' bray.

It always tugged on Andy's heartstrings.

He turned back to be met by a dozen sad-looking eyes watching him from over their stable doors.

"I'm going, niiiight!" Andy wasn't going to be sucked back in. He had to be firm with these boys or they'd run rings around him.

"Tough love," he muttered to himself.

He spotted Jess as he walked up the lane towards Sutton Park. It was a beautiful summer's evening. The path was dappled with sunlight that had filtered through the canopy of trees that lined the route.

"Settling in okay?" he asked, holding his hand up like a visor to shade the sun's glare.

"Like a duck to water." Jess grinned. The twenty-three-year-old had started out as a volunteer for the Sanctuary, but, when the vacancy arose to live on site, she jumped at the chance. "I love being surrounded by all this peace and quiet." She gestured towards the fields and trees and distant park.

"Peace and quiet ..." Andy raised both his eyebrows knowingly, thinking of the noisy brays of the donkeys in Jess's care.

The donkeys have a strict routine. They wake up around 5 a.m., but aren't let out until 7 a.m. In winter, it's a bit later, at 8 a.m. Donkeys tend to sleep standing up but they can lie down if they feel relaxed. It will only be for a few hours at a time though – a natural instinct to protect them from predators. The donkeys enjoy sunbathing in the paddock, but only if another donkey in the herd is keeping watch.

Later that evening, just as Andy had done with his 'children', Jess tucked her child, Phoebe, into bed, and then settled down in front of the TV with her boyfriend Marc.

She put her feet up on the coffee table and slouched into the worn sofa that bore the indents from previous wardens. Jess and Marc flicked through the channels, indecisive about what to watch. They settled for the classic RomCom *There's Something About Mary*.

Jess felt cosy and content tucked inside her house in the countryside. It was lovely to be in the peace and quiet. Aside from the background murmur of the television, all she could hear was the comforting hooting of the neighbourhood owl.

Her eyelids grew heavy, and rolled down like shutters. Jess hadn't realised she'd dozed off on the sofa until she was jolted awake by an ear-splitting siren.

"The donkeys!" she cried, jumping into her steel-toe-capped boots and throwing on her coat.

"I'll come with you?" Marc said.

"No, you stay here with Phoebe." Jess replied, half out the door.

The stables may look like something from a nineteenth-century novel, but they are actually equipped with a high-tech alarm system made up of lasers. Across every stable door is a laser; if the beam is broken, the alarm sounds.

Someone's stealing the donkeys. Jess panicked.

She sprinted through the car park and down the lane to the stables. The temperature had plummeted – the cold air burned her lungs. Her heart was pounding so hard she could hear it in her ears.

She screeched to a halt at the gate – and couldn't believe what she was seeing.

Three donkeys were dancing around the yard in the moonlight. They were having a whale of a time.

The hell-raisers had broken out of the stable and brought all their straw bedding with them.

"You rascals!" Jess shouted. She was seriously hacked off.

Shocks was standing on the sidelines, watching them. *Should I? Shan't I?* Jess could tell he was deliberating whether to join in.

"Don't you dare," she warned him.

Goody Two-Shoes Shocks took one step forward, and then another clop, and the next thing he knew, he was pulled into the chaos. Shocks kicked his hind legs in glee as Jess ran circles around the yard after them.

If the boys could speak, they would have been singing: "Na na nan naaaa na, you can't catch me!"

All the other donkeys were watching over their stable doors, cheering them on. There were brays coming from Jess's left, to her right; they were all riled up and wanting to play.

Bob was wearing a blanket to keep him warm, as his hair had only just been clipped. Mackenzie started to pull it off. Lob joined in.

"Oi no, leave that," Jess scolded them.

It fell on deaf donkey ears.

Jess threw her hands onto her hips and stared at the god-awful mess.

"No breakfast for you then," she muttered.

Jess grabbed a head collar and a lead rope and charged towards the ringleader – Mackenzie. She knew, if she had him under control, the others would fall into line.

"Come here, you." Jess lurched forward to grab him. Lucky she had steel toecaps on or she would risk a broken foot!

Mackenzie dodged her hand and made another victory lap of the yard. Jess suddenly had a much better idea. She rummaged around in her coat pocket.

"Ah ha! I knew I had it in there somewhere," she cheered, pulling out a ginger nut biscuit victoriously. The way to a donkey's heart is through his stomach, after all.

Jess waved it under Mackenzie's nose and the cheeky boy slowed to a gradual stop.

He sniffed the air and walked forward to claim his prize.

"Gotcha!" Jess celebrated, clipping the head collar and lead rope around Mackenzie's neck.

Jess was right; as soon as Mackenzie was back in the stable, Bob and Lob calmed down and did exactly as they were told. It was Shocks who was left stranded in the yard, surrounded by straw and mess. He didn't know what to do with himself.

Jess thought Shocks might feel frightened that he was going to be punished. The truth was, it was a good thing Shocks had run free with the bad boys. It meant he was growing in confidence.

It was similar to the situation Julian and Tracy were facing with Amber – how they didn't want to encourage her bad behaviour (in the form of her jealousy towards her sister and other children) but, at the same time, just as with Shocks, that bad behaviour was itself an indication of her progress along the road to recovery.

"I'm not going to hurt you, silly." Jess gently pulled Shocks back to his bed.

She fastened the locks, again, and double-checked them for good measure.

Jess left the straw on the yard; there was no way she was sweeping up after those boys at that time of night.

What time is it? Jess pondered as she walked in her front door. The red light on the cooker read: 1.54 a.m.

"Those bloody donkeys," she muttered, and then made her way to bed.

The night's events were discussed at length the following morning over a cup of tea.

Andy, who had just come in from sweeping up the mess, suspected the culprit was Mackenzie, who'd used a different trick to escape this time.

The donkeys that lived with horses before they came to the Sanctuary had acquired a unique set of skills from their equine friends. Horses are great escape artists: they can open stable-door locks with their teeth. Given Mackenzie's history of growing up around them, Andy was sure that was how he'd managed to get out. He'd broken out of every stable in the yard, except this one, until last night.

"I think he did it to show off to Shocks," Andy said. "Like naughty schoolkids."

He wiped his mucky hands on his trousers. Everyone else was hiding a smirk behind their mugs.

"I hope he doesn't pick up bad habits from those boys," Andy sighed.

Sara couldn't contain her laughter any longer. You couldn't help but find the whole thing very amusing. Sara set everyone else off into a fit of giggles.

"Well, at least someone finds it funny." Andy threw his arms up.

"Well, at least he's finally getting involved," she chuckled.

Sara was right, of course, and such a small thing as Shocks joining in the fun had led to a big change in the paddock, even overnight. Andy noticed how Shocks had become much more assertive with the breakfast hay nets that morning.

Of course he waited for the top dogs to have their feed first but, once they had finished pulling the net apart and chomping, Shocks dived in with the rest of them. It was as if he'd moved several rungs up the pecking order overnight.

"Good for you, boy." Andy grinned. He'd forgotten his grump about the morning's mess in the yard.

Like a smoking gun, Shocks wore the evidence of last night's crime – his brown coat was looking very grubby.

"You could do with a bath," Andy said to him.

Shocks stared back at him, dumbfounded. *A bath? What's that?* you could almost hear him think.

Considering Shocks used to bolt across the field whenever he saw Andy approach with a hosepipe, it was no surprise that the groom hadn't used it to wash him down.

But maybe we should give it a try today, Andy thought.

Andy ran through the variables in his head: the weather was still beautifully warm, so he didn't need to worry about Shocks catching a cold. Shocks was no longer scared of the hosepipe. And he let Andy brush him. So what was the worst that could happen? Shocks might actually enjoy it?

"Wait here, boy, I've got a treat for you," Andy instructed, as he went to fetch the blue hose and the bucket full of donkey-washing equipment. Just like people have sponges, and loofah brushes, and exfoliating mitts, donkeys have the squeegee. It's just like a car squeegee; only it's used to wipe down a donkey rather than a windscreen.

Andy wasn't sure if Shocks would let him use it; before then, he had to start with the basics – with the water.

Andy gingerly stepped towards Shocks, holding the hose out with both hands. The tap was only half open so there was a gentle trickle of water flowing across the concrete yard.

Andy gave the hosepipe a good tug, sending it to ripple like a rattlesnake.

Shocks jerked backwards.

"Easy, boy, I'm not going to hurt you, it's just water." Andy ran the cold stream across his fingers to show Shocks it wasn't harmful.

Shocks opened his nostrils wide, and sneezed – his answer to everything.

Andy tested the water, quite literally, with Shocks's legs. The donkey didn't seem to mind one bit, so Andy moved the hose a bit higher, to the tops of Shocks's long legs, and then across his back. Shocks closed his eyes and almost purred with happiness. It must have felt refreshing, like an ice-cold drink on a hot summer's day.

"You like that, don't you, my boy?" Andy chatted away.

He then pulled out the squeegee and got to work with ringing out the leftover water and mud. Shocks stood perfectly still for Andy. He clearly liked the attention.

Andy deliberated for a moment about whether he should run the water across Shocks's neck. His wounds had healed long ago, but the scars were still visible in the bright light of day. They looked like a silver lightning bolt slicing his head from his body.

Shocks gazed up at him through his long dark eyelashes, as if to say: "Why have you stopped washing me?"

"Sorry, sir," Andy joked.

Andy often caught himself drifting into deep thought about Shocks and his horrific past when he looked at the donkey's neck injuries.

"In those five happy years I worked here, you were in misery and pain." Andy tried to quantify how long Shocks had suffered for. "Time to wash away your past." Andy took the hose to Shocks's neck.

The giant donkey didn't flinch a bit. On the contrary, he seemed to love the feeling of the cool water across his shaggy fur.

Andy had goosebumps. He couldn't quite believe he was finally able to touch the whole of Shocks without Shocks being frightened.

It was a breakthrough moment. He'd finally won Shocks's trust. Andy felt like yelling, "Yee-ha!"

Instead, he settled for a shower of his own. Shocks shook himself like a dog, splattering Andy with water.

First he was mucky from sweeping the yard; now he was drenched in water ... good thing he loved the donkeys. It wasn't a job for anyone who couldn't stand getting their hands dirty!

On the other side of Sutton Park, Amber was also experiencing her first bath – physiotherapy-style. She'd of course had many washes over the past three years – which consisted of Tracy dipping Amber in a baby bath with only an inch of water in it, so as not to risk any liquid getting into her trachy. It was the one parental duty Julian just couldn't face. He found mixing water and Amber's tracheostomy nerve-racking. Julian couldn't even bring himself to watch Trace wash Amber.

So it was no surprise he was a little hesitant when Lucy, the physio, suggested Amber tried hydrotherapy. The very term conjured up scary images of Amber slipping underwater, her lungs filling …

He shook his head to shake away the horrific thought.

"It will be absolutely fine, we will stay in the shallow end of the pool," Lucy reassured the couple.

Amber had made incredible progress with her walking; however, she was still teetering on her tiptoes. Lucy wanted to try to get her left foot flat on the ground. The regular physiotherapy was hurting Amber, so that's why Lucy had suggested the pool. Hopefully, the weightlessness caused by the water might help.

"I'm just not sure," Julian said hesitantly.

Tracy shot him a look, in the way she usually did when she was pushing for something.

"Let's just give it a go," she urged.

It was the same dynamic every time. Tracy pushed Julian to try new things and, in turn, Julian calmed Tracy's nerves. It was the magic glue in their relationship. Most couples would have struggled to maintain a marriage with everything they had been through; the fact they were still going strong was a testament to their love and respect for each other.

Julian didn't mind coming along for the necessary shopping trip though – picking out Amber's first swimming costume would be fun. However, he should have known better than to think they would have some influence in the decision!

Amber's eyes lit up as her mum and dad pushed her in the trolley along the clothing aisle at Asda. Her head was swishing from left to right as she took in all the colours and designs. She was no doubt dreaming up a new party outfit to show off to Shocks.

They stopped by the kids' bathing suit section. Tracy and Julian had had no idea there would be such a selection, from bikinis to swimming costumes, some emblazoned with cartoon characters, such as Minions and My Little Pony. Tracy held up a selection for Amber's approval.

"Which one do you want?" Tracy asked.

Amber scrunched up her nose as she deliberated.

The early support worker, Barbara, had once told Tracy that she should always encourage the children to make their own decisions because it makes their brains develop more. It was a theory the Donkey Sanctuary also swore by, hence all the tasks during the donkey rides involved choices. *Which letterbox should I post it through? Which card should I pick up?* There were dozens of choices mapped out for the children, whether it be shapes or colours.

Now Amber had to decide – *Should I go for Peppa Pig, the Little Mermaid or Minnie Mouse?*

She pointed to the red Minnie Mouse costume with white polka dots.

"Good choice, Amber," Julian said encouragingly.

Amber couldn't wait to get home to try her bathing suit on. As soon as they walked through the door, she grabbed the bag and scuttled into the living room to get changed. There was a little pile of clothes on the floor to mark where Amber had been.

She paraded her new outfit up and down the living room, like a peacock showing off its feathers.

She was smiling from ear to ear. There was no way she was going to take it off any time soon.

Amber even insisted on eating her tea in her bathing suit.

She was just as keen to show off her new garment the following day. The swimming pool Lucy wanted to use was attached to Wilson Stuart School – where they had met Ms Christmas a year and a quarter ago. It was designed for children with assisted needs.

Amber was a real hit in the changing rooms. There must have been at least half a dozen other mums getting ready to go for a splash with their children. The kids varied massively in age and disabilities. There was a seventeen-year-old girl who was paralysed from the waist down. Tracy wondered how she was going to be able to swim. She remembered the first time they had visited the donkeys, how she and Julian had had so many questions about how the children would be able to ride.

Amber was by far the smallest there though, so she attracted quite an audience in her little Minnie Mouse swimming costume.

"She's adorable," all the mums cooed.

Amber looked coyly up at the adults – just like Shocks, some might say; they both had mastered the art of gazing through their eyelashes.

Tracy smiled proudly – not just because Amber was getting so much attention, but at the distance Amber had travelled since she last stepped foot in the school. A year and a half ago, Amber would have wanted to hide in a corner, but now she was lapping up the limelight.

Tracy carried the suctioning machine over one arm and held Amber's hand tightly with her other as they walked into the pool area. Julian and Lucy were waiting for them; poor Julian was looking nervous. The heat and the humidity in the room was sky high. It had to be warm for the children who couldn't move much, but it spelled trouble for Amber's lungs.

"Is she going to be able to breathe okay?" Julian worried.

"We can always leave if it gets too much," Tracy reassured him.

Meanwhile, Amber was blissfully unaware of the grown-ups' concerns. She was wearing a big grin; it was the most excited they had seen Amber about her physiotherapy!

Lucy guided the Austwicks to the ramp that led into the pool. It was where the wheelchairs went in and out. Lucy reassured them they would stay at the top of the ramp, where the water was at its most shallow and would only reach to Amber's waist.

Amber tested the water by dipping her little toes in first.

"Oh God, I can't watch." Julian panicked.

Lucy had a firm grip on Amber with both hands but that didn't stop Julian conjuring up scary thoughts.

One false move and Amber could go under. Her life was in Lucy's hands. It was too much to bear.

Julian, selflessly, didn't want Amber to pick up on his anxiety, so he swam away into the deep end of the pool.

"Is Julian okay?" Lucy asked, bewildered.

"Oh yes, he's fine, he just can't watch Amber and water together," Tracy explained.

Tracy sat on the side of the pool with her legs crossed, armed with the suctioning machine, ready to dive in at any moment.

Lucy made Amber hold onto the side and kick back into the water with her legs. She enjoyed making a splash. Next, Lucy tried bending Amber's knee up and moving her hip around. She was trying to loosen up Amber's muscles – it was the tightness that was causing Amber to stand on her tiptoe. Amber didn't like this so much.

Trace was tempted to use donkey bribes but she caught the words before they left her mouth. How long was she going to keep Amber and Shocks apart? Maybe Julian was right about it just being a jealous phase. It had been a week since they had been to the Sanctuary, and, if truth be told, Tracy was starting to have serious withdrawal symptoms herself! She pushed her thoughts to the back of her mind for now.

Lucy cleverly mixed up the not-so-enjoyable exercises with the fun ones. Lucy lined up a bunch of toys on the side so Amber would have to use her muscles to reach for them. Amber's favourite was the pink plastic watering can. Julian glanced over just at the moment Amber lifted it above her head and poured the water out like a mini waterfall.

"Oh God." He looked away.

Tracy chuckled. "Are you going to say that every five minutes?" she teased.

Julian was right to worry about the humidity though. It was the only downside of the experience. Tracy had to suction Amber's airways more than usual because the heat had loosened up the gunk in her chest.

Amber coped with it well though. She even had a smile on her face at some moments throughout the therapy, such as when the teenager, who'd been in the wheelchair in the changing rooms, waved to her from across the pool. Amber was mesmerised by the fact the girl was floating on her back. She looked at Lucy as if to say, "Can I do that?"

"No, Amber, you'll have to make do with your watering can for now," Tracy chipped in.

Even though it was much more enjoyable for Amber, she still carried that 'disgruntled look' in the session. And after about half an hour it was obvious she was exhausted, so they called it a day.

Amber still managed a little wave to her new friends in the pool before disappearing back into the changing rooms. Tracy re-emerged a short time later carrying Amber in her arms. Her head was heavy on her mum's shoulders, her eyelids half closed.

The school was just up the road from their house, but Julian made sure Amber was wrapped up warm. The last thing she needed was to catch a cold – it could set her back weeks. He wrapped several blankets around her; Amber looked like the Michelin man by the time she was bundled into the back of the car.

She was fast asleep by the time they pulled into their drive. Julian carried his little Eskimo to the sofa, where she slept until teatime.

Amber woke to find Hope next to her. What's more, she had a present for her sister – a picture she'd drawn at nursery. It was the first time Hope had wanted to give Amber something. The rest of her art collection had been for Mum and Dad.

"Ahhhh, that's lovely, Hope." Julian encouraged the new caring side in his daughter.

"What's it a picture of?" he asked. It was hard to decipher the squiggles on the page.

"Shocks," Hope said, grinning proudly.

"Of course it is." Julian smothered his laugh.

Amber wriggled her hands on her head to do donkey ears. She then turned to her mum as if to ask: "So when are we going to see Shocks?"

Tracy felt a pang of guilt.

How could she keep Amber and Shocks apart? What was she thinking?

The girls were getting on fine, there was no jealousy between them; quite the opposite in fact. Tracy was missing Shocks too. She had underestimated the impact the donkeys had on her mood. Her depression had been lifting and she had no doubt that was thanks to the Sanctuary.

It had only been a week, but Tracy had already missed that rush she got every time they entered Sutton Park. When she could breathe again, a long inhale and exhale of fresh country air.

They went back to the Sanctuary the very next day.

Tracy brought along a packet of ginger biscuits as a treat for the donkeys. The staff were very strict about feeding – only they are allowed to give the donkeys treat-buckets of apples, ginger biscuits and polo mints. If it were left in the hands of the visitors, the donkeys would be obese! But Tracy knew the staff would hand out her gift at an appropriate time on her behalf.

Amber wanted to go to the paddock as soon as they arrived. Tracy noticed Shocks's clean coat straight away.

Shocks, meanwhile, noticed Amber straight away – and walked over to the gate to say hello. There was a great big fence between them, but it didn't stop Shocks dropping his head so Amber could stroke his fur through the gaps in the wire.

"They've missed each other." Andy came up behind Trace. "It sounds a bit soppy," he continued, "but you can see the difference in Shocks's mood immediately. He'll have a smile on his face for the rest of the day now."

Tracy had to bite her lip to stop herself from welling up.

"It's not soppy," she said, in the end. "Amber is the same. She's lost without Shocks."

CHAPTER 19

A Cruel World

Sutton Coldfield, Birmingham,
Summer 2013

Tracy was so used to the kindness and the non-judgemental way people behaved at the Donkey Sanctuary, she'd forgotten how cruel the outside world could be.

She was reminded while at the supermarket one day. Amber was toddling alongside the trolley, pointing at things she thought her mum ought to buy. Tracy heard that familiar crackling noise in Amber's trachy tube and told her to slow down for a moment.

She crouched by Amber's side, inserted the catheter, switched on the noisy suctioning machine, and got on with removing the gunk.

Out of the corner of her eye, Tracy spotted a little girl, much the same age as Amber, looking at what was going on. She didn't seem frightened, just curious, like all children her age were.

Tracy was about to smile at the girl, when her mum grabbed her hand and pulled her along.

"Come on, she's poorly," she said as she yanked her away, as if Amber had some sort of disease.

It was such a blow, Tracy felt like she'd been punched in the stomach. "She's not poorly, she's just got a trachy," Tracy wanted to shout after the woman. She wanted to fight her daughter's corner, but the woman had already disappeared from sight.

They'd had a few instances when strangers had asked what Amber's trachy was; some mistaking it for a necklace, of all things. But this was the first time she'd been met with hostility. Tracy would rather people asked than stared. The reality was, Amber had lived such a sheltered life until now, to-ing and fro-ing between their family home and the Sanctuary.

"Come on, Amber, let's get home." Tracy cut short their outing. But the horrible feeling hung over her for the rest of the day, like a black cloud. *How will Amber cope by herself?* Tracy worried. *She won't have her mum and dad to protect her all the time against people who point and stare.* They were thinking about sending their daughter to nursery in September and Tracy was more concerned than ever about letting her baby go.

Her fears were about to explode out of her mouth by the time Julian asked her what was eating her.

"There is no way we are sending Amber to nursery unless she can speak," Tracy blurted.

Julian threw his arms up in the air with frustration, but Tracy wasn't finished.

"No way. She's got this big piece of plastic sticking out of her neck; she's got mild cerebral palsy; she has special shoes … I don't want Amber not being able to speak as well.

"I'm worried she'll be bullied." Tracy welled up at the thought of her baby being persecuted by the other kids for being 'different'.

Julian tried to reason with Tracy.

"It doesn't matter if she can speak or not, it's just nursery, we can think about her speech later. We don't want to do anything to set Amber back," he argued.

Tracy shook her head vehemently.

"She'll be left behind because she can't talk to express herself. No way."

Tracy had to leave the room to cool down.

"Lovie," Julian called after her, but Tracy was too overwhelmed with emotion to respond. The protectiveness she felt over her daughter was indescribable.

In some ways, this was the biggest challenge the Austwicks had faced – it was crunch time.

On the one hand, it was incredible they could even consider sending Amber to nursery with Hope in September 2013. If it hadn't been for Shocks, Amber would never have been strong enough to go. She wouldn't even have been walking.

That was always Julian's line of argument – 'let's just be happy she's alive'.

But on the other hand, Tracy knew how cruel other children can be and she didn't want her daughter to suffer more than she had already. If there was a chance Amber could speak, then they had to do everything in their power to make that happen. She wanted her daughter to have the best start in life possible.

After all, they'd never thought she would be able to walk, to eat food by herself – and look at Amber now. *Miracles can happen*, Tracy thought.

Once Tracy had steeled herself and taken a few big gulps of air, she returned to the lounge. Julian looked up at her, apprehensive of what was to come.

"I think it's time we went to see the surgeon, Mr Kuo," Tracy announced.

Julian flinched. He knew he was walking through a minefield of emotions when his wife became driven like this – anything could set her off. He was very concerned Tracy could be setting herself up for a fall. What if they couldn't find a way to make Amber speak? As much as he didn't want Amber's health to regress, he didn't want Tracy to become depressed again.

He reminded Tracy of what the surgeon had said two and a half years ago, when Amber was six months old.

"The chances of the operation being successful are slim," Julian warned her.

But Tracy didn't want to hear 'no' for an answer. She was determined. She picked up the phone and dialled Birmingham Children's Hospital. Thankfully, they didn't have to wait too long to see the surgeon as Amber was one of his outpatients.

Julian had a little word in Tracy's ear the morning of the meeting.

"Now look, lovie, we don't know if Amber's vocal cords even work. If there is nothing we can do, then it doesn't matter, we will still love her all the same," Julian explained. "We will find a way to make things work, whether that be sign language or …"

He trailed off. His words appeared to be falling on deaf ears. Tracy seemed a million miles away as she fastened the girls into their car seats.

Going to the hospital always stirred up a cocktail of emotions for the Austwicks. For one, Julian hated Amber going near the place for fear she might catch an infection – but that was only the start of it.

As they walked along the sterile-smelling corridors, remembering all they had been through, the couple was hit by a wave of grief. A moment later, they were on a high, as they looked down at their daughters, now toddling alongside them – how far they had come! Hope was fascinated by the people and the noises. Amber, however, marched with her arms gripped by her side, her face like thunder. Hospitals meant one thing to her – pain – and immediately made her slip back into her shell.

"You remember Mr Kuo, don't you, Amber?" Julian said, as the family filed into his office.

Amber peered over her glasses in her disgruntled, and slightly wary, way.

Mr Kuo humoured her by welcoming the twins with a huge smile.

"Come in, come in." He beckoned them inside with a sweeping motion of his arms.

Mr Kuo was a very confident man. Julian would never forget the time when he and Tracy were waiting by Amber's bedside for Mr Kuo to finish examining their daughter's airway. Another surgeon walked past and Mr Kuo stopped what he was doing for a moment to ask: "Are we still on for skiing?" Julian had admired the way he could switch from serious mode to chat about his hobbies in the blink of an eye.

Mr Kuo had always been honest and direct, which the Austwicks hugely appreciated. It was also reassuring to have a surgeon who'd been on the journey with them from the start, until hopefully the end.

God willing, there was finally a finishing line.

"So this is what we've come to speak to you about," Julian began.

Mr Kuo nestled back into his chair – he was all ears.

"We're considering sending Amber to nursery …"

"Twickenham Primary School …" Tracy added.

"Yes, Twickenham." Julian smiled lovingly back at his wife.

Julian went on to explain to the surgeon the story of Amber's friendship with Shocks and how she had come on so much they were now able to think about sending Amber to a mainstream school (part of which was the nursery).

"She's finally caught up with her sister and they can be together." Tracy smiled proudly.

The three of them paused for a moment to look down at the three-year-old twins who were playing at their feet. Mr Kuo acknowledged Amber had made a miraculous recovery.

"We are just in the process of arranging with Complex Care for someone to look after Amber. And because she's developed so much thanks to Shocks, we wondered if an operation to reverse her tracheotomy would now be possible." Julian cut to the chase.

Tracy quickly added: "We are worried about her being bullied. I know nursery isn't the same as school, but children can be mean to each other at any age. I don't want Amber to be left behind." Her voice wavered.

Mr Kuo could see the huge obstacle the Austwicks now had to face.

Tracy's heart was clattering. She gripped the side of her chair nervously as she waited for Mr Kuo to speak. Julian was much more calm. Ever since their meeting with the sonographer who'd told them in no uncertain terms the chance of their babies living was slim to none, Julian was rarely rattled by bad news.

Mr Kuo leaned on his desk, pressing two hands together.

He started to spell out to the couple how it was a complex operation drawn out over at least six months. To reverse the tracheotomy, the surgeons would have to stretch both ends of the airway, using cartilage from Amber's rib. And after all that, the risk of the airway collapsing was high.

Before they could even consider the operation, Amber needed to reach 10 kilos in weight. Amber was currently around the 7-kilo mark.

"But we could start fattening her up," Tracy interrupted.

Mr Kuo opened his mouth to speak, but Tracy battled on.

"We could feed her more of the nutrient-rich milk," she said, desperate to find a way.

Mr Kuo sighed deeply. He rolled the words around on his tongue, choosing the best way to deliver the bad news.

"To get to the long and short of it, there's only a 40 per cent chance of the operation being successful," he said, in his soft voice, his bedside voice.

Tracy felt as though someone had stuck a pin in her balloon. Well, more like a spear. Julian flashed her a look as if to say, "Stay calm."

Mr Kuo explained the percentage was low at the moment because Amber's airway was so narrow.

But the older she became, the higher the chance of success. He compared her airway to a 5p and a 10p piece.

"If we operated now, we'd be turning a five-pence piece into a ten-pence piece. If we were to leave it for a while and start with a ten-pence piece, we'll get a two-pound-coin-size airway." Mr Kuo waved his hand in an 'abracadabra' enthusiastic way.

What Mr Kuo was trying to say was, the longer they left it before doing the operation, the more chance Amber's airway would grow, so the more effective the operation would eventually be.

Julian and Tracy locked eyes – it was a huge decision to make.

Do we do this operation now, while she's less aware of what is going on, but there is a huge risk it won't work? If we wait, will Amber hate us for making her go through this when, say, she's a teenager? All these and more were the questions swirling around in their heads.

The irony was, if Amber hadn't met Shocks, it might have been an easier decision to make. Because she was coming on well, they didn't want to do anything that might seriously set her back.

But Julian and Tracy had to make the decision either way. And as much as Tracy wanted Amber to speak, she could see sense.

"We are not going to bother even trying with a percentage like that." Tracy was first off the mark. "I'm not going to cause her all that pain, and pressure and heartache, just to have the trachy put back in at the end of it." She shook her head. Just thinking about it brought tears to her eyes.

Julian nodded. "Anything under fifty per cent is just not worth consideration."

"I want one hundred per cent," Tracy blurted out.

Mr Kuo shook his head. "You'll never get one hundred per cent with an operation like this."

The couple had more questions for the doctor.

"But is there a chance the airway will grow by itself?" Julian asked the obvious.

"Unlikely," said Mr Kuo. "Because the airway is so small and scarred."

Another hope dashed. Tracy was growing more anxious by the second. An uncomfortable silence filled the room as everyone digested the information.

Mr Kuo broke the tension. "I think it's great that you've come to see me now though." He smiled sympathetically. "Normally, in this situation, I would suggest you give me a call whenever you are ready to think about having the operation, but I've done this before with another child. The problem was, by the time we came to take the tracheostomy out, the child had grown so accustomed to it that she was too scared to have the operation.

"So to avoid this, I think we should agree to review Amber's situation every year, and aim to remove it before she goes to school."

That was just the answer Julian was looking for. As much as he would like the operation out of the way while Amber was a baby and wouldn't remember it so much, he didn't want to rock

224

the boat. What Julian wanted was to get home and for things to resume as normal.

"Perfect, we'll see how she gets on at nursery," Julian said, pushing back his chair.

But Tracy had other ideas.

"What about a speaking valve?" she suddenly said.

Jo Matthews, the speech and language worker, had once mentioned it as an option to try, and Tracy hadn't really thought much more about it until now.

Julian looked puzzled. It was one of the first times he'd heard about it, and he didn't have much of a clue what it was. The word 'speaking valve' conjured up images of a metallic robotic voice.

It was actually a very simple device whereby a one-way valve attaches to the outside opening of the tracheostomy tube and allows air to pass into the tracheostomy, but not out through it. The valve would open when Amber breathed in. When Amber breathed out, the valve would close and air would flow past the tracheostomy tube, and up and over the vocal cords and out through the nose and mouth.

Mr Kuo looked hesitant.

"I don't think she'll get on well with a valve because of her airway being so small," he said, frowning.

Tracy's face dropped. Another dashed hope. The reality was, no one knew if Amber's vocal cords actually worked.

"Having said that, if the speech and learning woman says it's worth a try, maybe you should give it a go." Mr Kuo tried to lift the mood.

Julian was the first to thank the surgeon for his time. He could tell the meeting was getting to Tracy and he wanted to wrap things up quickly. He wanted to protect her as much as his girls.

Tracy held onto her thoughts until they had reached the car – which had become something of a swimming pool of emotions over the past three and a bit years.

Julian cleared his throat.

"Look, love, if there's a problem at the nursery, if Amber's being bullied, or the kids are pulling the trachy out, or the school are having problems with a carer going in, then we will have to reconsider the op. Otherwise, we'll just leave it and keep it in for the foreseeable future, until the time does come that we need to remove it," he said.

Tracy stared out of the car window; the words of Mr Kuo were swirling around in her head like a whirlpool.

"Okay." She nodded.

Phew. Julian was relieved Tracy wasn't going to fight him on this one.

"But …" she started.

He braced himself.

"But I think we need to give this speaking valve a go instead."

Julian sighed deeply. He knew he was fighting a losing battle.

CHAPTER 20

Amber Finds Her Voice

Sutton Coldfield, Birmingham,
August 2013

Julian and Tracy were going head to head in their approach to Amber starting nursery.

Julian researched courses in sign language (Makaton) for kids, while Tracy fixed a day and time for Jo Matthews, the speech and language worker, to come round to their house to try out the speaking valve.

Julian was so enthusiastic about *his* approach that he'd even spoken to the head teacher at Twickenham Primary about the possibility of the nursery running Makaton classes after school to teach the other children how to communicate with Amber. He simply didn't see the point in rocking the boat unnecessarily.

And so, when the day came for Jo's visit to their house, Julian sat stiffly, a tight ball of nerves on the sofa, as Jo breezed into the room. As usual, Julian was conjuring up a truckload of worst-case scenarios. He was worried the valve could upset Amber's breathing, that his baby girl could get upset, that they were about to open a whole new can of worms.

But whether Julian realised it or not, the biggest fear preying on his mind was the fact that they were all about to find out whether Amber's vocal cords actually worked.

The idea they may or may not be able to hear Amber's voice for the first time was nerve-racking.

"I wonder if she will have a Brummie accent …" Tracy joked.

Jo laughed out loud. But try as she might, Tracy couldn't get Julian to crack a smile. He had worry lines etched across his forehead.

Amber could mouth some words, like 'Mumma' and 'Dada', and food requests. So, if she was able to speak, what would she say? What would her voice sound like?

Julian was desperate for his wife not to get her hopes up. Jo, too, tried to be pragmatic about the whole thing.

"Let's just give it a quick go," she said briskly.

Jo beckoned Julian and Tracy to join her on the carpet with Amber. They sat cross-legged in a circle, with Amber nestled in her mum's lap.

Amber was none the wiser about the events that were unfolding. She looked at her mum and dad, smiling at the fact they were all together on the carpet.

"Let's show Mummy and Daddy what a big voice you have," Jo said, turning to Amber.

Amber grinned some more.

Jo rummaged around in her bag for a moment and pulled out a purple plastic box.

Julian's pulse was racing with nerves. Tracy's heart was pounding, but more from excitement.

Please let this work, please let this work, she was telling herself.

Meanwhile, Julian was having a very different conversation with himself.

Please don't let this cause more problems, please, he thought as he watched Jo open the box. It was more like opening Pandora's box as far as he was concerned.

The valve looked very different to how they imagined – like a little purple plastic mushroom.

"Okay, Tracy, I want you to divert Amber's attention for a moment," Jo said, signalling.

Tracy started clapping her hands to catch Amber's eyes, while Jo whipped the valve from the box.

Meanwhile, Julian held his breath.

"One, two, three!" Jo unscrewed the coil covering the trachy tube and replaced it with the purple mushroom.

Julian and Tracy froze. The room fell ghostly silent as all eyes were on their girl.

Amber's face started to turn red, tears swelled in her eyes, and she opened her mouth to cry out.

"Whaaaaaaa!" she bleated.

They all nearly jumped out of their skins, it was so loud.

Tracy clasped her mouth to stop herself crying.

"She can speak, I can hear her!" Tracy shrieked.

Julian was in shock.

"Come on, Amber, say 'Mummy', say 'Daddy'," Tracy coaxed.

But Amber was looking more and more distressed. Her lips were turning a light shade of blue.

"Take it off!" Julian panicked she was suffocating.

"Just a second more," Tracy pushed, desperate to hear Amber say something.

Julian had had enough.

"Now," he snapped.

Jo switched the coil for the valve, sending the air that had been building up whooshing out. It was much like the sound of Julian exhaling all his tension.

The moment was so emotionally charged no one knew whether to laugh or cry. Julian and Tracy were still in shock.

"Having that air pass through her mouth for the first time must have felt very strange for Amber," Julian said, worried.

He turned to his little girl.

"Are you okay?" Julian asked.

Amber nodded. Her eyes were still big and watery.

"I think we should leave the speaking valve for a while," he told Tracy and Jo.

Tracy nodded. Of course she didn't want to give up – Tracy wanted to hear Amber say her first word. But at the same time, she knew how to handle her husband. If Trace took her foot off the accelerator for now, she could go faster next time.

No mum likes to see their daughter distressed, but Tracy was confident the phase of Amber getting used to breathing in a new way would soon pass. She believed sometimes you had to be tough to be kind.

And, although Julian hated seeing Amber cry like that, he had to admit, it was a huge relief to know her vocal cords were working.

The next few weeks were a careful game of negotiating for Tracy. She would suggest they try the valve again. Julian would be overly cautious and say he only wanted to do it while Jo was there. Tracy would then barter for a few minutes of valve time, and so it would go on.

Hope was completely confused by the whole thing. Like her parents, she'd never heard a peep out of her sister for over three years, so she was a little disturbed by the new squeaking noises Amber was making. Hope would run across the room and sit next to Amber, protectively so. She was like a guard dog watching over her.

"It's okay, Hope, Mummy and Daddy just want to see what a big voice Amber has," Tracy said, gearing up to try again.

Hope watched with wide blue eyes as Tracy attached the valve to Amber's trachy tube. Amber was starting to get used to the purple mushroom, and, truth be known, quite liked the attention.

The problem for Julian was that the valve amplified all those crackling and gurgling noises in Amber's airway. He was on high alert whenever they tried it.

Amber's cheeks inflated like balloons as she coughed up a bit of gunk. The cough was as loud as thunder to Julian's ears.

"Take it off now," he said quickly, frowning.

"No, she's fine, look at her lips, they are not turning blue," Tracy reassured him.

"But you can hear she's struggling, take it off," Julian said more urgently.

Amber's head rolled back and forth, watching her bickering parents.

"No, just leave it for a while longer, just a few more seconds," Tracy haggled.

The couple had the same conversation every day. The purple box on the second shelf above the TV had become a bad omen for Julian.

Perhaps if I just hide it behind the books, Tracy will forget about it today, Julian caught himself fantasising.

In turn, Tracy found herself thinking up ways to try out the valve without Julian getting worked up – like when he wasn't there, such as when he was picking Hope up from nursery or going to the shops. She'd always tell him as soon as he got back though.

"We had the speaking valve on for ten minutes today," Tracy would say, grinning. Amber was grinning too so Julian knew Amber wasn't bothered. Secretly, he quite liked Tracy handling it this way; just as with the aqua physiotherapy, Julian found it easier to look away.

So the breathing through the valve was becoming easier for Amber, and they knew her vocal cords worked, but they still hadn't heard her speak. Why couldn't she connect the vocals with the words she liked to mouth?

"Maybe the vocal cords are too damaged to say actual words?" Julian wondered aloud.

"Nonsense," Tracy snapped. Julian scowled at her bad temper. "Sorry, I didn't mean to snap," Tracy apologised. "I just want this so much for her."

Tempers had been a little frayed over the past couple of weeks. In the end, Julian pulled Tracy aside. He told her how much he loved her and that he wanted Tracy to take it easy.

"You must look after yourself as well," he warned her.

Tracy looked down at her hands nervously; she knew her husband was right. She'd come a long way since that day she'd broken down in the car with her sister Debs, but anyone can take a step backwards on the road to recovery and she knew she could easily do so if she wasn't careful.

Julian and Tracy were still taking alternate nights to watch over Amber. It was Tracy's turn to sleep that night but, try as she might, she couldn't nod off. She found herself staring at the shapes on the ceiling, listening to every sound outside – the fox rummaging through the bins, a cat meowing, car engines. Each noise seemed to be amplified by 100 in the dark night.

She was searching for cures, raking back over memories and advice and tales of other children. She remembered Andy's story about the autistic boy who'd learned to speak. Suddenly, the answer popped into her head.

Maybe Shocks will help Amber to speak? she thought.

It would have sounded like madness to anyone else, but to Tracy it made perfect sense. The Donkey Sanctuary was a safe haven for Amber, a place where she felt totally relaxed. If she wouldn't say anything to her parents, maybe she would to her best friend?

Tracy couldn't wait to bundle Amber into the car the following morning and test her theory. Julian was all for the idea.

"Maybe you're right, Trace, maybe Shocks will help her," Julian agreed. He then chuckled to himself; he wouldn't have been caught dead three years ago suggesting an animal could help a person talk. How far he had also come!

Amber insisted on wearing a purple-and-white dress and having her hair in pigtails for her visit to Shocks. Julian took a picture just as mum and daughter were about to step out the door. Amber really did look cute as a button with her pink glasses and these two ponytails sticking out of the top of her head like antennae.

"Make sure you don't get any dust in the trachy when you change the coil over," Julian gave one last protective word as he waved them off. Tracy rolled her eyes playfully.

The staff were looking a little frazzled as they arrived at the Sanctuary. They'd had a busy morning with a busload of children, and a second coach was on its way. Plus, the farrier had been in to tend to the donkeys' hooves, which always made them a bit jumpy and difficult to deal with for the rest of the morning.

"What a day!" Andy pulled a silly face to Amber.

Amber giggled. Her face always lit up when Andy was around.

"We've had a bit of a tough time ourselves," Tracy sighed. That was another great thing about the Sanctuary: the staff were always ready to lend a listening ear. It was a bit like therapy sometimes.

"We are trying out this new speaking valve, but we haven't yet managed to get Amber to talk," Tracy explained, with a twinge of sadness.

Ever the optimist, Andy crouched by Amber's side and said with a smile: "I'm sure Shocks can help us with that."

Tracy and Andy were on the same wavelength!

"That's what I thought," Tracy said, beaming, relieved she wasn't completely loopy for thinking so.

Shocks was already saddled up in the arena with Bob and Jacko. A few other children had ridden him that morning but he was clearly delighted to see Amber at the gate. He could spot his friend a mile off. Amber waved vigorously; she couldn't wait to get back in the saddle.

Tracy kneeled beside her and pulled out the dreaded purple box. Amber grinned; she didn't mind it at all anymore. Off went the coil, and on went the purple mushroom speaking valve. Tracy stepped back for a moment, as if she'd placed a precious ornament down and was waiting to grab it if it wobbled. Amber was fine. In fact, the first thing she did was flap her hand in front of her nose to indicate something was stinky.

Tracy's heart exploded.

"You can smell?" She squealed with joy. Until that moment, they'd had no idea whether Amber would be able to taste or smell.

How funny that the first scent she picked up on was smelly donkey! Amber scrunched up her nose in a disgusted fashion.

"Yes, they are smelly," Tracy said, laughing, imitating Amber's 'poo' wave.

Andy came over to let them know Shocks was ready for his little rider.

"Do you mind if you carry Amber over today?" Tracy asked. "I'm just a bit worried about her new valve and the dust."

"I don't mind," Andy said, pretending Amber weighed a tonne as he lifted her into the air. Then he turned back to Tracy, worried. "I can hear some noises …"

Tracy smiled. "I know it sounds strange, but it's nothing to worry about; we're just not used to hearing them," she explained.

Andy didn't want Amber to miss out on saying hello to Shocks, so he held her by the donkey's face so she could give him a big kiss and cuddle. Their eyes were on the same level today, and Shocks gazed back at her adoringly.

Amber Brennan was on riding duty again and the two Ambers waved at Tracy enthusiastically.

As Jacko kicked off the circuit, Tracy's heart fluttered with nerves. She wasn't so worried about Amber needing suction, but more about whether her theory would work. Would Shocks help her to say something, anything? It could be 'ginger biscuit' for all Tracy minded.

"Come on, Amber, that's it," Tracy muttered, watching her daughter like a hawk.

"How are you today, Tracy?" Big Amber asked as they clopped past her.

"Fine," she lied, through a forced smile.

Amber looked back at her mum, completely oblivious to her mum's nervous energy.

The donkey train had to stop for a moment while the little boy riding on Jacko took his turn to throw the bright-yellow beanbag into the bucket.

While all the parents' eyes were on the boy, while Tracy's eyes were on Amber, Shocks did something nobody expected. He quietly, without any fuss or bother, walked past Jacko.

Big Amber and Andy smiled with happiness as they let him take the lead.

And in turn, Amber celebrated her donkey finally coming first by lifting both her hands off the saddle to cheer.

It was a magical 'blink and you miss it' moment.

"Well done, Amber and Shocks!" Andy cheered, as it was a first for both of them. Andy had been trying for months to get Shocks to lead the group, and Big Amber had been similarly attempting to get Amber to take a leap of faith by letting go of the saddle with both hands.

The best thing was, neither of them knew quite what they had done. Shocks carried on with his tasks, letting Amber take the time she needed, while Amber continued to smile and wave and pat her winning donkey.

As the ride came to an end, Andy mentioned to Big Amber that it was always those quiet moments when no one's watching when amazing things happen.

"I think you're right, Andy." Big Amber agreed with his theory on life.

She then turned to Little Amber and broke the news it was time to say goodbye to Shocks.

Amber looked sad and leaned forward to cuddle his furry neck.

"I love you, Shocky," she said.

Andy and Big Amber had to pinch themselves. Did they just hear Little Amber speak?

"Amber's just told Shocks she loves him," Big Amber cried out to Tracy.

Tracy wanted to pole-vault the fence.

"You're kidding?" she squealed, gripping the gate.

Andy led Shocks to Tracy so she might be able to hear.

"Go on, Amber, tell Shocks you love him. Mummy wants to hear." Andy encouraged her to take the stage.

Amber still had her arms wrapped firmly around Shocks's thick neck. She looked at her audience coyly.

And then, like a true performer, Amber delivered her lines.

"I love you, Shocky," she said, giving him a kiss.

Tracy burst into tears.

She set Big Amber off crying too. Little Amber hadn't just touched Shocks's soul; she had won the hearts of all the staff at the Sanctuary.

"I'm sorry," Tracy apologised, dabbing her tears with her sleeve. "I just never thought this day would happen."

Big Amber gave her a hug over the fence, while Little Amber carried on hugging her best friend.

Andy whispered in Shocks's ear.

"So when are you going to find your voice, old boy?"

They were still waiting for that magical moment when Shocks would bray.

CHAPTER 21

Twins At Last

Sutton Coldfield, Birmingham, September 2013

"We are not going to split them up again," Tracy said.

This time, there was no debating the matter; Julian agreed Hope and Amber would go to nursery at the same time, at the same place.

The discussion had arisen because it had taken a bit longer than they'd hoped to secure Complex Care for Amber. The endless paperwork wouldn't be signed off in time for the start of the school year, so they were forced to choose whether to send Hope to Twickenham Nursery in September, and Amber a month later, or hold them both back a month. Amber obviously couldn't go to the school without a carer by her side at all times.

The girls were separated at birth, and had pretty much led separate lives up until this point.

"Amber doesn't need to be left behind even more, she needs to be keeping up with Hope at the very least," Julian said as they discussed the matter over a cup of tea in the living room.

He just needed reassurance from Tracy that she agreed. A month didn't seem like a long time to them, but in children's terms it was a critical four weeks when friendships would be made.

Which was why the Austwicks thought it better the girls go together, because at least then they would have each other.

"Added to which, Amber understands so much more now; she would get ever so upset seeing Hope go somewhere she isn't allowed," Tracy offered.

"We'll just enjoy this extra month with them." Julian flipped it around to see the good side.

They both took a satisfied slurp from their mugs, happy they'd put the matter to bed.

The next few weeks sailed past. Amber's vocabulary was improving by the day and in particular she enjoyed saying: "Can I have more chocolate please?" Julian and Tracy tried their best to make the most of their precious time with the girls; however, a lot of it was spent worrying about 'letting Amber go'.

Would she be bullied? How would she interact with the other boys and girls? After all, her only friends up until then had been a donkey and other children with special needs.

They had a little test run a week before the girls were due to start. The family had decided to take a walk together around the block. It just so happened that the teachers at Twickenham Primary had had the same idea for the children in nursery – Amber and Hope's future classmates.

Julian, Tracy, Amber and Hope turned the corner and were almost mown down by the 30-odd kids walking by. They looked like ducklings waddling in one big wavering line. Their luminous vests swamped their tiny bodies.

Tracy was quick to recognise the teachers from their initial visit to the school.

"Look, there are your classmates." She pointed them out to Amber and Hope.

Amber grinned excitedly, while Hope frowned. She wasn't so sure about making a whole new bunch of friends. It was apparent that Amber was becoming the more confident and outgoing of the twins. There had been a complete role reversal.

Tracy and Julian put it down to another phase in the girls' lives. They were sure the tables would turn again in no time at all.

The moment was tinged with a little guilt though, as Julian and Tracy felt bad the twins couldn't be with their friends right away.

"You'll be with your classmates soon," Julian told the girls, as much to reassure himself as them.

He was right, of course; within no time, the big day had arrived in October 2013.

Tracy had been up since the crack of dawn preparing everything for the girls. Julian had made a list as long as his arm of all the things the carer would need to do throughout the day. The bag of essentials – containing catheters, nebuliser machine, suctioning machine, medicines – had been standing ready by the front door since 5 a.m.

The Complex Care worker, Jade Cooper, arrived early so she could run through the list with the Austwicks. She was a young woman in her mid-twenties, with purple-red shoulder-length hair and a tiny sparkling nose stud.

"As you can tell, we're a bit nervous," Julian said as he welcomed her inside, shoving his hands in his pockets to stop himself writing even more down on the list.

Jade, to whom Amber took an instant liking, reassured them everything would be fine. She explained this was a new experience for her too – to be caring for a child with such specifications in a mainstream school. She'd only ever looked after children in special-needs schools before.

And within those few sentences, Jade highlighted just how far Amber had come. The fact she was about to enter a mainstream school was an incredible achievement. It was also thanks to the head teacher of Twickenham, Mrs Mortiboy, who had agreed to accommodate Amber's needs.

Hope picked up on what they were discussing and shouted, "Mrs Naughtiboy!" at the top of her voice.

They all fell about laughing. Kids have a great way of innocently saying inappropriate things! It was a nice ice-breaker.

Julian and Tracy had chosen Twickenham Primary in part for its friendly atmosphere, but also for its convenient location, within walking distance from their house. At the appointed hour, Jade took hold of Amber's hand as they began their first of hopefully many walks to the school.

Tracy and Julian had a swarm of butterflies in their stomachs as they trod the pavements with Jade and their daughters. They hid it well, though, as they didn't want the girls picking up on their anxiety.

They turned the corner and their stomachs clenched. Suddenly it all seemed very real. They weren't worried about whether Hope would be okay; they'd been through this whole 'saying goodbye at the gates' thing with her before, they knew she could hold her own. But Julian and Tracy were fretting about walking up to the gates with a child who had a tracheostomy. Would the children pick on her? So many emotions were bouncing around.

There was a long line of mums and children snaking down the road from the school, queuing for the gates to be opened at 8.50 a.m. Tracy was about to introduce herself to the other parents in the line, but suddenly came over all shy. She wasn't used to mixing with mums outside the Donkey Sanctuary.

Julian and Tracy locked eyes and smiled nervously at each other. They daren't say anything in case they set the other one off worrying.

Julian was panicking about the other children knocking into Amber's trachy tube. Less than a foot away from him, Tracy was fretting about whether Hope and Amber would make friends.

Have we made a mistake sending them a month later? Will the other children have already made their best friends? Have we done the right thing? She agonised over the decision that had been made. It didn't help that Amber and Hope were the smallest there; they were half the size of all the other children.

They were shaken back to reality by the squeaking noise of the school gate opening. Children started running into the playground. Mums were shouting after them. It was time to go.

"Come on, girls." Julian took Amber's hand, while Tracy held Hope's. They braced themselves for the unknown.

They followed the river of mums to the nursery classroom. The river split into two streams as the children made their way through the doors at either end of the long room.

This was crunch time – the girls had to say goodbye to each other. Amber and Hope would be in the same room, but in different classes at either end. Julian and Tracy felt it would be best this way, so they could make their own set of friends.

"Say goodbye to each other," Julian encouraged.

Amber and Hope gave each other a cuddle.

Tracy wiped a tear from her eye. She was already welling up.

Amber was the first to let go; she couldn't wait to see what all the other children were doing. Hope grabbed hold of her mum's hand again; she was feeling a bit more shy and clingy.

"Come on, Hope." Tracy stroked her daughter's golden hair, taking her through the door on the left. Meanwhile, Julian chased after Amber, who'd raced ahead through the door on the right. He handed the suctioning machine and the medicine bag to Jade.

It was hard for him to let go. Especially when he saw one of the boisterous boys making a beeline for Amber.

"What's that?" The little lad pointed at Amber's trachy tube.

"It just helps her breathe," Julian explained, trying not to come across too protective.

"Oh, okay." The boy shrugged, and ran off to play with his friends.

Amber wasn't the slightest bit bothered; she'd become as resilient as the donkeys! She toddled off to take a closer look at the classroom pet – a tortoise. Julian flashed Tracy a look to say he was a little concerned, but Trace waved him back.

Jade patted Julian's arm and told him there was nothing to worry about.

"Everything will be fine, I have your number," she said confidently, ushering him out the door. The girls were now sitting cross-legged on the carpet at either end of the classroom, gazing up at the teacher.

Tracy joined Julian outside. They couldn't leave without taking one last look. They stood on their tiptoes to peer through the big window.

"Are you crying?" Julian poked her.

"No, don't be silly." Tracy wiped the tears from her eyes. "Anyway, *you* cried when you first dropped Hope off at nursery." She reminded Julian of how sentimental he could also be.

Jade caught them watching and fanned them off.

"Go," she mouthed from across the room.

"I guess that's our cue," Julian sighed, resigning himself to the fact there was nothing much else they could do.

The couple were lost in their own thoughts as they made their way home. The first thing that struck both of them as they walked through the front door was how ghostly quiet the house seemed. They hadn't been alone in each other's company for three and a quarter years.

"Well, what do we do now?" Tracy said, baffled by the silence.

Julian looked around at all the toys strewn across the carpet. Signs of where life had been only hours earlier. It was the weirdest feeling.

There had been so many occasions when they had wished for silence and time to catch their breath but, now they had it, Julian and Tracy were clueless as to what to do with their freedom.

"We could go to the Range?" Tracy suggested they take a trip to the home furnishings shop down the road.

Julian pulled a hesitant face.

"We better not go too far in case something happens," he said.

They both checked their phones to see if Jade had been in touch.

She hadn't.

Another half an hour passed. Tracy wondered what the girls were up to.

"It's 11 a.m., they are probably having snack time now," she pondered aloud.

They checked their phones again. They both had to stop themselves from texting Jade.

"This is ridiculous," Tracy said, jumping to her feet. She began scooping the toys off the floor and getting stuck in to some much overdue housework.

The truth was, she felt a bit lost without the girls being there. She even strangely missed the suctioning machine, even the drone of it, because it gave her a purpose – to care for Amber.

It was Julian who caved in first and texted Jade.

"'The girls are doing great, they are playing in the sandpit.'" He read the message out loud.

Tracy smiled at the thought of Amber and Hope having fun with the other children.

"I hope Jade's watching Amber so she doesn't get sand in her trachy" was Julian's next response.

And that's how they spent the rest of the day – worrying about the girls, imagining what they might be up to, fantasising about things they could do as a couple, such as go into Birmingham.

"No, we better not ..." They'd always talk themselves out of it seconds later.

Before they knew it, it was nearly 3.15 p.m. – time to pick up Amber and Hope.

Julian and Tracy recognised a few faces at the school gates this time around. Just as you might imagine, there was a lot of gossiping going on and Tracy couldn't help but overhear some of the conversations. She chuckled to herself, making a note to tell Julian later.

The gates creaked open and the mums and dads made their way into the holding pen – the playground – where they waited for the classroom doors to open and the sea of children to spill out.

Julian and Tracy craned their necks, trying to spot the girls.

Hope was the first to run out; she was so excited to see her mum and dad that half her coat was still hanging off one arm. Her lunch box was bouncing against her little legs.

"Hi, Hopey! Have you had a good day?" Tracy asked.

Hope didn't say much, she just thrust a picture with scribbles on it into her mum's hand. She then clung to Tracy's legs like ivy.

A few seconds later, Amber emerged, beaming.

"There it is again, the swagger." Julian poked fun at the way Amber strutted towards them. She still had her limp but it wasn't half as pronounced – she was a lot more solid on her legs.

"Have you had a good day, Amber?" they asked.

Amber nodded her head enthusiastically.

"Can I go back tomorrow?" she asked, grinning. Amber was proudly wearing the speaking valve all the time now.

Julian and Tracy smiled at each other – with relief.

"Of course you can." Julian took her hand to begin the walk home.

It was such a weight off their shoulders. All day they had been sweating about whether Amber would fit in, whether she would enjoy herself, so to hear her wanting to go back to nursery was music to their ears.

They turned to Jade for a rundown of the day's events. The carer explained she'd only needed to suction Amber half a dozen times, that she'd had a nebuliser at lunchtime, and a little snooze in the afternoon.

It was nice for Julian and Tracy to hear about what went on in class – parents don't normally get to find out what their children get up to.

Hope may have been shy in the playground but, as soon as she walked through her front door, she transformed into a little extrovert.

Julian told her off for leaving her shoes, coat and bag in the middle of the floor.

"She's behaving like a teenager." He scratched his head, confused by her turnaround.

Hope might have been turning into a little madam in the house, but she'd become a lot more caring and protective over her sister. They had only spent one day at nursery and already something had shifted.

Amber was on the sofa that afternoon, watching cartoons, when she started coughing. She'd grown so much stronger it wasn't always necessary for Julian and Tracy to suction her; she could now bring up her own gunk.

But Hope saw her sister struggling and raced over to her side. She patted Amber's back lovingly.

Julian would have taken a photo if the moment hadn't passed so quickly.

Hope then tried to coax Amber into playing 'schools' in the garden. It was a beautiful October evening so Julian and Tracy opened up the patio doors for the girls. They laid a rug out for them, which Hope and Amber proceeded to sit cross-legged on, just like they had done earlier that day in the classroom.

"I'm the teacher," Hope announced, waggling her finger.

Amber rolled her eyes in an accepting way. Julian and Tracy were in no doubt that Amber's laid-back 'take things as they come' attitude was thanks to the Donkey Sanctuary.

She pretended to listen to Hope bossing her around – for a while. Of course, there is a limit to a toddler's attention span, and Amber soon found herself wandering off, looking for a new adventure. She seemed happy and confident in her own company.

"Come back," Hope called after her, but Amber was already bustling into the kitchen to see what her mum was preparing for tea.

The next couple of weeks just flew by. With every passing day, Amber grew in confidence, and Hope and Amber's relationship evolved into something much more 'sisterly'.

They even played donkeys – where Amber would be the donkey and Hope would be doing all the activities like posting bits of paper. Julian stopped Hope from posting a bit of food through the DVD player just in the nick of time.

Jo, the speech and learning worker, had also noticed the dramatic differences. Amber's voice had become clear and pronounced, and Jo suggested Tracy and Julian stop by the hospital to show Dr Kuo how miracles can happen.

"Oh, I don't know, if we can avoid going to the hospital we should," Julian said, worrying about all the germs.

Tracy was all for Jo's idea though. She believed it was important Amber's surgeon saw how they'd managed with the speaking valve. As always, Tracy had the last word.

The family took a detour past the Children's Hospital on the way back from nursery the following day. It was incredible to watch Amber's change in behaviour. Within seconds she had gone from grinning to grimacing as she recognised the familiar sights and smells of the wards.

It was a nice feeling for Julian and Tracy to whizz through the outpatients' waiting room, though, as they headed straight for Jo's office.

Jo was over the moon that they had taken her up on her suggestion.

"Come in." Jo beckoned them into the room. Amber and Hope immediately scampered off to the play mat. "I'll get Mr Kuo on the phone, I know he's about somewhere," she said, picking up the receiver.

The adults were deep in conversation, telling stories of what had been going on in the nursery, when they heard the sound of the blinds banging against the doorframe. Mr Kuo made his usual larger-than-life entrance.

"Hello, Amber!" he cheered, with his arms wide open.

"Hello!" Amber smiled up at him. "What's your name?"

Julian and Tracy chuckled. That was her latest thing – to ask everyone, even people she knew, what his or her name was.

"Wow, you're doing very well," Mr Kuo exclaimed. He seemed lost for words.

Julian and Tracy stood back and let Jo explain how Amber had been wearing the valve without any problems. How she was now speaking to all her friends at nursery.

The couple weren't trying to prove a point; they merely wanted the surgeon to see how their daughter had overcome adversity. It also raised the question – if Amber had defied all odds up until now, maybe the chances of her operation being successful were much higher than originally predicted?

Mr Kuo agreed it was imperative the Austwicks return within the next year to review the situation.

Julian and Tracy couldn't quite believe how everything was falling into place.

"Pinch me," Tracy said to Julian later that evening.

"Huh?" he said. "Why?"

"Because I want to know this isn't a dream," Tracy laughed.

Another week skipped past and Julian and Tracy turned to Jade for their usual feedback.

As the carer handed over the heavy suctioning machine, and then the bag full of catheters, she casually asked: "Who's Shocks?"

Julian and Tracy looked stunned, like an alarm had just gone off.

They'd been so consumed with the girls going to nursery they hadn't had time to think about anything else.

"He's a donkey, why do you ask?" Tracy said. She couldn't say why, but she could sense a storm brewing.

"Ah, that makes sense." Jade explained that the teacher had gone around the class asking everyone if they had a pet and Amber had said hers was Shocks.

Julian and Tracy smiled at the thought of Amber proudly speaking about her best friend.

But there was more.

"I've noticed, as Amber's got used to me, she's opened up a bit more, and she keeps telling me she loves Shocks, and misses him," Jade revealed. "And I've noticed that, although she's happy in class, she's not really making friends."

Julian and Tracy recoiled in horror, concerned their worst nightmares about Amber not fitting in were being realised.

"No, no, don't worry," Jade tried to reassure them. "She's not being bullied. Amber plays with the other children, but she's not forming any bonds with anyone – and I wonder if that's because she's missing Shocks."

Tracy's face turned to ash as it suddenly dawned on her that her daughter was feeling heartbroken.

She was annoyed at herself for not seeing this coming. From going to the Sanctuary three times a week, to not once in three weeks – it was not surprising this had happened.

"We should take the girls to Saturday Club this weekend," Tracy said, turning to Julian with urgency.

Julian made a 'calm down' motion with his hands.

"It will be fine, love," Julian said confidently.

But Tracy wasn't so convinced. If keeping Amber from Shocks was going to be detrimental to her daughter's wellbeing, they needed to plug that hole as soon as they could, before it caused a massive setback to Amber's recovery.

What's more, Tracy was worried that Shocks might also be suffering from not seeing his friend. They'd all grown so close she felt equally responsible for his wellbeing.

She knew she wouldn't sleep a wink until the problem was sorted.

CHAPTER 22

Stable Girl

Sutton Park, Birmingham,
November 2013

Shocks had lost his appetite.

"Yep, there's no doubt about it, something is bothering him." Andy scratched his head as his attempt to throw a carrot Shocks's way was met with a disgruntled look.

They had never known the donkey to be off his food. Even the veterinary nurses in Liscarroll had joked about how, despite Shocks's life-threatening injuries, he still managed to eat his sandwiches smothered with ginger nut paste.

"Let's try a biscuit." Amber Brennan rooted around in her pocket.

Ginger nut biscuits are the ultimate test as to whether a donkey is sick or not.

"Here, boy." She held out the treat.

Shocks sniffed the air and rolled back his lips as he took in the sugary scent. He then gave a look, not too dissimilar to the ones Amber was giving her sister, as if to say: "If I must."

He clopped over and hoovered it up in one vacuuming mouthful.

"I think he misses Amber, you know," Andy said, as he watched Shocks swan off to the other side of the paddock.

His theory was put into practice later that day as the Sanctuary received a surprise visit from the Austwick family.

"We've missed you!" Big Amber stretched her arms out wide to welcome Little Amber back.

Andy, Sara and the rest of the staff working that Saturday crowded around. Hope also wanted some attention, so she stretched up her arms, looking for hugs.

"What's your name?" Little Amber asked Big Amber, and Andy, and all the other people she already knew.

"It's her latest thing," Julian said, rolling his eyes playfully. He'd lost count of how many times he'd explained Amber's latest quirk.

Tracy pulled a bag full of carrots and apples and ginger nut biscuits out from behind her back.

"Present for Shocks and the rest of the boys," she said as she passed it over.

As Andy walked them along the lane and down to the paddock, he explained how Shocks had lost his appetite.

"I'm a little bit worried about him," he said gravely.

Tracy in turn explained how Amber had been missing Shocks, and how she had been drawing pictures of him at nursery and telling the other children he was her pet donkey. Tracy said she had been concerned Shocks was also missing Amber.

No sooner had they arrived at the paddock fence, Shocks lifted his head as he honed in on the familiar smells and sounds. He sniffed the air, much in the same manner as he would for a biscuit, but this time he looked very happy with his treat.

"Shocks, Shocks," Amber called out, her voice croaky as she was trying to shout so loudly.

Shocks made a beeline for his best friend. He didn't give a second glance to all the other donkeys, who were watching where he was marching. He might as well have been shouting:

"Coming through!" His ears were pricked up, his eyes were bright and alert – he couldn't wait to greet Amber.

"Awww, isn't that lovely?" Julian watched in awe as Shocks lowered his snout for his daughter, and she patted his nose through the gaps in the fence.

"Why don't we make this a bit easier?" Julian lifted Amber into his arms so she could get closer to Shocks. Amber carefully combed the fluff on his big ears with her fingers.

"Oh, he never lets anyone touch his ears, he must have missed her," Andy said, surprised.

He then revealed the bad news – unfortunately, that was the closest the pair were going to get for quite a while, as there was no riding school on Saturday until the next school holidays in December.

Amber's face dropped. Tracy could feel her heart breaking from just a foot away.

Suddenly, an idea popped into Andy's head.

"We don't normally do this ..." He pretended to glance around him, as if he was about to unveil something top secret. "But why doesn't Amber, and Hope if she likes, help clean out Shocks's stable?"

Amber's face lit up like a Christmas tree. She jumped up and down on the spot chanting, "Shocky, Shocky!" Hope didn't look quite so enthusiastic, but she was a little intrigued.

If they were all worried Shocks and Amber's rehabilitation might be affected by their not spending time with each other, then they simply were going to have to find other ways around it, Andy surmised.

"Such as cleaning duties." He winked at the parents.

Despite sounding like hard work, it was a very prestigious job to be given, as none of the other children who'd visited the riding centre had been asked to help in that way before.

"Could you imagine? We'd be besieged by kids wanting to get into the stables." Andy shuddered at the thought of how they'd cope.

Amber's swagger returned as Andy led her over to the stables. She clearly felt immensely proud of her special duties. Hope followed behind, a little more wary of what was about to happen. She didn't know the day-to-day running of the Donkey Sanctuary like Amber, so cleaning out stables was a bit of a mystery.

"Wait here for a moment." Andy held his hand up like a stop sign.

The whole point of the exercise was to make sure Amber and Shocks could spend time with each other, so Andy grabbed a lead rope and went to collect him from the paddock. Shocks still had his head pressed up against the fence, listening to and watching everything Amber was doing.

"Here you go, boy, you can keep a closer eye on Amber from here." He tied Shocks up in the yard, metres from his stable. Jacko was nearby, dozing on the spot.

Amber waved to Shocks as she waited for her instructions.

Andy would clean away the donkey poo while the girls would lay down fresh hay. Amber couldn't believe the smell when she stepped into the stable.

"Poo!" She pinched her nose with her thumb and forefinger. She turned and gave her mum and dad a cheeky grin.

Hope wasn't impressed with the smell at all.

"Come here, Hopey." Julian beckoned Hope over, saving her from a fate worse than death judging by her face. He took her hand as they went on a wander around the grounds.

Tracy couldn't help but think how adorable Amber looked, mucking out a stable in a party dress and leggings and flower-patterned Wellington boots! She also marvelled at how strong her little girl had become. No tool was too big or too heavy for

Amber, as she lifted the spade and shovelled the hay around in Shocks's stable.

The whole while, Shocks stood only a few feet away, peacefully watching over her.

"He's checking to see if she's doing a good job of it," Andy joked.

Tracy was also impressed with how much work went into making sure the donkeys had a clean bed to sleep in. After the dirty hay had been mucked out, new hay was spread out in a thick 'mattress' to make a comfy home for the donkeys. After that, even more work was required, as Andy had to fill up the water troughs.

In turn, Andy was so impressed with his stable girl that he awarded her some extra duties – feeding Shocks.

This really was an honour, as dozens of children ask every week if they can feed the donkeys. Sadly, the staff can't allow it as the donkeys have strict feeding times and otherwise they would have bellies as big as barrels.

But Amber was in the right place at the right time and her special relationship with Shocks made her an exceptional case. As she looked on excitedly, Andy grabbed a bucket to fill it up with treats such as carrots, apples, ginger biscuits and polo mints. He rattled the ingredients around loudly.

"Why do donkeys and horses like polo mints?" Tracy asked, baffled by what she'd thought was a myth.

"They don't just like Polos, they *love* them. Mackenzie will practically push me over trying to get into my pockets," Andy laughed. Then he answered Tracy's question. "It's because they are so sugary and tangy."

They also feed them Polos because they are the only sweet manufactured with a hole – so the donkey could still breathe if it were to become stuck in his windpipe.

Amber was so excited; she was clapping and dancing on the spot.

Andy told her that she had to carry the bucket over to Shocks and leave it under his nose. He held one side of the handle as she gripped the other. Shocks's eyes grew wide as saucers as he got a whiff of his feast.

Amber placed the bucket down in front of Shocks and proudly stood back as he gobbled the contents in five seconds flat. He lifted his wet nose out of the bucket and then licked all around his mouth with his very long tongue. Amber covered her eyes with her hands, as if she was trying to tell Shocks he had bad table manners.

"He seems to have his appetite back," Andy chortled.

Julian and Tracy also noticed a change in Amber that evening. She appeared to have more spring in her step. It was hard for them to put their finger on what was different, but Amber simply radiated a glow of happiness and contentment.

The couple agreed it was essential they kept taking Amber to see Shocks at the weekend, even if she couldn't ride him. To stop her missing him too much in the week, Julian came up with the next best thing – a picture of Shocks, so she could carry him with her at all times.

He printed out a head shot of the donkey, which he'd taken at one of their riding classes, and presented it to his daughter.

Amber was so pleased with her present. She gave the picture a kiss, and waddled off clutching it in her hand, as if it were a trophy.

Amber and her picture of Shocks were inseparable for the next week. Jade joked how Amber kept it with her at all times, tucked away in her cardigan pocket. The carer explained how every now and then, Amber would show Jade the picture, and say she loved and missed 'Shocky'. Sometimes, she would give it a kiss.

Amber even insisted on taking the picture with her when she had a bath.

"Why don't we put the picture next to the bathtub, otherwise it will get wet?" Tracy reasoned.

Amber wouldn't hear of it. She shook her head fiercely, insisting Shocks remained with her at all times.

Tracy hung the drenched picture on the radiator once Amber had nodded off to sleep, ready to take with her in the morning.

It had practically disintegrated into nothing by the end of the week. Luckily, it was time to see Shocks again by then.

Just as Amber missed Shocks during the days she was at nursery, Tracy was experiencing a similar sensation. But because Tracy wasn't brilliant at understanding her own feelings – by her own admission – it took her a while to put two and two together. Nonetheless, eventually, one evening when she was snuggled up watching the TV with Julian, it suddenly dawned on her.

"I miss Shocks too," she confessed.

Julian looked startled; he had no idea where that had come from.

"I miss the mums, I miss the staff, I miss the brilliant work they do – I miss everything about the place ..." she tapered off.

Tracy realised the Donkey Sanctuary had given her a purpose to her days, aside from being a mum and wife. She missed her little oasis of calm.

"Why don't you become a volunteer there?" Julian suggested. It would also be a wonderful way for the Austwicks to give something back to the Sanctuary – a little 'thank you' for all they had done for their family.

Tracy felt a weight lifting off her back just talking about the idea. She set the wheels in motion the very next day.

The staff were naturally over the moon to hear the news that Tracy wanted to become an official member of the team. It was agreed she would help with the riding school one morning a week.

"What better way to mark the occasion than by getting Tracy to bring Shocks in for the class this morning?" suggested Amber Brennan on her first day.

"Me?" Tracy tapped her chest in surprise. She knew all too well that Shocks was quite choosy about who he liked.

"You'll be fine." Big Amber handed her the lead rope. She plunged Tracy into the deep end, just like she would with the kids whom she could see had potential but needed encouraging.

Tracy felt a flutter of nerves whip through her as she made her way down to the paddock. Shocks was hanging out near the sandpit with Jacko. She leaned on the gate and wondered what her best move was.

Shocks was two steps ahead. To Tracy's surprise, he'd spotted her coming. His head was up, his big furry ears tuned into her footsteps.

He probably thinks Amber is with me. Tracy explained away his enthusiasm.

That may have been true but, when he realised she wasn't, Shocks still seemed genuinely pleased to see Amber's mum.

He took a few steps forward, intrigued by why Tracy was there without his friend.

Tracy felt a surge of confidence. She grabbed her chance.

"Come on, Shocks, here, boy," she called out.

I am probably going to have to go into the paddock to fetch him, but it is worth a shot, she thought.

Shocks tilted his head, as if trying to work out what was going on, and then clopped over to say hi.

Tracy's heart nearly burst with happiness.

"Oh my goodness," she squealed. She couldn't believe he was coming over to say hi to her.

She held out her hand for him to have a good smell. The hairs on his chin tickled her palm.

"I bet you can smell Amber," she said.

He let out one of his head-shaking, almighty sneezes.

"That's a yes," Tracy laughed, wiping his snot on her jeans.

He stood there patiently as Tracy attached the lead rope to his head collar. He then calmly trailed behind her as she led him into the riding arena.

The whole while, Tracy chatted away about Amber. She told Shocks Amber was doing well at nursery, that she missed him dearly.

"She played with the water yesterday …" Tracy prattled away.

It was almost therapeutic for Tracy to tell Shocks all her news, and he in turn looked comforted by her voice and her stories.

There was a whole gaggle of children waiting to ride Shocks. He was fast becoming the most popular donkey to ride at the Sanctuary due to his size and calm nature.

Tracy handed the reins over to Andy so he could commence the morning's riding school. She waved goodbye to Shocks and imagined he gave her a look as if to say: "Say hello to Amber from me."

She had only been in the company of Shocks for 15 minutes or so, but Tracy already felt 'lighter'. It was a hard emotion to describe, probably not dissimilar to what people feel when they cuddle their pets. *No wonder Amber feels so happy being around him*, Tracy thought.

The healing power of animals never ceased to amaze her.

CHAPTER 23

Tragedy Strikes

Sutton Coldfield, Birmingham, February 2014

Julian and Tracy were going on their first 'date' since the girls were born. Well, more of a 'day date', but still a special time, reserved just for the two of them.

It was a cold February morning in 2014. Amber and Hope were at nursery, well settled in to their second term, so Julian and Tracy decided to slip off for a snuggle in the cinema.

"This feels a little bit weird," Tracy whispered to Julian, giggling like a teenager.

It had been so long since the couple had felt relaxed enough to step away from the house and take a moment for themselves that it almost seemed strange to be out together. Saying that, they couldn't entirely let go. Their faces kept lighting up comically as they checked their phones every now and then to see if Jade had been in touch.

"Nothing," Julian whispered as he looked at his screen. "You?"

"No, I haven't got a message either," Tracy replied.

Julian held his arms open, beckoning Tracy in for a cuddle. She manoeuvred herself around the armrest and positioned her head against the warmth of her husband's chest.

For an hour and 45 minutes, Julian and Tracy forgot everything else that was going on in their lives and enjoyed their break from reality.

They came out of the cinema holding hands and laughing.

It was an hour before they were due to pick the girls up from nursery when the bubble burst.

Jade had noticed that Amber was a lot quieter than normal. She texted Tracy with the news that Amber was drowsy, wanting to fall asleep.

"That's strange. Maybe she didn't get a good night's sleep and is a bit tired?" Tracy wondered aloud to Julian.

The couple had trained themselves not to divert to panic stations whenever there was a slight change in Amber's behaviour. They had to, otherwise they'd be constantly on tenterhooks.

So what followed was a shock to everyone.

Amber's health took a sudden nosedive. As Julian and Tracy arrived at the school gates, Jade was running along the pathway, clutching Amber in her arms.

"She's really hot, her temperature is sky-high," Jade said, panicking. The carer hadn't seen Amber poorly before so she was very worried.

Tracy felt her daughter's forehead. Amber was burning up.

"Let's get her home quickly." Tracy put her in the back of the car, while Julian fetched Hope.

Amber had suffered colds in the past. Sadly, she was prone to bugs because of her trachy tube. The best thing Julian and Tracy could do was stay calm.

As soon as they got through the front door, they took her temperature.

"Jesus, it's thirty-nine degrees." Julian stared at the thermometer in shock.

Tracy whipped off all of Amber's clothes in an attempt to cool her down. She propped Amber in the corner of the sofa in just her underpants. Julian used a magazine to fan her.

He checked the thermometer again – 38 degrees.

"She's cooling down a bit," he reported back.

Tracy dashed off to fetch some paracetamol and cold flannels. She wrung out the water and lay the cool flannels across Amber's forehead and chest. Her little body was limp. She barely had the strength to keep her eyes open. Her head was rolling from side to side.

Julian stood back, his hands on his hips, as he tried to work out what they should do.

It could just be a cold. We don't want to take her into hospital if we can help it, he thought.

Another hour passed and thankfully her temperature had dropped to 35 degrees. Tracy tried to get Amber to drink some water but she pushed the cup away with her fist.

"See if she wants a bit of fruit." Julian handed Tracy a banana.

Amber turned her cheek; she didn't want to know.

More time passed and it was now 7 p.m., the girls' bedtime. Julian carried Hope up to bed and left Amber on the sofa with Trace. Hope looked a little distressed. She'd become very in tune with her sister and could sense something wasn't right.

"Amber will be fine, go to sleep, Hopey." Julian tucked her under the duvet.

He was making his way back down the staircase when he heard Tracy cry out for help.

"What's wrong?" He raced into the lounge.

Amber was being sick everywhere. Tracy was trying to catch the vomit in her hands; petrified it might go down her trachy tube and drown her lungs.

Amber's face was crimson. She was literally red-hot. Something was seriously wrong.

"Call the ambulance," Tracy cried out.

Julian dialled 999. His heart was pounding. His speech was strained as he explained to the operator how his daughter was burning up, she was being sick everywhere, she was barely conscious.

"She has a tracheostomy," he blurted, feeling completely helpless.

Those seven minutes it took for the First Response officer to screech into their drive felt like an eternity. They'd left the front door wide open for him so they wouldn't have to leave Amber's side.

He rushed into the living room wearing his fluorescents and carrying a bag full of medicines and equipment.

"What's her name?" the paramedic asked Julian and Tracy, as he ripped open the Velcro seal on his bag.

"Amber," Julian said, stepping out of the way.

The paramedic rooted around in his bag and pulled out some more equipment. It was like a Mary Poppins bag, Tracy thought; she couldn't believe how much stuff he had in there.

"Amber, can you hear me?" the paramedic asked, in a calm voice, as he flashed a light into her eyes.

Amber didn't say a word; she looked like she was slipping off into some coma-like sleep.

The paramedic immediately radioed for an ambulance.

And then a ghostly silence fell on the room. Julian and Tracy watched in horror as Amber's chest stopped moving up and down. Her eyes glazed over. Her lips turned blue. Amber stopped breathing.

"AMBER," Julian shouted at the top of his voice. "AMBER, BREATHE!"

Julian was frozen to the spot.

The paramedic calmly put his hand on Julian's shoulder.

"Do what you normally do with the suctioning machine," he instructed.

"Just suction her," Tracy echoed the paramedic.

Their words jolted Julian into action.

He fell to his knees beside Amber. Julian pulled the coil off her trachy, inserted the catheter, and switched on the machine. A great big lump of gunk chugged up the pipe, and then Amber let out a great big sigh as the air poured back into her lungs.

Julian's whole body also sighed – with relief. It wasn't as if he'd forgotten he had to suction, but Julian had panicked for a moment because he'd never seen Amber stop breathing before. He didn't know what to do.

A moment later, the ambulance pulled up outside the house.

"You go," Julian directed Tracy.

Tracy took to her heels – she ran up the stairs and grabbed the bag they always had ready in case of an emergency. It contained overnight essentials like a toothbrush set, clean clothes and a pair of slippers.

She grabbed a warm blanket on her way down to wrap Amber up in.

"You're going to be okay, Amber," Tracy whispered to her little girl as she bundled her up into her arms and carried Amber into the back of the ambulance.

Things were moving so quickly Tracy barely got a chance to say goodbye to Julian. The plan was for Julian to stay in the house and look after Hope while Tracy rushed to the hospital.

"I'll text you what's happening when I get there," she called out.

They locked eyes for a moment, and then the ambulance doors slammed shut.

Julian was left alone with his thoughts.

His mind was in overdrive. Every worst-case scenario was racing round in his head. His chest felt tight. His breath grew short and strained.

He pulled himself away from the loneliness by going to check on Hope. Julian peered through the gap in the door to find her fast asleep, none the wiser to any of the drama that had just exploded in the room beneath.

He crept back along the landing but came to a stop at the top of the stairs, where the large window overlooked the neighbourhood, and beyond. He imagined he could see Birmingham Children's Hospital and his eyes welled up with tears.

Julian was relieved Amber was now in the safe hands of the surgeons, but he was worried sick about whether she was going to be okay.

That worry had a horrible familiarity to it.

Oh God, he cried helplessly to himself, looking out, unseeing, at the dark city. *How did we end up back here?*

CHAPTER 24

Back to Square One

Birmingham Children's Hospital, Birmingham, February 2014

The ambulance doors opened and Amber was raced through into A & E.

Tracy was running behind the stretcher as the paramedics pushed Amber through the next set of double doors.

Amber had an oxygen mask over her tracheostomy. Each inhale and exhale looked painful. Her lungs made a horrid rasping noise.

The doctor on duty wanted to get Amber on an IV drip immediately – she needed fluids and antibiotics loaded into her system. He suspected she might have caught a virus of some sort.

He reassured Tracy it was probably nothing serious. The problem was, her tracheostomy made Amber much more susceptible to bugs.

Despite his comforting words, Tracy wasn't so sure. She had a terrible feeling in the pit of her stomach, which was screaming at her that something was seriously wrong. She told herself not to panic though. She needed to hold it together for the sake of Amber.

The idea was to monitor Amber overnight, to see if her temperature would drop thanks to the penicillin.

By 11 p.m., Amber's condition was stable enough to move her onto a ward. Tracy kept Julian updated with a constant stream of text messages.

Tracy didn't leave her daughter's side all night. She held Amber's little hand in hers, praying for her temperature to continue dropping. Every now and then Tracy's eyes would start to close, her head would feel heavy, and she'd rest it on the side of the bed until she was shaken awake by the sound of Amber coughing, or straining for air.

"You'll be okay." Tracy rubbed Amber's back soothingly.

As soon as Julian had dropped Hope off at the nursery the next morning, he came straight to the Children's Hospital.

"Hi, lovie." He gave Tracy a big hug. "How is she?"

He pulled up a chair by Amber's bedside. Amber was so out of it she couldn't even muster up the strength to smile for her daddy.

"Her temperature is the same, nothing's changed," Tracy said, her voice wavering. Tracy's eyes were puffy from tiredness and tears.

"It's going to be fine." Julian squeezed her arm tenderly.

They held a vigil around Amber's bed for the rest of that day as nurses came and went, taking temperature readings, giving her more paracetamol and antibiotics.

Amber's condition wasn't getting worse – but she wasn't improving either. Nobody really knew what was wrong with her.

Keep calm and carry on, Tracy kept telling herself. She'd barely said a word to Julian all day; she was locked away with her despair.

"Do you want me to take over?" Julian asked as the time came to pick up Hope from nursery.

Julian had to repeat the question because Tracy was so distant in her own thoughts.

"Tracy?" he repeated. Julian was worried his wife needed a break.

But Tracy insisted on staying with Amber. She was settled; she needed to see it through.

"Okay. I'll pick Hope up and I'll speak to you in a bit." He kissed her forehead as he left.

As the afternoon wore on, Amber's temperature went up and up.

Tracy's fears grew stronger and stronger.

It was time for lights out on the ward at 7 p.m., but Tracy didn't want her baby to be left to sleep for the night. They'd been kept in the dark for too long.

"She's getting even hotter," Tracy said, cornering a nurse. She was feeling desperate.

"Okay, we will give her one more nebuliser to slow her breathing down," the nurse suggested, hoping the heat of the machine would break down the gunk in Amber's lungs.

But it didn't help. Nothing was helping.

"She's getting worse, you need to get the doctor." Tracy's voice was on the cusp of shouting.

The ward doctor came to Amber's bedside. He instructed the nurses to rev her treatment up, and give her a nebuliser every hour.

By 10 p.m., Amber was wheezing. Her body was red and sweaty. Her eyes kept rolling into her head.

"We need to get another doctor to look at her, *now*." Tracy had had enough. She wasn't taking 'no' for an answer.

Her pushiness worked, as a harassed-looking doctor from intensive care came down to check on Amber's condition.

One thing was clear: whatever the virus was that was attacking Amber, it was leaving her with no energy to breathe.

"We need to get her up to intensive care."

The doctor signalled to the nurses. And with that, the bars on the bed were raised, the brakes were taken off and Amber was wheeled up to the unit where she'd started her life.

Julian's heart almost stopped when he received the news. Intensive care meant things were really serious. There was nowhere to go after that, other than the morgue. It was a terrible thing to be thinking, but he couldn't help it. He was scared for his daughter's life.

Amber was given a stronger dose of antibiotics intravenously, and an oxygen mask. She was still having sugar water pumped through her system as she couldn't hold down any food or water.

They were both relieved Amber now had her own nurse watching over her twenty-four-seven. Julian tried to persuade Tracy to come home, as there was nowhere for parents to sleep in the intensive care unit.

"I want to stay," Tracy insisted. She told Julian she'd wait in the corridor if needs be; she wasn't going anywhere until she knew Amber was out of a critical condition.

From experience, Julian knew it was futile to argue with her.

Tracy lost count of how many coffees she drank over the next six hours. Her body was running on empty, her brain was in overdrive. She'd get up, have a walk around, and then return to the hard plastic of the hospital chair that bit into her back.

Julian wasn't sleeping a wink either. Every couple of hours, he'd nervously text Tracy for news.

I haven't heard anything. Still don't know what's wrong with her, she'd reply.

They were on tenterhooks.

Julian returned to the hospital the following morning, as soon as he'd dropped Hope off. He was carrying a bag full of food and snacks for Tracy.

"Here, eat this." He thrust an energy bar into her hand.

"I can't, I feel sick with worry," Tracy said, clutching her stomach.

Minutes later, the doctor who had rushed Amber into intensive care appeared with his clipboard of notes, calling them away from Amber's bed for a consultation. He was a young guy with bright-ginger hair and a night's worth of stubble on his chin.

Julian and Tracy both stared up at him, holding their breath as they waited for him to speak – to put them out of their suffering.

"We took an X-ray during the night," he started.

They listened intently.

"And we found that Amber has pneumonia in her right lung."

There was a moment of shocked silence. They weren't expecting that.

Tracy put her hand over her mouth to stop herself blurting out something she'd later regret.

"Pneumonia?" Julian repeated, stunned. "Well, how did she get that?" he asked.

The young doctor explained it was just one of those things; unfortunately, Amber would have been susceptible to the bug with an open airway.

Julian and Tracy looked at each other, neither really knowing what to say, or how to feel.

On the one hand, there was a mild sense of relief that they finally knew what was wrong with Amber, so the doctors would now be able to treat her accordingly, such as by giving her the correct antibiotics. However, they also knew pneumonia was serious and life-threatening.

Julian and Tracy couldn't bring themselves to ask the doctor how serious the situation was. They knew it was bad or she wouldn't be in intensive care. *Sometimes, it's better to be an ostrich and stick your head in the sand. Sometimes, no good comes from knowing too much*, they thought.

The doctor told the couple they could now return to Amber's bedside. They nodded, asking for a moment to themselves.

Julian took Tracy's hand and gave it a squeeze. Neither of them said a word to the other, but the message was clear. They were going to get through this together.

Bad memories came flooding back as they trudged the familiar steps down the long corridor to intensive care, the glare of the strip lights illuminating the way. They covered their hands with disinfectant, took a deep breath, and pushed through the double doors.

Julian had forgotten the noise of the place. Machines bleeping. Lights flashing. Doctors flying past. Dozens of beds filled with sick children. It was heart-breaking.

Amber was tucked away in the corner, looking very poorly. Her skin was the colour of ash. Her blonde fringe was glued to her forehead with sweat. She looked so tired and helpless.

Her breathing sounded like a dying man taking his last gasps of air.

"We're here, Amber," Julian said, touching her arm. It was burning hot.

There was a lot of noise and commotion around the bed next to Amber. A little boy had just been wheeled in after having open-heart surgery.

"Oh no." Julian looked away. He felt so sorry for the child, and for everyone in that room with Amber. The whole experience was horrific.

Everything was happening so quickly. The next moment, the doctor was checking Amber's vitals. He nodded as if he was having a conversation with himself. He then turned to Julian and Tracy.

"Her lungs are working too hard, so we are just going to give her a rest. Just so she can build her strength back up so as to get over the pneumonia," he explained.

"Oh, okay," they said, nodding without comprehending. Julian and Tracy were back where they started when the twins were born, trying to decipher medical terminology.

The nurse picked up on their uncertainty, and stepped in.

"Do you understand what the doctor is telling you?" she asked sweetly.

Julian and Tracy looked at each other, bewildered.

"Um, we think so," they said, confused.

The nurse explained that they were going to put Amber back on the ventilator. Julian and Tracy had understood the doctor, but it was as if the reality of the situation hadn't sunk in until the nurse spelled it out for them.

"Oh God, no," Tracy gasped.

It was their biggest fear to have a machine breathing for Amber. They were terrified if she was put on the ventilator, they might never be able to get her off it again.

Amber had come all this way, only to go back to square one. Julian and Tracy were devastated.

And then, as if the moment couldn't have been any worse, the machines next to them started screaming. The little boy's heart was going into arrest.

An army of doctors and nurses came rushing over. They pulled the curtain around the bed and everyone was asked to leave the room.

Mums and dads were herded into the family room. The atmosphere was so tense you could have cut it with a knife. No one really knew quite where to look. Everyone felt sorry for the poor boy, as well as feeling the severity of their own circumstances keenly.

That's what was racing through Julian's mind at any rate.

Something like this brings home where I am – that my daughter is in a critical state. He closed his eyes, wishing his family was a million miles away.

They didn't have to wait too long though. Luckily, the doctors managed to stabilise the boy's condition and Julian and Tracy could return to Amber's bedside. The curtain was still drawn around the next bed, to give the boy's family some dignity.

The couple's anxiety levels were now rocket-high as the doctor approached to put Amber on the ventilator.

Saying they'll put her on the ventilator sounds less harsh than the reality, Julian thought: *that they are going to stop Amber breathing and let the machines take over.*

His hands were clenched so tightly you could see his knuckles protruding.

"Don't panic, the machine will pick up the breathing straight away," the nurse reassured them as she started the process. First, they needed to sedate Amber, because they couldn't have her moving while she was on the ventilator.

Julian and Tracy stood in silence at the end of the bed, their eyes glued to Amber's chest, watching it heave up and down.

Her breathing slowed, and slowed down some more, and then it stopped.

Even though the room was filled with noise, Julian and Tracy could have heard a pin drop in that very moment. Their eyes and ears were tunnelled on their daughter.

The machine made a clanking noise as it kicked in, and Amber's chest rose.

Julian and Tracy made a whooshing noise as the air they'd been holding onto flew out.

"Oh thank goodness," Julian whispered.

The difference was instantly noticeable: Amber wasn't struggling anymore. It was as if she'd been covered in a veil of calmness.

Julian stepped outside for a moment to take in his own dose of oxygen. He then pulled his mobile out of his pocket and scrolled through the list of names until he reached Debbie.

There was no way he was going to be able to leave Amber and Tracy's side. He asked his sister-in-law if she could look after Hope for the night.

Debs wanted to race down to the hospital but Julian said there was nothing she could do at the moment. Amber was sedated; they were hoping the new batch of antibiotics would calm the fever soon.

Okay, call me if anything happens, she texted back. She'd pick Hope up from school, she promised.

Julian took one last breath of air, and then thrust his hands deep into his pockets as he marched back into the hospital – back into the warzone.

Amber's condition remained stable over the next few hours. The sound of the ventilator pumping air filled the long silences between Julian and Tracy. They were too tired to enter into any conversation, and they were concerned that saying something might bring the other down. Julian would reach over and squeeze Tracy's hand every now and again. She'd muster a smile and blink away her tears.

It was getting late and the nurse pushed for them to take a break and go home for the night. The nurse looked at her watch as she approached the couple keeping vigil by their daughter's side. It was close to 11 p.m.

"There's nothing you can do," she told them. "Amber is sedated, the ventilator is working. Go home and have a rest. If anything happens, we will ring you," she added.

Julian agreed; it made sense to go home. They were only 20 minutes away if anything were to happen. Tracy was on her last legs – she needed to rest.

"Come on, lovie." Julian held his hand out. He had to prise Tracy out of the chair.

Of course, neither of them would get a wink of sleep, but at least they could have some sort of rest. Tracy curled herself into a ball under the duvet and stared numbly at her bedside table. It had been some time since she'd laid her eyes on the little angel by her bed, but the angel was still there, watching over them. Tracy wasn't religious, but she said a prayer for Amber that night.

She thought about everything the twins had been through, all the obstacles they'd overcome. She found herself thinking about the Sanctuary, and about Shocks.

"Shocks …" she whispered.

As if she'd seen the clearing in the woods.

CHAPTER 25

Shocks to the Rescue

Birmingham Children's Hospital, Birmingham, February 2014

Tracy had had an idea. If Shocks had healed Amber before, what was to say he couldn't make her better now?

She mulled it over all night, and the following morning, back at the hospital, Tracy turned to Julian with purpose.

"Uh oh, I know that look," he said with a wary grimace.

They were sitting side by side, next to Amber. Her condition was stable, but she wasn't improving. Tracy knew she needed an intervention.

"Can you go down to the Donkey Sanctuary and take a few pictures of Shocks on your phone?" she asked.

Julian's eyebrows nearly hit his hairline.

"If he doesn't come over to you, just talk to him," she carried on, ignoring his surprised expression.

"Are you serious?" he laughed.

"Oh, just get on and do it. I think hearing about Shocks and seeing pictures of him might speed up Amber's recovery," she said, patting him on the leg.

Not being the world's greatest animal lover, it was hard for Julian to believe that a donkey could make such a big impact on Amber's recovery but, somewhere in his heart, he knew she was right.

After all, Shocks had healed Amber before.

"I'll see you in a bit," he said, sighing deeply as he rose to his feet.

As Julian drove through beautiful Sutton Park, he had to admit it was nice to step away from the hospital for a short while. He could finally see what Tracy had meant by her stories of the park being an oasis where you could breathe properly.

He wound down the window and drank in the cold air.

Julian was met by some confused faces as he pulled into the Sanctuary car park. He'd never visited on his own before.

"Is everything okay?" Big Amber asked. She could see the worry etched on his face.

Julian had to try hard not to cry as he told Amber – and Andy and the rest of the staff who gathered around – how Amber had contracted pneumonia. How she was back on a ventilator. And how he needed all the help he could find to get her better. He explained Tracy's idea about the photo.

"That's a brilliant idea," the Sanctuary team said in chorus, not batting an eyelid at the premise of it.

"He's in the paddock," Andy said. He walked Julian down to see Shocks.

Luckily, he was grazing not too far from the fence.

"Do you want me to fetch him?" Andy asked.

Julian declined, not being one to make a fuss over things. Andy could sense Julian needed a moment alone, and tactfully backed away.

Julian pulled out his mobile and started snapping some shots of Shocks grazing. Frustratingly, the donkey wouldn't lift his head, so the pictures weren't looking very good. Julian moved along the fence, hoping a new angle would throw up some new shots. But Shocks was just that little bit too far away.

Julian sighed deeply. He didn't want to bother the staff, as they were now getting ready for the riding school.

He remembered Tracy's words – *If Shocks doesn't come over to you, talk to him.*

Julian shook his head with disbelief. He couldn't believe he was about to have a conversation with an animal.

"Shocks," he called out.

No reaction. Although Shocks had become much more approachable, he still didn't like men that much.

Julian cleared his throat, ready to give it another go.

"Shocks, I need your help," he said. "Amber is in hospital and I know she misses you and I need to take a picture of you to show her."

Julian leaned on the gate. He suddenly felt overwhelmed with emotion.

"I have no idea if it will help her get better. But I need your help now. I need you to help Amber." His voice cracked. "Please come a bit closer."

Shocks turned his head and looked at him with one eye.

"Ah, you're listening to me now." Julian felt a surge of excitement. "Come on, boy, come a bit closer."

He beckoned the donkey over.

"It's for *Amber*." Julian kept saying his daughter's name, hoping Shocks understood.

Shocks finished grinding the last straws of grass he had swirling in his mouth – and then started to walk over to Julian.

"That's it, Shocks. Come here, boy." Julian wanted to jump up and down with excitement, but he couldn't in case he scared Amber's friend away.

Click. Click. Click. Julian snapped away like a photographer on a photo shoot. He took some lovely close-up shots of Shocks's big fluffy head and ears.

"Amber will love these," he muttered to himself, grinning.

Julian paused for a moment, as he realised the enormity of what had just happened. Shocks had given him a break just at the moment he needed him most.

"Thank you," he said simply.

Shocks must have sensed Julian's grief and wanted to reach out to him, as he'd done for Amber when she'd needed him most. He put his head over the fence so Julian could stroke his nose.

It was the first time the pair had made a connection.

Julian couldn't quite believe he was welling up as he petted Shocks.

He ticked himself off for being a big softy. However, as Julian made his way back to the car, he felt a bit more positive about things. Some of his worry seemed to have been lifted from his shoulders. Was it Shocks who had helped him?

He popped his head into the riding arena to say a quick goodbye.

"Send our love to Amber!" Andy and Big Amber funnelled their hands around their mouths, hollering across the big arena.

Julian nodded and gave them a thumbs-up. He'd enjoyed his visit much more than he'd expected to. Not only had it been a getaway from the pressure of the intensive care unit, but he wondered if he'd also made a friend.

"Did you get them?" Tracy asked urgently, as soon as she saw Julian approaching her back at the hospital.

"I got them." He smiled at her, holding up his phone like it was an Olympic gold medal.

"Oh thank God." Tracy patted her heart with relief.

"I felt a bit bad sending you down there once you'd left," she confessed. "I thought you wouldn't stand a chance of getting Shocks to pose for you."

As Tracy flicked through the pictures, she could see that Shocks had made a special effort.

"Don't you start welling up," Julian teased. He could see the effect the donkey was having on her.

He changed the subject.

"How's she been doing since I've been away?" Julian held Amber's limp hand.

"Still the same." Tracy pursed her lips together wearily.

Although Amber was sedated and looked as if she was sleeping, Julian and Tracy thought talking to her would help; she might absorb some of what they were saying.

"I saw Shocks today. He misses you and can't wait for you to get better." Julian started on Amber's favourite subject.

"That's right, Amber, if you get better we can go and see him," Tracy said, joining in. She hoped the thought of seeing Shocks would spur on Amber's recovery.

The rest of the afternoon consisted of the couple chattering across Amber's bed. Occasionally Julian would step out for some air. He'd stand where the ambulances zipped in and out until another cold blast of February chill forced him to retreat into the overheated hospital corridors. He couldn't help reliving the nightmare of when the twins were born.

Shocks was never far from their thoughts or conversation though, and, strangely enough, Amber's special friend kept them going. He was a happy thought Julian and Tracy could divert to when they were struggling to remain positive.

Shocks was thrust into their thoughts again come early evening, when Julian and Tracy received a surprise visitor.

Intensive care rules specify only two relatives by a bedside at any one time. Julian stepped out to see who had arrived.

It was Big Amber.

"I'm sorry, I hope you don't mind me coming. I just couldn't bear to think of Amber lying there and wanted to stop by." She smiled sweetly. "She's become like family to us," she added, clutching a bag full of gifts.

Julian was too moved for words.

"Julian, are you okay?" Amber tried to meet his gaze.

Julian shook himself free of his thoughts.

"Yes, go through. I'll wait here." He pointed to the double doors to show her where to go.

Big Amber gave his arm a gentle squeeze and then made her way into intensive care, swinging her plastic bag full of goodies.

Tracy was over the moon to see her friend. Big Amber spread her arms wide like an eagle's wings and pulled her in for a big hug. How Tracy had been missing that connection – with the Donkey Sanctuary, Shocks and all her friends there!

"How's the little one doing?" Big Amber craned her neck to look at the tiny figure lying in the bed.

"She's stable." Tracy sighed with helplessness.

Big Amber delved her hand deep into her plastic carrier and pulled out a present.

"Everyone at the riding school thought she must be missing Shocks, so, if she can't see him, we have the next best thing." Amber Brennan handed over a little crocheted donkey.

"Oh, that's beautiful." Tracy fanned away her tears. The slightest thing was setting her off.

It was the best gift she could have brought Amber, as it kept the thought of Shocks alive. Tracy believed, wholeheartedly, that Shocks was the key to her recovery.

Big Amber rustled around in the carrier again and pulled out a present for Tracy – a box of chocolates.

"To keep your energy levels up," she said with a wink.

Big Amber couldn't stay long because she wasn't an immediate relative, but her visit had given all the Austwicks a lift. Of course, they had another sleepless night, but they weren't filled with such dread and worry as they had been. Tracy couldn't explain how or why, but she could sense things were about to get better.

She was right. The next morning, the ginger-haired doctor announced the good news – Amber's temperature had dropped so significantly during the night that they were going to take her off the ventilator.

"She's going to be just fine," he said, his smile lighting his big freckled face.

"Oh thank God," Julian and Tracy muttered under their breath.

Of course, Amber's parents now had to go through the horror of watching the ventilator stop … and Amber's own breathing take over. It was the reverse of everything they had been through 48 hours ago. But at least they knew Amber was getting better. They had that hope to cling on to.

Tracy picked up the little crocheted donkey from Amber's bedside. She gripped it tightly in her hands as she waited at the end of the bed with Julian.

"It will be fine," the nurse said, smiling reassuringly.

The familiarity of the situation was horrible. It was like they were suffering from déjà vu.

Perhaps a recurring nightmare would be a better description.

The clanking and whooshing noise of the ventilator slowed to a silence.

Julian took Tracy's hand.

The silence carried on.

Julian squeezed his wife's fingers tightly.

And then little Amber's chest rose.

The croaky rasping sound was still there, but not a fraction of what it had been. The most important thing was that Amber was breathing for herself.

"Oh thank God," they both muttered again.

It took a while for the sedation to wear off. It was dark and bitterly cold outside by the time Amber came round.

Both parents were hunched over her bed, coming at her from either side.

"Amber, can you hear us?" Julian asked as he watched her stir.

Amber smacked her lips together, like she had just chewed something bitter.

"Amber, we love you." Tracy's eyes were welling up again.

Amber could definitely hear what her mum and dad were saying, as the corners of her little mouth curled up with happiness.

"You had us scared for a moment ..." Julian carried on chatting. He had days of catching up to do.

Amber lay there, breathing heavily, as Julian and Tracy recounted the story of how they had sent her dad to see Shocks. How her best friend had even come over to say hello to him.

"He's waiting for you," Julian said, showing her the photo.

Amber barely had the strength to open her eyes, but those precious few seconds of seeing Shocks brought a smile to her face.

Back on Her Feet

Children's Hospital, Birmingham,
February 2014

Amber was a little fighter.

As quickly as Amber had gone downhill, she bounced back. Once she had that fire in her belly, there was nothing stopping her recovery.

Julian and Tracy walked into the hospital the following morning to find Amber sitting up in bed chomping on a bag of Monster Munch while watching the TV the nurses had set up for her at the end of her bed.

"Someone's better," Julian chuckled.

Amber beamed at her mum and dad. She had clearly missed them.

She held up her little palm to give her parents a high-five.

"How are you feeling?" Tracy started fussing over her little girl.

Amber wouldn't be able to have her speech valve on for some time until the pneumonia had completely cleared, but that didn't stop her communicating.

She made donkey ears with her hands.

"Did you hear me tell you about Shocks?" Julian asked.

Amber nodded enthusiastically.

They both pulled up a chair, ready to tell her the story again.

"Well, I went down to see Shocks yesterday," Julian started. He knew Amber would be eager to hear every last detail about her friend. "I told him you weren't very well."

Amber pulled a sad face.

"But as soon as you are better you can go down and see him," Tracy promised.

Amber hit her fists together, the way she used to do when she knew they were off to the Donkey Sanctuary.

Julian proudly showed her the pictures he'd taken again.

Amber's eyes grew wide with happiness. She clutched her dad's phone so she could get a closer look.

"Love you, Shocky," she mouthed and gave the screen a little kiss.

"Ahhhh," Julian and Tracy both cooed.

Amber grew better by the hour. The antibiotics combined with her sheer determination to go home, to see Shocks, were driving her miraculous recovery.

The nurses had really taken to Amber. They fussed over her endlessly; they even made her a pink crown out of paper which matched her pink 'I LOVE NY' top and tied balloons to her bed.

Princess Amber they wrote across the front of the crown.

Amber couldn't stop smiling.

She became so much better by the evening that the doctors decided to move her back onto a hospital ward as they needed to make space for more emergency cases in the intensive care unit.

She was given a royal send-off.

A few of the doctors and nurses gathered by the door to say goodbye. Amber, wearing her pink crown, waved regally from her bed as the nurses wheeled her out. She turned back and the whole of intensive care was waving.

It was like she was the Queen.

Julian and Tracy looked through their hands; they felt so embarrassed.

They also felt a little bad for all the poorly children she was leaving behind.

"Bye, Amber, hope we *don't* see you again soon!" the nurses said.

The Austwicks thought that was a very thoughtful touch.

And even though they thought it was a cringeworthy moment, it was also very funny. Julian had to pull out his camera and take pictures of Princess Amber.

Amber's parents walked behind the 'royal carriage', carrying all her gifts, chuckling to themselves.

Amber had to spend a while on the ward until the doctors were convinced she was well enough to go home. She'd been in hospital for ten days by the time they were given the all-clear.

It had also been nearly a fortnight since Amber had seen her sister. Julian collected Hope from nursery on the way to the hospital to bring Amber home.

Hope was very excited about seeing Amber. She kept asking if her sister was better the whole car journey there.

"She can't wait to see you, Hopey," Julian told her.

On arrival, father and daughter were met by the sight of Amber toddling up and down the hospital ward, a big mischievous grin plastered on her face. Tracy was trying to keep up with her.

"Look who's come to see you!" Julian announced.

Hope let go of her dad's hand and started running towards her sister.

"Amber! Amber!" she called out, her arms outstretched.

Amber was delighted to see Hope. She held out her arms too. It was like a scene from a film, where two long-lost friends are finally reunited.

They cuddled each other, resting their heads on one another's shoulders. Julian took some pictures for the family album.

"Miss you, miss you," Hope kept saying. "Are you coming home now?"

Amber nodded. She held Hope's hand as they toddled over to their parents, each with a look of: "Can we go home now please?"

Julian had of course brought a thousand and one layers with him to wrap Amber up like an Eskimo. He wasn't risking her getting sick again.

"You can barely see her," Tracy chuckled as the scarf covered half her face. Just her big blue eyes were peeping out.

"Come on, it's home time," Julian announced. He'd been waiting a long time to say those words.

Julian and Tracy went a little over the top about sanitation when they arrived back at the house. Tracy couldn't stop spraying the surfaces with disinfectant. She washed her hands before every suction. She even wiped the door handles.

They never wanted to go through that experience again. Of course there was no way of stopping Amber from falling ill, that was out of their hands, but they just needed to feel they had some control back, even for a little while.

It was only once they were all at home, relaxing in front of the TV, that the enormity of what they had been through hit them.

"You think everything is getting better, and then something like this knocks the wind from your sails," Julian sighed.

Tracy was determined it wouldn't set them back.

"I know, but look how quickly she recovered. We can't let this get the better of us," she said gently, spurring him on.

Julian nodded. He knew his wife was right; and they wouldn't have got as far as they had if it hadn't been for her pushing them forwards to try new things. But tonight, he just wanted to cuddle on the sofa and forget their worries.

It was a couple of months before Julian and Tracy considered sending Amber back to nursery school. They wanted her immune system to be as strong as a fortress before they allowed her to play with other kids who were snotty with winter colds.

They were well aware they couldn't keep her wrapped in cotton wool forever, though. In fact, they agreed the bugs would actually help Amber's immune system improve.

Naturally, Julian found it harder to let go than Tracy.

Tracy decided a trip to the Donkey Sanctuary was in order – to gently ease Amber into the outside world.

Julian looked at her with furrowed brows.

"I just don't know, Trace, it's cold out there." He pointed to the grey sky, which was threatening rain.

"Don't be silly, we will wrap the girls up warmly," she said, jumping off the sofa.

Shocks must be missing Amber as much as she is missing him, she thought. It had been a whole two months since the pair had been together. They'd kept Amber's spirits up with pictures of her friend, and every now and then they'd give her a Donkey Sanctuary postcard signed 'love from Shocks'. The postcards took pride of place on Amber's bedside table.

Tracy couldn't wait to break the news to Amber.

Amber, who had her speaking valve back by now, galloped around the living room with pure joy.

"I want to wear a dress," she announced.

"Of course you do." Tracy could have seen that coming.

Julian stepped in. There was no way Amber, who'd just recovered from pneumonia, was going to wear a frock to ride a donkey on a cool April day.

"No." He wagged his finger.

But Amber had already darted up the staircase and was choosing from her vast collection.

Tracy reassured Julian she'd be wrapped up warm, but she didn't have the heart not to let her wear a dress. Apart from it being Amber's little ritual, she hadn't seen her friend in months, and she would be heartbroken if she couldn't wear her best outfit for their reunion.

Amber chose a blue dress with a picture of Queen Elsa from Disney's *Frozen*. Tracy accessorised it with purple leggings, pink Wellington boots, a fleece and two scarves.

"No bugs will be getting in here," she said as she showed Julian.

"Alright, alright," he agreed with a smile. He herded the twins towards the car.

He had to admit, it was nice to get out on a family outing again.

Amber recognised the familiar sights and sounds as they travelled away from the suburbs and burst into the green of Sutton Park. By the time they juddered over the cattle bars, Amber was on the verge of breaking out of her car seat.

Hope crossly held her finger up to her mouth to tell Amber to 'shhhhh'.

There was nothing that could bring her to silence though.

"Shocks Shocks Shocks!" she chanted.

The girl who once couldn't speak was now shouting from the rooftops about how happy she was to be returning to the Donkey Sanctuary.

As soon as they had parked and unclipped the girls from their seats, Amber was off.

She headed straight for the paddock. There was no stopping to say hi to the gang, no waving to the other donkeys. Amber wanted to see Shocks, and only Shocks.

Julian got his camera ready.

Although Tracy and Julian had seen it with their own eyes, Shocks's reaction to Amber continued to amaze them.

He saw her coming and started heading over to the fence.

Andy also saw them coming and waved enthusiastically.

"Hello, strangers," he shouted.

And then something amazing happened.

Shocks was so happy to see Amber he let out his first bray.

Andy shook his head as if he couldn't quite believe what he'd just heard. He then scrambled across the grass, practically pole-vaulting the fence, as he went to get the others.

Meanwhile, Julian had lifted Amber up so she was eye level with Shocks. Tracy was a few feet back, holding Hope's hand.

Shocks let out another giant hee-haw. Amber covered her ears, it was so noisy.

Shocks waited patiently for his strokes. Amber patted the spiky hair between his ears and then brushed her hands along his nose.

They had clearly missed each other.

"I love you, Shocky," she said as Julian lowered her to the ground.

She then swung around and grabbed her dad's leg.

"I love you, Daddy." She beamed.

"We all love you too, Amber," Julian replied, feeling quite sentimental. He turned and looked at the donkey standing patiently by the fence. "And we love you, Shocks, for everything you have done for Amber," he said.

Shocks looked at all the Austwicks, and then let out a big sneeze of appreciation.

The Three Musketeers – Zebedee, Mackenzie and King – were lurking close by, no doubt wondering what all the commotion was about. Zebedee boldly walked over to where Amber was holding onto the fence.

Back in the day, Shocks would have frozen as the leader approached, but not anymore. He was fiercely protective of Amber. He eyeballed Zebedee as the white donkey drew closer. Shocks flashed him a look as if to say, "Get lost."

Zebedee ignored Shocks's warning shot and cheekily carried on. He must have been only a foot away from Amber when Shocks turned. He drew back his lips in a snarling manner and nipped Zebedee in the neck.

"Take that," he seemed to say as he swished his tail.

Zebedee was so startled by Shocks's assertiveness that he staggered backwards, almost tripping over his own hooves.

He gave Shocks a filthy look. His ears were pinned back.

"Okay, boys, break it up!" Andy stepped in. He'd watched the whole thing unfold on his way back. It was like breaking up boys fighting in the schoolyard.

Amber wasn't in the least bit fazed by the squabble. In fact, she found the whole thing quite exciting.

"You little hooligan," Andy teased her as he crouched to his knees to give Amber a welcome-back hug.

"Me too," Hope screeched as she came running over to join the reunion.

Poor Andy literally had to prise the girls off, they were that happy to see him. They clung to his legs like wheel clamps as he explained to Julian and Tracy that Shocks's behaviour towards Zebedee was not a one-off.

Shocks's newfound confidence had caused a massive reshuffle of the pecking order amongst the donkeys.

"He's gone from number twenty-one to about number nine," Andy said proudly. "He doesn't wait to be thrown a carrot anymore, he's one of the first at the hay nets in the morning, and nips at the other donkeys to wait their turn."

But Andy quickly reassured the Austwicks that Shocks hadn't turned into a thug. In fact, he remained very loyal to his original group of friends – Jacko and Rambo. He'd just become a bit braver. It was everything the staff at the Sanctuary had been hoping and longing for.

With that, Andy suggested they take a wander, as he knew someone who would be over the moon to see Amber back on her feet.

Big Amber was busy in the office sifting through a mountain of paperwork. That was the problem with the donkeys; they were so all-consuming the staff barely got around to filling out admin.

She looked up from behind a stack of paper and files as the office door opened. And then …

"Amber," she squealed, her chair screeching as she pushed it backwards.

Big Amber took Little Amber into her arms and told her how much she'd been missed.

"What's your name?" Little Amber asked cheekily.

"Oh, not that again!" Julian rolled his eyes, laughing.

Big Amber suggested they grab a cup of tea and a plate of chips and sit on the picnic benches in the outside play area.

Amber and Hope immediately scampered off to investigate what toys had been left out ready for playing with.

As the adults took their seats at the picnic bench, Big Amber looked like she had something on her mind. She drummed her fingers on the wooden table thoughtfully.

Julian and Tracy waited for her to speak.

"You'll never guess what I've gone and done," she finally blurted out.

Julian and Tracy looked at each other and then back at her – they had no idea.

"I've entered Shocks for the Animal Hero Awards," she said.

And then, without taking a breath, she rattled on.

"It's the first time the Sanctuary has ever done anything like this, but we thought Shocks's transformation has been so miraculous we just wanted to share it with the rest of the country. I have no idea if we stand a chance, but …"

She paused to catch her breath.

" … We'll find out soon enough."

Julian and Tracy were speechless. They had no clue such awards existed. But they had a good feeling about it. Ever since Shocks had been rescued, people had noticed how he had a sparkle in his eye, that he was special. So there was no reason that was about to stop now.

CHAPTER 27

Animal Hero

London, Summer 2014

Big Amber had never seen the bright lights of London.

So for her first visit to encompass a champagne dinner at the prestigious Langham Hotel, attended by celebrities such as Amanda Holden, Queen guitarist Brian May and boy band McFly, was almost too much to take in.

Shocks had been nominated for the *Daily Mirror* and RSPCA Rescue Animal of the Year Award at its Hero Awards ceremony.

Big Amber couldn't believe it.

"I wish I could take you with me, boy," Amber had said to the donkey, when she'd shared a moment alone with Shocks before she caught the coach to the city.

But Amber told Shocks that he probably wouldn't like London much because it was noisy and dirty and there wasn't much grass to munch on.

Instead, she'd be going to the awards with Suzi Cretney and Dawn Vincent from the Donkey Sanctuary's communications team.

Amber had given Shocks a scratch behind his ears and apologised that she had to run, but she needed to choose a dress for the big event and, as usual, was leaving everything to the last minute.

"Good luck!" Andy and the rest of the team had cheered her on as she'd rushed to her car to take her to the bus station.

They had all gathered in a little semi-circle in the car park to see her off. Amber had craned her head out of the window one last time and kept waving all the way up the drive, until the team had turned into specks in the distance.

It was showtime!

Suzi and Dawn were just as excited and nervous when Amber met them in the lobby of their hotel later that day. They too couldn't quite believe Shocks was in the running for the award, that in a few hours' time they would be part of a very special ceremony that recognises the wonderful work done by animals and their owners.

After checking in, Amber summoned the elevator to take her to her room. She stepped into the lift wearing a blue Donkey Sanctuary fleece, jeans and boots, and re-emerged an hour and a half later in a beautiful black-and-white figure-hugging dress and black stilettos.

Suzi and Dawn told her how stunning she looked. Being press officers, they were a little more used to getting dressed up, but this was a rare occasion for Big Amber. She spent most of her time in mucky overalls.

Amber had butterflies in her stomach for the whole of the taxi ride to the Langham Hotel in central London. She was nervous about meeting lots of new faces; but most of all, she was nervous about whether Shocks was going to win the award. Amber knew there would be some tough competition.

They stepped out in front of the grand building – one of the oldest hotels in London. Police had cordoned off the area in front with cones. Black limousines were negotiating their way through the gridlocked traffic. There was a large crowd of onlookers trying to get a glimpse of the celebrities arriving.

Even Big Amber felt dwarfed underneath the eight-storey building and the towering white pillars. There were Union Jack flags swishing in the wind above the arched entrance. The door was guarded by half a dozen men, all very smartly dressed in tailored grey suits and top hats.

"Wow-wee," Amber gasped. Her eyes lit up like a firework.

Over to the right was a pack of paparazzi photographers, their bulbs flashing as a host of celebrities made their way up the red-carpeted stairs leading into the building.

Deborah Meaden, one of the judges from the TV show *Dragons' Den*, was having her photo snapped as Amber arrived. But, being an animal lover, Amber was more taken by *who* she was having her photo taken with – two giant police horses. Their coats were perfectly clipped, and their tails had been braided for the occasion.

"Ahh, they are beautiful," she sighed in admiration. And then, naturally, she found her thoughts turning to the donkeys.

Time some of our boys had a haircut, she found herself thinking, making a mental note to arrange for the donkeys to be clipped on her return to the Sanctuary.

Amber, Suzi and Dawn were directed along the perfectly upholstered corridors, all lined with white lilies and huge bouquets of flowers. All three women gasped at the same time as they emerged into the grand ballroom.

It was a sight to behold – an enormous, pristine white room lined with colonnades of gold-encrusted pillars. There were so many chandeliers on the ceiling you couldn't see for all the light sparking off them.

Big Amber wondered if it was time they gave their office a spring clean.

"How the other half lives," she chuckled to her colleagues.

Luckily, the ladies weren't sharing their table with anyone in their category – that could have been quite awkward. There were so many other awards being handed out that night, such as Hero Animal of the Year and Caring Animal of the Year and Public Service Animal of the Year, for animals who work in extreme conditions to protect and serve.

"Oh look!" Amber pointed to the dog bowls discreetly placed at the edges of the room. She hadn't spotted them at first for all the glamour and grandeur but it was becoming obvious why they were there. The room was filling up with dogs and small animals that owners could carry in transportable cages.

It was a wonderful sight to see one of London's finest hotels turned into an animal farm.

They took their seats. Amber was busy chatting to the man sitting next to her about the work he did training police horses when the room was hushed into silence.

Presenter Amanda Holden sashayed onto the stage wearing a floor-length, white, diamond-encrusted dress. Her hair was pinned up, leaving just her blonde fringe sweeping across her face. The outfit was finished off with a very large pair of diamond earrings.

Amber glanced across the room. She couldn't believe how many celebrities were there – Anita Dobson, Ashley and Pudsey, McFly, Sarah Harding, Bill Oddie, Helen Worth, Ben Fogle and Peter Egan were just some of those who caught her eye.

Unexpectedly, her stomach somersaulted with nerves. Suddenly the stakes seemed sky-high. Luckily, the Rescue Animal of the Year Award was the second to be announced. Suzi and Dawn both agreed with Amber that it was a massive relief they wouldn't have to bite their nails all night worrying.

Amanda Holden read out a little description of the award and a biography of the other rescue animals that were nominated in the category. As she began to describe Shocks, Amber's eyes immediately started to well up.

Pictures of Shocks flashed up on the big screen as Amanda recounted his horrific past.

"Shocks was found with horrendous wounds to his neck due to his previous owner deliberately pouring industrial bleach over him; how anyone could do this is beyond me," she said.

There were gasps of horror coming from every direction.

"It took more than a year for the Birmingham team to gain Shocks's trust and restore his faith in people. His rehabilitation wasn't quick – he received extended veterinary care to recover from his physical and mental wounds," the presenter carried on, with a lump in her throat.

"After such an ordeal, I was speechless to learn that Shocks now offers rides to children with special needs and disabilities at Birmingham's Assisted Therapy Centre. Shocks is able to trust again and not only put a smile on a young person's face, but help them learn to walk and communicate."

A great stillness fell across the room. Amber had tears streaming down her face. She hadn't realised how emotional the journey had been until someone else had spelled it out for her like that.

"And the winner is ..." Amanda daintily pulled the crisp white card from the envelope.

Amber's stomach clenched. Suzi and Dawn were frozen to their seats. Amber heard a drum roll in her head.

"And the winner is Shocks."

Amber let out a glass-breaking scream of happiness.

"Yes!" She leapt to her feet with her arms in the air.

The room erupted into clapping and cheering.

Amber suddenly felt a little self-conscious. *Behave, Amber, you're in a posh hotel.* She ticked herself off as she slithered back into her seat, but she couldn't help the enormous grin that split her face from ear to ear.

Dawn, as the granddaughter of Dr Elisabeth Svendsen (the woman who founded the Sanctuary), was the one who would formally collect the award. She gave her dress a little tug as she made her way to the stage. The award was presented to her by former Pussycat Dolls singers Ashley Roberts and Kimberly Wyatt.

The head of communications tucked her blonde strands of hair behind her ear as she addressed the crowd. She spoke of how proud she was of Shocks and how the Donkey Sanctuary had worked as a team to save his life.

She finished simply. "Thank you." She held the engraved blue and white plaque in the air to a thunder of clapping.

Amid the applause, Amber discreetly pulled her phone out from her clutch bag. She tweeted and Facebooked the incredible news so everyone waiting on tenterhooks in Birmingham would know the happy result right away.

Bleep bleep. Bleep bleep. Her phone was inundated with text messages from Andy and Sara and all the rest of the staff and volunteers, who were gobsmacked.

After that, the Donkey Sanctuary's table was quite possibly the noisiest of the night, as a couple of the other charities sitting with them also won awards.

And if the evening hadn't been magical enough, the team was cheered on by boy band McFly.

"Yay, donkey ladies," they chanted, as they made their way past their table en route to the stage to sing.

Amber felt her cheeks turn pink – she was a little starstruck.

The perfect evening was rounded off with a press photo. Brian May's wife, Anita Dobson, took a moment to congratulate them.

The *EastEnders* star asked the women where they were off to next.

"We're back to work tomorrow, mucking out the stables," Amber laughed.

"You do a great job. I'm so jealous you get to work with donkeys all day," Anita replied, with sincerity.

And with that, the soap star said her goodbyes and stepped into the blinding flashes of the paparazzi.

The Donkey Sanctuary women joked that there weren't quite so many people wanting to take their picture as they made their way back to the hotel. Big Amber couldn't wait to take her high heels off; she was used to wearing steel-toe-capped boots. She fell onto her bed like a starfish, the ceiling spinning from the champagne. She couldn't remember the last time she had slept so well.

The morning after was another story – Amber was grateful for the quiet coach to Birmingham! Even though her head throbbed a little, she still had a very important call to make. She scrolled through her phone, searching for the name.

But Tracy was already two steps ahead.

"We won!" She answered Amber's call with a high-pitched squeal.

Big Amber could hear Little Amber in the background, mimicking her mum.

"We won, we won, we won," she cheered.

Tracy revealed how she and Julian had been glued to social media all night, watching the updates.

"We couldn't have done it without Amber, without your whole family." Big Amber became emotional.

She told Tracy how the local paper – the *Birmingham Post* – wanted to write a feature on the award and that she would really like it if Little Amber could be there for the interview and photo shoot they wanted to do.

Wild horses wouldn't keep Little Amber away from such a celebration.

"We'll pick out her party dress now," Tracy said, grinning from ear to ear at the thought of her daughter and Shocks starring in the paper.

With the long journey ahead of her, Big Amber had a few hours to kill before she'd be back at the Sanctuary. As the hype of the evening wore off, her thoughts turned inward.

The coach window had become foggy with early morning condensation so Amber rubbed a porthole to the outside with her sleeve. As she stared at the life on the other side, Amber reflected on Shocks's journey. She remembered the night he'd arrived in that terrible thunderstorm – a frightened wreck who'd stood shivering with fear and cold. *Now look at him.* She couldn't help but smile.

How a donkey that was left for dead could transform into a confident, caring creature – the most popular to ride of all the donkeys at the Sanctuary – was nothing short of a miracle.

And all it had taken was for someone to believe in him. All he had needed was someone to trust. That someone turned out to be a very special girl called Amber.

The staff and volunteers had hung balloons and streamers from every pinboard in the riding school by the time Big Amber arrived back.

They were cheering and clapping as she paraded in, holding the award above her head like it was a football trophy. She was reliving the celebration from the night before; only this time, she was surrounded by all the people who'd donated hours of their time and masses of love to help with Shocks's recovery.

Julian and Tracy couldn't have timed their arrival better. They'd picked the girls up from nursery and taken a mini detour via the supermarket. Little Amber emerged from the car clutching a bag full of apples.

She was wearing a long-sleeved cream fleece, and over the top of that, a white dress sprinkled with bright flowers. She had on matching cream leggings and, of course, her pink Wellington boots – the perfect outfit for a photo shoot.

Hope looked at her proudly, as if she knew this was her sister's crowning moment, and didn't mind Amber taking centre stage. Hope toddled across the parking lot to give her a hug. Amber returned her embrace with a quick squeeze – and then she was off. Amber couldn't sit still for a moment; she was always looking for the next adventure. In this case – feeding Shocks his treats.

"Amber, wait!" Hope shouted out, distressed at being left behind. Amber spun around, pushing her pink spectacles up her nose. She took Hope's hand and the twins wobbled down to the paddock together. It was a lovely moment for Julian and Tracy to see – Amber was finally sharing her donkey world with her sister.

Andy and Big Amber had a treat bucket ready for their arrival. It had an extra helping of polo mints and ginger biscuits as a reward for the award. Amber popped a few of her own apples into the mix.

Andy gave the bucket a big noisy shake. Amber jumped up and down on the spot; she couldn't wait to help carry it over.

The photographer and the reporter from the *Birmingham Post* were waiting at the gates to the paddock. Amber grinned broadly as the warm glow of the flashbulb lit up her face. She couldn't have been further from the shy girl who used to hide behind the sofa. Amber loved the camera! If she hadn't been carrying the bucket, she probably would have struck a series of poses like a model.

Shocks was delighted with his treats. He gobbled the contents up in less than ten seconds. Julian and Tracy wondered if he'd actually chewed or just swallowed the lot whole.

Shocks had quite an audience watching, but he didn't seem to bat an eyelid. He looked innocently through his lashes as if to say, "What's all the fuss about?"

The photographer took some shots of Big Amber holding the award, and then rounded off with Little Amber riding Shocks. Like a true professional, Amber reached forward and wrapped her arms around Shocks's neck.

Snap snap snap – that was the winning picture.

The reporter turned to the Austwicks to ask a few questions. She was in her mid-twenties and came across as if she was just starting out in the industry. She was polite and a little nervous.

Julian and Tracy recounted the story of how Shocks had helped Amber to walk and talk. How Amber wouldn't be able to do either if it weren't for Shocks.

"Amber used to hate people. All of this could have gone the opposite way. She could be reclusive and sad if it wasn't for meeting Shocks," Tracy added, with tears of happiness in her eyes.

"So Shocks saved your daughter?" the reporter asked.

Julian paused for a moment, mulling over his words.

"I'd say they healed each other."

How You Can Help

During the last 45 years, the Donkey Sanctuary has made a profound difference to the lives of donkeys and people all over the world. This is down to the drive and belief of its founder, Dr Elisabeth Svendsen, MBE, its staff and volunteers, and of course the charity's fantastic supporters and partners worldwide.

However, there is still much to do. By 2018, the Donkey Sanctuary wants to be able to give a helping hand to two million donkeys each year in 40 countries, to double the number of donkeys in foster care to 3,000 and to expand its donkey assisted therapy programme in the United Kingdom and internationally.

There are a multitude of ways you can help from a donation as small as £3 (which covers the cost of looking after a rescued donkey for half a day), to gift aid and fostering or adopting a donkey.

The adoption scheme is the perfect way to get your daily dose of donkey capers, and you'll be part of the donkey's life forever. The donkeys come to the Sanctuary for many different reasons, such as neglect, abandonment or just because their owners can no longer care for them. By adopting your donkey, you'll guarantee their future where they will never want for warmth, care or food again. Your adoption pack includes a framed portrait, four beautiful postcards, a certificate and your donkey's story, plus you'll receive regular updates about your donkey. You can also follow their antics on Facebook and Twitter (@AdoptADonkey) pages.

If you'd like to find out more, please visit www.thedonkeysanctuary.org.uk or call 01395 578222.

Acknowledgements

This book couldn't have happened without the help of so many wonderful and supportive people.

Firstly, we'd like to thank the staff at the neonatal unit at Heartlands Hospital, who kept our children alive for those painstaking months.

The incredible Birmingham Children's Hospital nurses, doctors and consultants. The fantastic staff of BCH Intensive Care Unit. Special mentions to the greatest ENT surgeon Mr Kuo and paediatrician Dr Vin Diwakar.

Thanks also to Barbara Tumulty (Early Support), Jo Matthews (Speech and Language), Sam Ridley (Health Visitor) and Ros Blackmore (Dietician).

A big thank you to Wilson Stuart School Physiotherapy Department – Lucy Weardon and Pauline Christmas.

Thanks also to the carers from Complex Care especially Jade, Jess, Aga and Amina.

Thanks to Twickenham Primary School, Kingstanding, especially Head Teacher Mrs Mortiboy.

Big thanks to the wonderful Michelle Snipe (now O'Neill), Children's Community Nurse, for all your help and support over the past five years.

Thank you to the Donkey Sanctuary. Thank you to all the wonderful staff and volunteers that have become a big part of our lives at the Birmingham Sanctuary in Sutton Park. Enormous thanks to Andy Perry, Amber Brennan, Sara Gee, Sue and Phil

Brennan, Jessica O'Grady, Gill Warner, Jo Jo, all the donkeys and especially Shocks!

Special thanks to Susan Smith at MBA, for starting the ball rolling.

A huge thank you goes to our ghostwriter Ruth Kelly for all her hard work bringing our story to life.

Massive thanks also to the publishers, Ebury Press, for the opportunity to get our story out there. We hope it will inspire and bring happiness and hope to others.

Thank you also to our family. But especially Lee, Debbie, Nat Nat and Yar Yar. Nanny Di and Nanny Rene. And thanks to friends, old and new, especially Sam, Liz and Abbie Hardman just for being there!

Also available from Ebury:

Toby & Sox

Vikky and Neil Turner

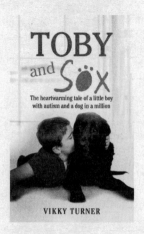

When Toby Turner was excluded from school for hitting and kicking his teachers, he felt so upset by his own aggression, he told his parents they would be better off without him. Until Sox came along. This is the heartwarming tale of a little boy with autism and a dog in a million.

ISBN 9781785032004

Order direct from www.penguin.co.uk

Lucca the War Dog
Maria Goodavage

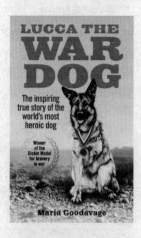

The incredible, true story of K-9 Marine hero Lucca, winner
of the Dickin Medal for bravery in war, and her adventures on
and off the battlefield. Heartwarming and inspiring, Lucca the
War Dog is a compelling portrait of modern warfare.

ISBN 9781785035173

Order direct from www.penguin.co.uk

Buster

Will Barrow

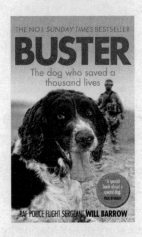

Thousands of lives have been saved by this spaniel. He is a brave dog who has served his colleagues and his country with true devotion. This is the story of the partnership of Buster and Will, describing how each came to save the other's life.

ISBN 978073555798

Order direct from www.penguin.co.uk